# Stringing
## the Pearls

# Stringing the Pearls

## How to Read the Weekly Torah Portion

JAMES S. DIAMOND

The Jewish Publication Society
Philadelphia
2008 • 5768

JPS is a nonprofit educational association and the oldest and foremost publisher of Judaica in English in North America. The mission of JPS is to enhance Jewish culture by promoting the dissemination of religious and secular works, in the United States and abroad, to all individuals and institutions interested in past and contemporary Jewish life.

The Jewish Publication Society
2100 Arch Street, 2nd floor
Philadelphia, PA 19103
www.jewishpub.org

Design and Composition by Sandy Freeman

Manufactured in the United States of America

08 09 10 11    11 10 9 8 7 6 5 4 3 2 1

Library of Congress Cataloging-in-Publication Data

Diamond, James S.
  Stringing the pearls : how to read the weekly Torah portion / James S. Diamond.
      p. cm.
  Includes bibliographical references.
  ISBN 978-0-8276-0868-9 (alk. paper)
  1. Bible. O.T. Pentateuch—Criticism, interpretation, etc.  I. Title.
  BS1225.53.D53 2008
  222'.10071—dc22
  2007042243

JPS books are available at discounts for bulk purchases for reading groups, special sales, and fundraising purchases. Custom editions, including personalized covers, can be created in larger quantities for special needs. For more information, please contact us at marketing@jewishpub.org or at this address: 2100 Arch Street, Philadelphia, PA 19103.

For Shifra, Gila, Alan, Judy, and Etan,

five books bound as one.

. . . צוָּארֵךְ בַּחֲרוּזִים.

— שִׁיר הַשִּׁירִים 1:10


ר' לוי בשם רבי חמא ברבי חנינא אמר:
אלו פרשותיה של תורה שהן חרוזות זו בזו ומושכות
זו בזו ומדלגות זו מזו ודומות זו לזו וקרובות זו לזו.

— שיר השירים רבה 1:54


*" . . . your neck [is comely] with a string of pearls"**

—Song of Songs 1:10


**Rabbi Levi said in the name of Rabbi Hama son of Rabbi Hanina:
These are the portions of the Torah, which are strung together, and
which draw upon each other, and which jump back and forth
among each other, which resemble each other, and which share
affinities with each other.**

—Midrash Rabbah on Song of Songs 1:54


*The JPS TANAKH renders this "your neck with strings of jewels." The Anchor Bible notes that the Hebrew word *haruzim* "does not occur elsewhere in the Bible, but in postbiblical Hebrew it is used of [sic] stringing pearls or fish." *The Anchor Bible: Song of Songs*, trans. Marvin H. Pope (Garden City, N.Y.: Doubleday & Co., 1977), 344.

# Contents

# Preface

The seeds of this book were planted long ago, in my childhood, when my grandfather, at my mother's behest, would pick me up every Saturday morning and take me—I should say drag me—to shul (synagogue) with him. Those were long mornings. I had no idea what was going on. What I remember most is that when they took out the Torah, everyone cleared out, leaving the near-empty synagogue to the old men as the Torah reader droned on.

Later in life I came to understand how pernicious this mass exodus was in the scale of Jewish values and aspirations. As the years went by and I began to appreciate the gift we Jews unwrap and open each *Shabbat* morning, I came full circle: the Torah reading became for me the main event of the shul experience. And I vowed that one day I would do something that might help others feel the same way and prevent them from being bored in shul. That is one of my impulses for writing this book.

A related one, more positive in its outlook, is my belief that what Jewish life today needs most are serious Jews. I stand with those who hold that in our time the decisive distinction in Jewish self-definition is between Jews who are serious and deliberate about the content of their life as Jews and those who are casual or apathetic about it, between those who aspire to be substantial Jews and those for whom "Jewish" is an empty signifier. All other criteria by which Jewish identity is calibrated—affiliation, denomination, level of observance, support of Jewish institutions and causes, or even level of Jewish literacy—all flow from this distinction. This book is for all who strive to be serious Jews. Ultimately they—you—will be the only ones who matter.

In the writing of this book there is a "before" and an "after" that I wish to note. The "before" is the time, some years ago, when I began actively pondering what is involved in reading the Five Books of the Torah and tried my hand at writing about it. I was fortunate to show some of what I had put down to my colleague Ira Stone. In our discussion of what I had attempted, he noted that implicit in it was a book on how to read the weekly parashah, and that in all the voluminous material written about the Bible and the Torah there was no such book. As soon as he said this, this book formed in my mind. Shortly thereafter, on a delightful spring day in Princeton, I had a seminal discussion of the project with Ellen Frankel, the editor-in-chief of JPS. Her ideas about it were, as always, fruitful, and her encouragement of it was instrumental in catalyzing the process of my putting it into words and sentences and paragraphs and parts.

That process, otherwise known as writing, went on for several months in 2006. When it had finished, at least when I thought it had finished, I asked a number of friends and colleagues to read the resulting manuscript: Lenny Gordon, Martha Himmelfarb, Lori Lefkowitz, Mitchell Marx, Gary Rendsburg, Esther Schor, Reena Spicehandler, Max Ticktin, and Judy Walzer. Each of them gave unstintingly of their time, their knowledge, and their reading acuity. The insights that accrued from their reading led to the "after." After I had reflected on and incorporated many—most— of their comments and suggestions into the manuscript, it improved far beyond the one I had given them. It was also purged of many errors of many kinds. For those that, alas, may have persisted, only I am responsible.

I wish, therefore, to record here my thanks and lasting appreciation to all the aforementioned for their advice and, above all, for their friendship. Their role in bringing my original project to fruition, from its conception to its actualization, was crucial.

One more vector on the pages that follow needs mention. It consists of two experiences I have had prior to and between and following the "before" and the "after" events I have noted. One is my regular participation in a *Shabbat* morning minyan that meets at the Center for Jewish Life at Princeton University. This is a singular community of cherished friends who each week grapple together with the Torah portion. The other is my involvement in

Me'ah, the adult Jewish learning program sponsored by the Hebrew College of Boston in which I have had, and continue to have,
the privilege of teaching the TANAKH module. The discussions of
Bible and Torah, and much else, in both those venues have nur-
tured and shaped much of what you will read here. My gratitude
to all who were and are a part of those discussions is boundless.
They are too many to name here; they know who they are.

The same is true for the editorial and production staff at The Jewish Publication Society. It has been a privilege to have benefited
from their expertise and savvy.

I dedicate this book to my children and their life companions.
They each read the *Humash* in their own ways, and they will each
read what I say about it likewise. I will pay attention to what they
will tell me, for they are serious Jews.

James S. Diamond<br>
Princeton, New Jersey<br>
Tishri 5768 September 2007

# How to Read This Book

Of all the texts of Jewish tradition none is more frequently read and discussed than the weekly Torah portion, the *parashat hashavua*, as it's known in Hebrew. The volume of material commenting on and analyzing the 54 slices of the Five Books of Moses is immense and, happily, continues to proliferate.

But abundant as this interpretative material is, there is a surprising paucity of books that attempt to provide a methodology of **how** to read the weekly Torah portions. This book aims to begin to address that deficiency. It is a "how to" book, not an interpretive or an exegetical one. It is not a commentary on each week's parashah, nor does it seek to advance novel readings of them. I have conceived of it as an instruction manual on how to approach the 54 weekly Torah portions, how to read and hear them. It is offered to all who would like to upgrade the nature and quality of their experience with the Torah, that is, the Five Books of Moses.

Specifically, I have in mind three kinds of readers:

- Synagogue-goers who want to sit in synagogue during the Torah reading, not in boredom or in a less wakeful state of consciousness, but as involved listeners in what for 15 centuries has become the centerpiece of the *Shabbat* morning service: the millennial reenactment of the Sinai experience through the public reading from the Torah scroll.

- Jewish readers for whom synagogue services are not the focal point of their Jewish life but who, nevertheless, whether in the

privacy of their homes or in study groups, want a better understanding of how the five books work together to make the
Torah or, to put it somewhat differently, the core text of the Jewish narrative.

• Non-Jews who want to attain deeper insight into how Jews
  read the Five Books of Moses and relate to it as Torah. A note to
  Christian readers follows below.[1]

The movement of the five parts of this book is from the theoreti-
cal to the operational, from a discussion of some of the ideas and
principles that underlie our reading of the Five Books to a presentation of a methodology of working through a weekly Torah portion.[2]

• Part I sets out the context. It explains some basic terms and out-
  lines the overall structure of the Hebrew Bible into which a
  weekly Torah portion fits.

• Parts II and III identify some key issues and approaches that inform our reading of a weekly portion.

• Parts IV and V present an operational guide to reading a
  weekly portion and commentaries.

The five parts do not have to be read sequentially. Nor do they
have to be read together or all in the same year. Readers in each
of the three constituencies for whom this book is intended will approach and handle it differently at different seasons of life, as they
will the Torah itself. A "one size fits all" approach to the following pages is, therefore, not indicated; an individualized and lon-
gitudinal one is. In the Jewish scheme of things, reading Torah is
a lifelong project. If you cycle through the 54 weekly Torah portions year after year, you will see that your understanding of each
of them will steadily deepen.

• **If you regard yourself as a novice** at reading the Five Books,
  Parts I and IV may suffice for now, and maybe Part V, too. You
  can always pick up the parts you skip at some future point, after you have taken your first steps in engaging with a weekly
  portion.

- **If you have had some experience in reading the Bible**, you could safely skip Part I and begin at Part II. Or, again, you could read the remaining four parts in any order you choose.

- **If your level of biblical literacy is high** and you are experienced at handling biblical text, this book may not teach you anything you don't already know. But it might give you some ideas to think about, offer you some new ways to delve into the text you haven't tried before, ways that you can share with your study partners or your students. And it may help you situate yourself more precisely on the interpretive map.

Regardless of the readership you belong to and where you are in your spiritual life, my hope is that this book will help you chart your own path as you develop your skills in meeting the piece of Torah that awaits your presence each week.

# A Note to the Christian Reader

The prophet Isaiah counsels: "Look to the rock whence you were hewn . . ." (Isa. 51:1). For Christians this could be understood to mean that the path to one's self-understanding as a Christian runs through an inquiry into Judaism and an encounter with its canonical texts and key ideas. This book hopefully can serve as a gateway to such an inquiry and a facilitator of such an encounter.

Most Christians know that Jews read from their Scripture during their services. The New Testament furnishes among the most important documentations of this ancient practice: "For Moses from ancient generations has in every city those who preach him, since he is read in the synagogues every Sabbath" (Acts 15:21). This is not a trivial observation, for the entire Christian lectionary tradition of including weekly readings and lessons (lections) in the church service stems from the Jewish practice of reading a portion of the Torah each week over the year.

This book will help you understand this practice and, in doing so, will help you better understand and appreciate your own tradition. While my agenda here is to outline for Jews a method of how they can approach and read the weekly Torah portions, the method itself may have relevance for you in your own reading. Taken as a whole, this book will illuminate for you the nature of the Jewish transaction with the Pentateuch and give you some idea of the hermeneutics that this transaction involves. Old Testament texts that are familiar to you may, in the following pages, come to look somewhat different.

Reading the Bible and about the Bible is always a challenge. It is a challenge when we do this within the comfortable confines of the assumptions we hold about God, man, and the world, and even more so when we look at Scripture outside these parameters and see how it is read from under a different interpretive horizon. I applaud your willingness to accept this challenge.

As I invite you into the pages that follow, I cannot improve upon what Martin Buber said to a group of German Protestant missionaries in Stuttgart in 1930:

> **What have you and we in common? If we take the question literally, a book and an expectation. To you the book is a forecourt; to us it is the sanctuary. But in this place we can dwell together; and together listen to the voice that speaks here. That means we can work together to evoke the buried speech of that voice; together we can redeem the imprisoned living word.[1]**

# What Is What:
# Some Basic Terms

**The Five Books of Moses** are often referred to as **the Pentateuch**. In Hebrew the Pentateuch is called **the *Humash***, from the Hebrew word for the number five, *hamesh*. That is how I shall mostly be calling it. The *Humash* comprises:

- Genesis, in Hebrew B'reishit בראשית
- Exodus, in Hebrew Shemot שמות
- Leviticus, in Hebrew Va-yikra' ויקרא
- Numbers, in Hebrew Be-midbar במדבר
- Deuteronomy, in Hebrew Devarim דברים.

The Hebrew names are taken from the first word or the first key word in the book's opening verse. The anglicized names come from Greek, from the titles given them by the Septuagint, the oldest Greek translation of the Torah, done by the Jews of Alexandria about 250 B.C.E.

Sometimes the Five Books are called **the Torah**. This is where it gets confusing. For "Torah," which literally in Hebrew means "teaching" or "instruction," has over time acquired other meanings as well:

- Torah can denote the scroll upon which the Five Books are written—handwritten, letter by letter, by an authorized scribe.

- Torah is sometimes used to signify the status of a Jewish text or teaching as divinely revealed, holy, revered.

- Torah in its broadest sense can refer to the totality of Jewish religion, that is, Judaism.

In this book I use the term "Torah" variously in all three senses.

The Pentateuch or *Humash* is part of a larger collection of books that comprise **the Hebrew Bible**. In Hebrew this is called **the TANAKH**.

I shall say more about all this in Part I.

PART I

# Preliminaries: What Are We Talking About?

# 1.
# Starting Points

Long ago our Rabbinic forebears divided up the *Humash* into 54 consecutive units. Each week, starting in the fall at the end of the Sukkot festival, one unit or portion would be read starting with the beginning of Genesis and progressing, over the succeeding weeks and months, to the end of Deuteronomy, so that in the course of a luni-solar year the entire five books would be traversed.[1]

Thus did the annual cycle of weekly Torah portions come about. In Hebrew these weekly portions are called variously *parshiyot* or *parashiyot* (singular parashah) or *sidrot* (singular *sidrah*). This practice of reading through the entire *Humash* annually began in Babylonia and has since become normative for much of Jewry. An alternative cycle was developed in Palestine that spanned three years (some sources speak of three and a half years). In that system, which itself has variations, the weekly readings are of course shorter and only about a third of the five books are read within a calendar year. Modifications of that practice obtain today in some Conservative synagogues. This book is pegged to the annual cycle, though everything in it applies and is easily adapted to the triennial system.

Here we come to a basic question: Was the Torah and its weekly portions meant to be read or heard? Is the public reading of the Torah in synagogue on *Shabbat* and holidays, not to mention Monday and Thursday mornings, a liturgical act or an intellectual endeavor, a kind of group study session?

The indications are that it is both. Hearing and reading, reading and hearing, are not mutually exclusive acts. The Torah addresses

both the heart and the mind—though not necessarily in that order. It is meant to be heard and it is meant to be studied. Indeed,
Judaism presumes a synergy between the two, between what the
auditory nerve and the optical nerve each transmit to the brain.
To hear the weekly Torah portion read aloud without having
some idea of what it is that is reaching our ears is, in the Jewish
scheme of things, as problematic as knowing a great deal about
the Bible without hearing the voices that are speaking in and
through its text and pondering the import of what they may be
suggesting or implying to us.

What you are holding now is a guide and a handbook, the goals
of which are:

- to tell you what kind(s) of texts you are looking at—and hearing—when you are reading or following along any one of the
  54 weekly *parshiyot;*
- to map out for you the textual terrain of the Pentateuch;
- to identify for you an array of strategies you can use in your
  own encounter with the text, as you struggle to make sense of
  it from year to year;
- to furnish you with some basic tools and resources, both in
  books and on the Web, that can help you develop your knowledge and your reading acumen. This is a book that will send
  you off in many directions depending on where you will want
  to go in your spiritual and intellectual search.

One more preliminary point. This is not a book about the Hebrew
Bible (TANAKH) . But I will certainly have a lot to say about it, for
it is difficult, if not impossible, to talk about the *Humash* in isola-
tion from that larger corpus of text.

There are many ways to read the *Humash,* many lenses through
which its depth and breadth can be seen. The oldest ones, which
originate as far back as the very early Rabbinic period (2nd century B.C.E.), are *peshat* and *derash. Peshat* derives from the Hebrew
verb root *p-sh-t,* פשט "to lay out" or "to explain," and is related to
the Hebrew word *pashut,* "simple." To read for *peshat* is to read for
the meaning that the plain sense of the words, the grammar, and
the syntax of a verse furnish. *Derash* derives from the Hebrew
verb root *d-r-sh,* דרש, "to seek" or "to inquire." It involves putting
some kind of interpretive move on the text whereby a word or a

phrase or a verse is understood to say something that goes beyond its literal meaning. The Rabbis developed a whole menu of such interpretive techniques, the generic name for which is **midrash**. I'll have more to say about all this below in Parts III and V.

But for now we may note that by the close of the Rabbinic period in the 6th century, Jewish interpretive tradition had developed four levels or modes in which the Torah can be processed by the mind of the reader:

- *Peshat:* the apparent, surface meaning of the text;
- *Remez:* the meaning that is only hinted at by the text;
- *Derash:* the meaning that has been ferreted out of the text after various interpretive techniques have been applied to it;
- *Sod:* the hidden mystical meaning(s) encoded in the text and available only to trained kabbalists.[2]

These kinds of reading served our ancient and medieval forebears brilliantly, as a look into the traditional commentaries on the Torah will show. They still suffice for many traditional Jews today. For many contemporary readers, however, the optics have changed and we need a new set of lenses through which to view the Torah text. I would identify these lenses as follows:

- the lens of the **historical,** which renders visible to us the social, political, and geographic context in which a given parashah or chapter or verse or even word needs to be understood. Such reading brings to bear the findings of archaeology, anthropology, and comparative religion, and it also makes visible the linguistic and cultural and legal matrix out of which the *Humash* comes.

- the lens of **art,** specifically literary art, which illuminates the beauty and the brilliance of how the text works literarily or poetically, its verbal and formal artifice. Such reading avails itself of the learnings furnished by comparative literature and literary and esthetic theory.

- the lens of **midrash,** which highlights the multiple ways in which the Torah text can be explicated so as to reveal its religious or theological or moral insights and implications. I say multiple ways because midrash is not only or merely a noun re-

ferring to classical collections of biblical interpretation bequeathed to us by the Rabbis of the talmudic period. Midrash
is also a *process* whereby readers in all ages and of all ages and
of both genders unpack the text out of their own cultural moment. There is Rabbinic midrash from the past and there is
modern midrash of the present.

- the **spiritual** or **existential** lens, which allows the text to dis-
  close to us truths that address our deepest personal concerns.
  These are the truths that nourish our souls and infuse our lives
  as Jews with meaning.

These are by no means the only prisms through which the multi-
layered text of the Bible can be refracted. There are many others,
to be sure, as I shall explain in Part III. But these are the ones that
I think are most immediate and relevant to readers who do not
come to the text with a more specialized perspective or concern.
Even those who do will not gainsay the relevance of the four with
which I shall be working.

Here I hasten to add: **none of these interpretive modes necessarily excludes the others**. In any given reading situation each one
can function by itself. Or they can all be in play together. And
when such synergy occurs, reading and contemplating the biblical text can be a thrilling and formative experience. Then we are
no longer merely reading biblical text; we are studying and expe-
riencing Torah. If in the following pages I disentangle each lens or
mode of reading from the others, from the thick interpretive mix
that is the Torah text, it is only to help the reader understand and
deploy each of them at different times. For just as no two different moments in time are identical, so no two reading experiences
are the same.

Take, for example, the Flood story in Genesis. One year you may
want to understand it historically, against the background of earlier, prebiblical accounts of that primordial event in
Mesopotamian mythology, specifically in the great Epic of Gilgamesh.[3] Or, if you are struck by what look to be duplications and
contradictions in the story, you may want to look into commentaries that show how the Flood narrative is really a combination
of two different versions that come from two different writers or
sources reflecting two different viewpoints.[4] The next year you

may want to read it midrashically, focusing on how the Rabbis understood Noah and his behavior both before and after the Deluge. And in still another year you may want to probe into the spiritual and metaphysical implications of global destruction, and of God giving up on the very world He took the trouble to create.[5] In Part III I will describe more fully these various ways in which the *Humash* can be read.

This book is written from the perspective of a Jew who understands himself as a non-Orthodox religionist, and it is written primarily for those readers who identify themselves as Jews in such terms. Some Orthodox and secularist Jews may not readily assent to the premises on which such an approach to Jewish religion rests, though I certainly do not wish to read them out of the discussion. In my attempt to understand what Torah is and what the *Humash* is, one of my starting points is the body of knowledge attainable and attained by that large, multidisciplinary enterprise known infelicitously as biblical criticism. I say starting point and not ending point because there is much more to the study and the comprehension of the Bible than source or higher criticism, valuable as I think it is. I call the term "biblical criticism" infelicitous because it smacks of a negative, even anti-Semitic attitude to the Hebrew Bible that characterized German biblical scholarship in the 19th century and is still visible in some Christian and secular Old Testament studies in the 20th. The reality is that most Bible scholars today, Jewish and non-Jewish alike, in Israel, North America, and Europe, would concur that "critical" and analytical scholarship of the TANAKH and other canonical Jewish texts, too, does not necessarily translate into a denial of their power, their insights, their values, and their authority. But anyone who finds higher criticism of the Bible objectionable or even repellent on theological grounds can safely skip my discussion of it in Part III and avail themselves of the parts of this book that they judge to be more relevant to their own interests.

Having said this, let me add that, engaged as I am by the Torah's religious ideas and their implications, I am not a theologian and I have not written this book to advance a particular theological agenda. While the reader will find in the following pages elements of a theology, it is one that is eclectic and decidedly non-systematic. In the words of Tennyson's "Ulysses," I am part of all that I have met. I have clearly been influenced by and draw on a variety of currents in modern Jewish thought, currents that on paper and in a classroom can be seen to contend with one another. Martin Buber's ideas are as formative for me as Mordecai Kaplan's, both of which I can accommodate within the broad canons of poststructuralist theory. In this I take my cue from my talmudic forebears who were quite nonsystematic in the construction of their Jewish worldviews. My own ongoing attempt to understand Judaism and the Jewish experience on this planet is grounded in what is for me an elementary fact: that Judaism and its core texts, the Bible and the two Talmuds (Babylonian and Palestinian), among many other books, did not materialize out of thin air. They were formed and developed within the purview of lived human history, not outside it in the supernatural realm to which our forebears, and the biblical text itself, were wont to ascribe them. They are, to be sure, the product and the textual record of our people's experience of the divine, but they were written by discrete human beings in discrete languages (Hebrew and Aramaic) with discrete vocabularies, terminologies, literary conventions, and biases; and they were written inside, and often in debate with, discrete social, cultural, and political contexts and codes. We need all the help we can get in ferreting out the meaning and implications of the received texts of Jewish tradition and the contexts in which they live and breathe. If comparative linguistics and comparative literature, history, archaeology, cultural anthropology, and phenomenology of religion, among other modes of inquiry, can furnish us with tools to see into and through and behind these texts, we should use them. Ismar Schorsch, the former chancellor of the Jewish Theological Seminary, has stated this point compellingly:

> **The sanctity of Scripture demands of the faithful nothing less than the vigilant retention of an open mind to unlock its meaning. In the quest for *peshat*, truth and faith are not bitter adversaries but wary allies, a set of polarities to be held in creative balance.**[6]

These words articulate the stance that I hope the following pages will reflect. If the approach is not that of Orthodoxy, neither is it that of a doctrinaire secularism. All the conceptual and analytic tools noted in the previous paragraph are, as I say, a starting point, a means to a larger end. They are not an end in themselves.

That larger end is to sharpen and deepen our understanding of the texts that comprise the five books of the Pentateuch, as Torah, as the bedrock on which our entire understanding of Judaism and our self-understanding as Jews rests. We can trace the method by which such understanding can be attained back to one Rabbi Ammi, a late 3rd- or early 4th-century Palestinian rabbi who was the head of the Rabbinic academy in Tiberias. R. Ammi enunciated the method this way:

> **One should always complete one's [private] reading of the weekly Torah Portion . . . twice in Hebrew and once in Aramaic translation [lit. *Targum*] by the time that it is read publicly by the congregation in the synagogue. . . . (Babylonian Talmud, *Berachot* 8a)**

Ultimately this is a book not so much about Bible study as about Torah study. It is a book that I hope will help you, the reader, as you make your unique and unduplicated passage through this world, read your way, from out of your time and your place, into a conversation with the Torah that has been going on among our people for centuries. And as you do so, may you, too, behold its transcendent beauty and take hold of it as a life-sustaining tree.

# 2.
# The Weekly Torah Portion:
# What Is a Parashah?

We open the *Humash* and turn to the portion of the week. Then what?

We are puzzled. What are we looking at? A finely crafted literary unit? An amorphous chunk of text?

Bible scholars would affirm both views and would not regard them as mutually exclusive. But they would not call the text amorphous. They would say that a weekly reading of a portion of the *Humash* is an assemblage of pieces of texts that are often diverse in kind and frequently speak in different voices. They would add that these pieces were not randomly assembled but arranged in an order that is meaningful and has a logic to it by an unnamed super-editor or editors they call the redactor(s). I will write more about them presently. There are, in fact, some commentators, ancient and modern, who would insist that if one knows how to look and looks hard enough, one can find some formal or esthetic principle or principles that serve to bind up and integrate a parashah into a more or less coherent unity.

Perhaps. But I must immediately make two things clear. First, when we speak of a weekly Torah portion **we are not referring to a group of chapters**. As everyone knows, the five books of the Pentateuch and the entire Hebrew Bible are divided into chapters, and verses, too. Such demarcations in the text are completely beside the point as far as this discussion goes.

> The division into chapters was made by Stephen
> Langton, later to become the Archbishop of Canter-
> bury, when he was a doctor at the University of Paris
> towards the end of the twelfth century. The division
> into verses was first made . . . by Rabbi Nathan, in
> 1448, as a help in Jewish debates with the Christians.[7]

For anyone trying to get a bearing on a weekly Torah portion, this
division into chapters and verses does not help. It may actually
hinder. The slice of Torah to be read each week presents itself to us
as a discrete unit, to be sure; but it is not a unit defined by the good
Dr. Langton's markers. Many weekly portions break right in the
middle of a chapter. So in reading Torah, the chapter and verse divisions serve only one purpose: as a reference tool. They help us
locate a particular passage or verse or word—no more than that.

Second, though Jews have for a long time now called the weekly
Torah portion a parashah, that was not the original meaning of
the term. In Rabbinic times a parashah (sometimes called a
*parashiyah*) referred to a shorter unit of text, what we would today
call a paragraph. It is paragraphs that constitute the textual units
of the *Humash*, and what breaks them up and marks the dividing
point between them is empty space. Look at a Torah scroll and
you'll see this layout (see photo on the next page).

Look very closely and you'll see that not all paragraphs, that is,
*parshiyot*, are uniform in appearance. Some are what we call
"open" and some are "closed." When a parashah ends in the middle of a line, the scribe leaves a blank space equal to the width of
nine letters, and if there is still some room left on that line, the
scribe begins writing the next section on that line. The paragraph
just completed is called a "sealed" or "closed" parashah (Heb.
*parashah setumah*). When, however, a paragraph ends in the middle of a line and the blank space extends all the way to the end of
the line, the scribe starts the next section at the beginning of the
next line. In that case the paragraph just completed is called an
"open" parashah (Heb. *parashah petuchah*). Exactly which *parshiyot*
are to be written "open" and which "closed" was stipulated by
scribal tradition a very long time ago. According to Rabbi Menachem Leibtag, "As a rule of thumb, [an open parashah] usually
indicates a major change of topic, while a [closed parashah] indicates a more subtle one, but . . . there are many exceptions.[8]

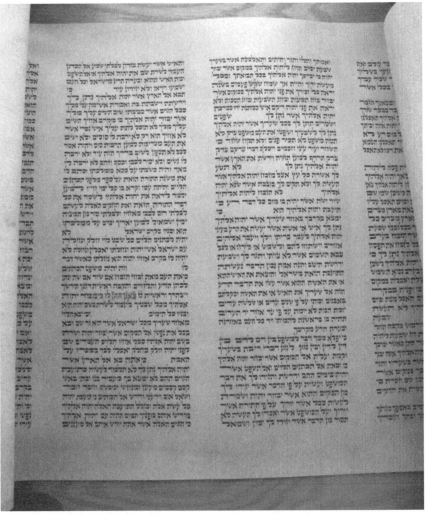

*Parashiyot* on a Torah scroll

Now none of these details has any direct bearing on what we are focusing on in this book. What we today call a weekly parashah is really a whole series or clump of *parshiyot*, that is, paragraph units (some "open" and some "closed") that have been designated as the portion of the Torah to be read during that particular week.

The chapter divisions, then, obscure our view of the weekly parashah. So, too, do the translations we read, because they preserve the division of the text into chapters.

## How many weekly portions are there in each book of the Humash?

- 12 in Genesis
- 11 in Exodus
- 10 in Leviticus
- 10 in Numbers
- 11 in Deuteronomy.

## How did the parshiyot get their names or titles?

Like the five books of the *Humash*, the Hebrew names of each weekly portion are taken from the first word or the first key word in the parashah's opening verse.

---

So we begin reading. We go from one section of the parashah of the week to the next section, and now a new perplexity arises. We notice that the textual units are quite heterogeneous. For example, we start reading a narrative and pretty soon there are detailed some laws. We keep reading and the textual scenery changes: a genealogical or some other kind of list pops up, or maybe a piece of poetry. The portion Be-ha'alotekha in Numbers is a good example of this. It is a collage of disparate kinds of texts, lists that are followed by narratives that are interlaced with laws.

Yet sometimes, when we look at other *parshiyot*, we find that they seem to be cut from whole cloth, with little apparent disturbance in the flow of the text, and they may even continue directly into the ones that follow. The portions Lekh Lekha and Va-yetse' in Genesis, which contain narratives about Abraham and Jacob, are like that. The textual units that make them up tend to be relatively large, though close inspection will show that even these seemingly smooth landscapes are dotted with little sentences and phrases that break up the narrative surface. The story of Joseph spans the last four *parshiyot* in Genesis (chapters 37–50) and is the longest sustained piece in the entire *Humash*—indeed it could almost be considered a kind of short novel. But even its unity is broken by the apparent intrusion of the story of Tamar in chapter 38 (in the portion Va-yeshev) and by the inclusion of the poem of Jacob's deathbed blessing of his sons in most of chapter 49 (in the portion Va-yeḥi). Contemplating why these chapters intrude, why the redactor(s) who put the *Humash* together spliced them in at just those places, is part of what makes reading the *Humash* so interesting.

## What kinds of texts do we find in these 54 weekly portions?

A wide variety. A general list of them is found on p. 17.

## How is one to make sense of this apparent textual hodgepodge?

In helping us answer this question we are much indebted to modern Bible scholarship. Drawing on the learnings of 20th-century textual criticism and literary theory, this voluminous body of knowledge gives us a clearer idea of what the heterogeneous parts of a parashah are and how they relate to the larger whole.

These learnings are not entirely new; they were already anticipated by the Rabbis of the Talmud and Midrash. Because they were on intimate terms with virtually every verse—indeed, every word—of the Torah, the Rabbis knew that any given parashah, discrete unit though it may be, is a part of a larger entity, namely the book in which it is situated. Every parashah has connections with what came before and with what follows—even if these connections are not immediately apparent.[9]

Consider Rabbi Levi's comment in the quotation from the Midrash on the Song of Songs cited at the beginning of this book. In expositing the verse " . . . your neck [is comely] with a string of pearls" (Songs 1:10), Rabbi Levi follows the approach to the Song of Songs that Rabbi Akiva laid down, that it is a poetic allegory of the relationship between God and Israel. In the verse in question God, the male lover, is praising the beauty of the woman who is his beloved, that is, Israel. Her fair neck, he says, is bedecked with a string, or possibly strings, of pearls (some translate this simply as jewels), which Levi interprets to represent the sections of the Torah strung together. Picking up on what I said earlier about what the word "parashah" originally meant, Rabbi Levi is probably talking about the paragraph units as he saw them arrayed on the parchment scroll. He was probably not referring to the weekly Torah portions.

But we can read him to mean that each one of the 54 portions, from the beginning of Genesis to the end of Deuteronomy, is in itself a precious and exquisite pearl, and that each of them has its place on the necklace—the Torah—which, in its totality, is an exquisite adornment on the body of Israel.

The metaphor of the five books of the Torah as a necklace, or perhaps five concentric necklaces, and the *parshiyot* as the individual pearls strung on them, works beautifully in pointing the way for how we are to read and relate to each weekly portion. There is, first of all, the implication of circularity. Reading Torah, while it seems and feels linear, is in reality a circular process. Each year on the festival of Simḥat Torah we reach the end of the book of Deuteronomy and immediately turn back to the opening of Genesis, and a new annual cycle of weekly Torah portions begins—again.

But look what else Rabbi Levi's metaphor tells us about the weekly *parshiyot*. They are:

• **strung together**

• and they **draw upon each other**

• and they **jump back and forth among each other**

• and they **resemble each other**

• and they **share affinities with each other.**

It's not clear exactly what Rabbi Levi means in this enumeration of the different ways in which the sections of the Torah interrelate. I'd parse them as follows:

The weekly Torah portions
• are strung together in a specific order;
• draw upon each other so that if you start dealing with one of them, the others will perforce assert their presence;

- jump back and forth among each other in content or style, both when they are contiguous and when they are not;
- resemble each other in spite of the fact that they differ in size and in form (i.e., narrative, law code, poetry);
- share affinities with each other in locution or phraseology or implication.

In other words, the weekly Torah portions are
- interrelated
- cross-referential
- intertextual
- and they form a continuity.

Like pearls on a necklace, each parashah is part of a larger book. And each of those larger books is part of an even larger one, namely the Pentateuch. And, as we shall soon see, the Pentateuch itself is part of a work larger yet: the TANAKH.

## Who wrote these texts and why?

Various authors over various centuries before the Common Era. As the diversity in form and content of the texts shows, the material and the books of the Pentateuch originate from several different sources or documents. This idea is what Bible scholars call "the documentary hypothesis," their educated conjecture that the *Humash* is an amalgam of different accounts and understandings of the Israelite experience, of Israelite religion, and even of the nature and nomenclature of the Israelite God. These sources are not so much the work of individual authors as they are the result of a collective effort on the part of our forebears to preserve the story of God and Israel as told by different schools of thought from different times and places in Israelite history and culture. We know these variously as the J source or school, the E source, the P source, and the D source. I will discuss them more fully in Part II. The point of knowing about them is to be able to recognize and hear their different voices in the text, and to appreciate the perspective that each one contributes to the multivocal symphony that is the *Humash* and to the TANAKH as a whole.

That said, as we read each parashah we must never lose sight of the fact that the *Humash* as a book is greater than the sum of its constituent parts and voices. The unsung and unidentified human hero or heroes of the *Humash* are not J or E or P or D but R, the redactor, whoever he—or she? or they?—may be. It was the redactor(s) who synthesized the various strands and sources of the *Humash* and infused the work with its overarching and subliminal unity. There is every possibility that this work was done by more than one individual but Bible scholars tend to speak of him in the singular. So important is his work that they often bestow on him a proper noun and speak of him as the Redactor.

## *Why five books?*

It's not clear that the Torah was always five books. Some Bible scholars think that the core is the story of the people Israel, from their beginnings in Egypt to their entry into the Promised Land. This would comprise the books of Exodus, Numbers, and the last narratives of Deuteronomy (which really are the conclusion of Numbers). At some point a collected instruction manual for *Kohanim*, that is, the book of Leviticus, was inserted between the two, as if to underscore that central to the Torah is the idea that Israel as a whole is a "kingdom of priests and a holy nation." Everett Fox calls Exodus, Leviticus, and Numbers "a trilogy in the middle of the Torah."[10] To this core an introductory collection of founding stories was, or might have been, added, telling of how the world came to be, how the human family evolved, how and where the People of Israel originated, and how—and why—they got to Egypt in the first place. The Torah thus in its earliest form may have consisted of four books—the Tetrateuch.

In time—and remember, these are educated conjectures of trained scholars based on their careful analysis of the language, style, and content of the text—these four might have been expanded to a total collection of **six** books. Deuteronomy, we believe, was written much later than the other four, perhaps in the decades just preceding the destruction of the First Temple in 586 B.C.E., and it may have been appended to them during or just after the Babylonian exile. The book of Joshua may also have been included, because by relating the details of the entry of the children of Israel into the land, the conquest, and the settlement of the 12 tribes, it provides the logical and happy ending to the whole story. In this construction some scholars believe that what we had was a Hexateuch.

## KINDS OF TEXTS FOUND IN THE *HUMASH*

- narratives emerging from ancient Near East mythology and epics (e.g., the stories in Genesis 1–11)

- narratives reflecting the collective experience and memory of the Israelite people (e.g., the stories of the Patriarchs in Genesis, the stories of the Israelites in Egypt and the desert in Exodus and Numbers)

- codes of law and morality (e.g., Exodus 21–23, Leviticus 18–19, and Deut. 12–26:15)

- textual blueprints for the *mishkan* (the Tent or Tabernacle constructed in the wilderness) (e.g., Exodus 25–40 except for the Golden Calf episode in Exodus 32–34)

- a procedural regimen for *Kohanim* (or for Moses and Aaron) on how to do sacrifices and perform other sacerdotal functions and stay pure (e.g., Leviticus 1–7)

- poems (e.g., Jacob's tribal utterances in Genesis 49, the Song of the Sea in Exodus 15, the poem of Moses in Deuteronomy 32)

- genealogy lists (e.g., the line of nations in Genesis 10, the line of Esau in Genesis 36)

- census figures (e.g., the demography of the 12 tribes in Numbers 1)

- purification procedures for impurities (e.g., after childbirth and leprosy in Leviticus 12–15)

- calendars of festival observances and sacrifices (e.g., Leviticus 23, Numbers 28 and 29, Deut. 16:1–17)

- snippets and quotations from ancient epics that have vanished (e.g., battle song from an Amorite saga in Num. 21:27–30)

- Moses' retrospective speeches (e.g., Deuteronomy 1–11)

How and why the six were reduced to the five we have on the Torah scroll that we read through annually, that is, why the book of Joshua was ultimately excluded from the Torah, is a long story. Suffice it to say here that it was not accidental that the unknown scribes or teachers who consolidated Israel's national literature wanted to end the Torah with the people still outside the land. Perhaps it was because they wanted to hold up the incompleteness or the unfulfillment of the Israelite experience as the paradigm of Jewish and human experience in history, in a world still unredeemed. After all, they themselves were in exactly that condition, in exile in Babylon after the destruction of the First Temple, which is when most scholars believe the Torah as we know it was collected. In any case, the Pentateuch or the *Humash* is what resulted and what we have today. It is the first part of what in time became the TANAKH.

**3.**

# What is the TANAKH?

TANAKH is a Hebrew acronym for the three collections of books, 39 in all, that comprise the Hebrew Bible (the Old Testament in Christian parlance).[11] Spelled out, the acronym denotes the three parts as:

- **Torah**, that is, the Five Books of Moses, a.k.a. the Pentateuch or the *Humash*
- **Nevi'im**, Hebrew for "Prophets"
- **Kethuvim**, Hebrew for "Writings" or "Scriptures."

## What books are contained in each part?

Here is the breakdown:

1. **Torah**
   Genesis
   Exodus
   Leviticus
   Numbers
   Deuteronomy

2. **Nevi'im**
   Joshua
   Judges
   1 Samuel
   2 Samuel
   1 Kings

2 Kings
Isaiah
Jeremiah
Ezekiel
Hosea ⎤
Joel
Amos
Obadiah
Jonah
Micah        The 12 Minor Prophets
Nahum
Habakkuk
Zephaniah
Haggai
Zechariah
Malachi ⎦

3. **Kethuvim**
Psalms
Proverbs
Job
The Song of Songs ⎤
Ruth
Lamentations        The Five Megillot (Scrolls)
Ecclesiastes
Esther ⎦
Daniel
Ezra
Nehemiah
1 Chronicles
2 Chronicles

## When were these books written?

They came into existence over a long period of time, perhaps a thousand years. The earliest ones, the narratives of Genesis and Exodus, go back, as written works, as far as the 8th or 7th century B.C.E. and probably originated even before then as oral tellings of ancestral tales. The poems in Exodus 15 (the Song of the Sea) and Deuteronomy 32 (Moses' swan song) are also very old. The latest parts of the TANAKH are parts of the book of Daniel that come from the time of the Maccabean wars of 165 B.C.E. There is a range of scholarly opinion on these matters.

The 39 books make up what we call the biblical canon. Canon is the technical term for their status as the historically sanctioned and acknowledged collection of texts that together present and preserve the national experience and culture—stories, teachings, and laws—of the people of Israel as they accumulated and solidified over the centuries we now know as the biblical period. Canonization seems to have been a gradual process, not an event. The Pentateuch was canonized first, quite possibly during the Babylonian exile (586–ca. 539 B.C.E.) or just afterward, and the Nevi'im and Kethuvim sections of the TANAKH in succeeding centuries. There were several other books that could have been included and, in fact, were considered, but in the end did not make the cut. These are such books as 1 Maccabees, Judith, Tobit, and Ben Sira. These books became part of an extrabiblical collection called the Apocrypha. They are included in the Protestant (and, more selectively, in the Roman Catholic) canons, that is, the Old Testament. The biblical canon was finally closed by the Rabbis at the end of the 1st or sometime in the 2nd century of the Common Era.

### Do we ever get to read from the second and third parts of the TANAKH?

We do, but only selectively, that is, certain parts on certain occasions.

On every *Shabbat* and major festival day we read a passage from one of the Nevi'im books at the conclusion of the Torah reading for that day. This is the **haftarah** ("finishing up") that, when the occasion warrants, bar and bat mitzvah celebrants or honored guests chant.

It is not clear just when or why this practice originated. Some scholars think it began early in the Second Temple period, when the returnees from the Babylonian exile faced the challenge of the local Samaritans who held that only the Torah was divine. By selecting a passage from the prophets to be read each *Shabbat* along with the weekly Torah portion, the Judeans (or Jews, as they now can be called) countered the Samaritan claims.

Another view locates the institution of reading a passage from the prophets in the synagogue on *Shabbat* later in Second Temple times, when the Seleucids occupied Judea. In their drive to stamp out religious and cultural particularism and promote a universal Hellenistic polity, the Seleucids forbade the weekly public reading from the Pentateuch but permitted it from other parts of the TANAKH. Accordingly, the Jewish religious leaders—we don't know exactly who they were—selected for each *Shabbat*, and for each major festival, a passage from the Nevi'im that had some connection with the portion of the Torah that would have been read on that particular day. Sometimes the connection was obvious, because it was either literal or thematic, and sometimes it was more subtle. Later, when the prohibition against reading from the Torah was rescinded, the prophetic portion was retained and read at the conclusion of the Torah reading as a supplement, just as we do today.[12]

From the Kethuvim we read only from Psalms during parts of the service, and, in most synagogues, from the five *megillot* (scrolls) as follows:

- The Song of Songs on Passover
- Ruth on Shavuot
- Lamentations on Tisha b'Av
- Ecclesiastes on Sukkot
- Esther on Purim.

Proverbs and Job are left to be read privately, as are Daniel, Ezra, Nehemiah, and 1 and 2 Chronicles. My hunch is that in this regard the former two fare only a little better than the latter four (or five), which is a shame.

### What does all this mean for where we're going in this discussion: how to read a weekly Torah portion?

It means that if you take an aerial view of any given parashah within the context of the whole TANAKH, you see that it is the innermost of three concentric anthologies:

1. the book within which it is situated, that is, Genesis, Exodus, etc.;
2. the five books within which that book is situated, that is, the *Humash*;

3. the 39 books within which those five are situated, that is, the TANAKH.

The operative word here is **anthology**. That's how we should think about the TANAKH and its constituent parts. The TANAKH is the grand anthology of the 39 canonical books. The *Humash* is an anthology of five books. The book in which a given parashah is situated is an anthology of *parshiyot*. And the parashah itself is an anthology of diverse textual units.

What is an anthology? Think of the Norton anthologies of poetry or the series of collections that Oxford University Press puts out regularly: *The Best Short Stories of* . . . or *The Best Essays of* . . . of the year or of a certain writer. An anthology is an assemblage of written items that someone decided to

- select
- collect
- and place or present in a specific order.

The ultimate challenge in reading an anthology—any anthology—is to know the guiding principles that inform the collection:

- to know what the anthologist had in mind when he or she selected just those pieces or works for the anthology;
- to know where he found them or took them from;
- and to know why she arranged them in just that way.

It certainly helps when the reader knows who the anthologist is. Sometimes, in contemporary anthologies, the anthologist tells up front what her criteria for selection were and how she made her decisions about inclusion and presentation.

But in the case of the anthologies we are talking about here, whether parashah or *Humash* or TANAKH, we don't know exactly who did the selecting, collecting, and presenting. We have only scholarly conjectures. One of the foremost students of Jewish anthologies, David Stern, holds that "unlike beauty, which lies in the mind of the beholder, the meaning of an anthologized text always lies in the mind of its compiler."[13]

**Always**? Then we are in an impossible situation when we read a parashah. For to know the meaning of the complex of words and verses and textual units we see on the page, and the order in which we find them, we need to know who the compiler was—and we cannot know this. I'd quibble, then, with this "always." In Part II I will discuss whether it's possible that meaning also lies in the mind of the reader who, the anthologizer notwithstanding, is driven to discover on his or her own the cords that bind an anthology like a parsahah together.

So when we read a given parashah we should ideally employ a double-barreled perspective:

- a **microscopic** one that looks at the parashah in its individuality, not as an amorphous mass of text but as a series of units set out in a sequence that is not random;
- a **macroscopic** one that sees it in the larger context of the anthological circles of which it is a part and which encompass it.

The macroscopic approach is admittedly a tall order. It is probably only achievable after years of both Bible study and weekly shul-going—and I would emphasize the both/and. My focus in this book will be mostly on the microscopic aspects of each parashah, though it will be hard to overlook totally the macroscopic dimension.

# 4.
# Bible and Torah:
# What Is the Difference?

Perhaps you have noticed that throughout this discussion so far I have freely interchanged the terms by which I have referred to the texts we are concerned with here. Sometimes I have called the five books on the Torah scroll the Pentateuch and sometimes the *Humash* or the Torah. Sometimes I have called the whole collection of the 39 books "the Bible" and sometimes "the TANAKH." The time has come to note that these different terminologies bespeak two very different ways of talking about the same material, two different discursive modes. Each one has its own set of assumptions about this material and each one has its own separate way of dealing with it.

Can you sense the difference between referring to the five books as the Pentateuch and calling them the Torah? The former has a more objective ring to it. It puts some distance between us and the material. This is appropriate for a discipline like academic Bible scholarship that seeks to read and examine and understand the text dispassionately. Like any text, the books of the Pentateuch, and the entire Bible, are susceptible to critical analysis. All questions about them are admissible: their authorship, their authority, their meaning and implication.

But calling or understanding these books, be they the five or the 39, "Torah" is to assign to them a special status and to read them in a different light. Now there is a distinct preunderstanding about them: that they are not secular but holy texts. They have, in one way or another—and there is substantial and profound disagreement among different Jews and Jewish reading communities on this point—a claim on our Jewish self-understanding, on our values, and, above all, on how we live our lives from day to day. To be sure, in this discursive framework these texts can be analyzed and interpreted, too. But here the analyses and the interpretations are all governed by the overriding conviction that they represent the will and/or concern of God, specifically as they pertain to the Jews as a collective entity and to the Jew in his or her individuality. Jewish tradition and Jewish thought, ancient, medieval, and modern, have many differing, and sometimes conflicting, understandings of this central belief. Briefly put they range from

- a certainty that God revealed His[14] will in the Torah and/or initiated His covenant with Israel at Mount Sinai as described in chapter 19 of Exodus (Torah portion Yitro)

- to an affirmation that there was at Sinai an encounter and a covenant between God and Israel, but that it may not have happened exactly as the account in Exodus tells it

- to a hallowing of these texts not because they were divinely revealed but because they represent the collective memory of the People of Israel and their millennial self-understanding, values, and aspirations.

This is, of course, a capsule description of very complex matters that are beyond the scope of this discussion. But even in this shorthand version, note the progression, the ratcheting down of assumptions made about the role of God and, correspondingly, what religious thinkers would call the ontological status of Torah. The trajectory is from an unabashed supernaturalism to a principled humanism. In the first view God is the preeminent agent in the divine-human encounter; He revealed His will to the People of Israel. In the third view, man is the preeminent agent; he discovers God's presence in the text by his own lights. In the second view there is a conscious equivocation about the nature of the interplay between God and man.

Yet these differences—and they are profound differences—notwithstanding, all these perspectives share the conviction that the books and the texts that make up the TANAKH are Torah, are holy, and have a claim on us as Jews. They may differ in the nature and the details of that claim but they are all clear that the TANAKH is something more, much more, than a great and abiding work of literature. In the end, when the supernaturalists and the humanists and the equivocators all assemble in their respective and diverse synagogues or prayer groups on *Shabbat* mornings, it is a reading of a portion from the *Humash* that they see and hear in their respective ways and not a performance of one of Shakespeare's plays.

In sum, there are two ways we can approach the unit of text we are bidden to read each week. We can locate it by picking up a book that is a Pentateuch and at the same time is also a *Humash*. We can look at the text both as a specimen of biblical literature and as a portion of Torah. The two approaches are not mutually exclusive. As I noted in the preface, they are mutually inclusive, even synergetic. For we read with our whole being, with mind and heart.

Let's now see what this entails.

# PART II

# Reading and Hearing

# 1.

# On Reading

What happens when we read? A lot. More than meets the eye. What happens is an ongoing exchange between three parties: the text, the author, and the reader. (There is also a fourth presence hovering silently in the background, but I'll come to that later.) In any act of reading each of these three "players" asserts itself and, in doing so, presents specific issues and problems. When we are reading the weekly Torah portion, there are some particular ones to note. Let's consider them.

## The Text

It's one thing to read a text that is part of our universe of discourse, like an article in the *New York Times* or *Newsweek*. It's quite another to read a parashah. For when we do we are tricked by an interesting optical illusion. We perceive the stories of Genesis or the laws of Deuteronomy within the covers of a bound book mechanically produced in the 20th or 21st century. The text sits there on a neatly printed page, set in contemporary typescript. And so, though we know we are reading the Bible, we begin to think, however subliminally, that the words and sentences we are taking in are much like the words and sentences we'd read in the *New York Times* or *Newsweek*, and the chapters we see are of the same order as the chapters in a novel by Toni Morrison or Charles Dickens. We lose sight of the fact that what faces us on the page is very, very old.

We wouldn't be deceived in this way by ancient buildings or monuments. We wouldn't, for example, look at the Western Wall in Jerusalem or the ruins at Megiddo or Jericho and think that they are of the same age and architecture or built of the same material as such modern structures as the Empire State Building or the Golden Gate Bridge or even the Eiffel Tower. Yet the stories in Genesis and the laws in Deuteronomy, not to mention the very words out of which they are made, are no less ancient than the stones of the Western Wall or Megiddo, however contemporary they may look typographically. Most of us probably read them with the conventions and expectations we have been conditioned to bring to the reading experience from our familiarity with more recent literature. The Joseph story cycle, for example, which occupies nearly the last third of Genesis, feels novelistic in the sweep of its plot and its intimations of character, and so we are blithely attuned to reading it more or less as we would read *A Tale of Two Cities* or *Crime and Punishment*. We make assumptions about the narrative and we ask questions about it similar to those we would ask about novels.

But is making such a facile literary connection warranted? Is the connection itself workable? The Joseph story, indeed Genesis as a whole, is not a novel in the formal sense of what, after the 17th century, came to be known as the novel. In fact, each of the five books of the Pentateuch defies formal definition within modern literary categories. Genesis and Exodus are two very different kinds of works. Both are radically different from Leviticus, and Deuteronomy has its own distinctiveness. Numbers is something else again. These works have no precise formal equivalents, neither in the literatures of modernity nor of antiquity (although in the latter case there are some broad affinities).

Then there is the matter of translation. It is one thing to read the *Humash* or the TANAKH in Hebrew. That alone presents a wide array of interpretive problems, to say the least. But to read a biblical text in translation creates a whole new tier of concerns. Nuances are lost (and sometimes gained, erroneously) because of lexical differences between Hebrew and English and the disparities in syntax between the two linguistic systems.

I note all this not to throw up roadblocks to novice parashah readers. My point here is that when we open to a Torah portion we need to take into account the antiquity and the distinctiveness of what we are looking at.

# The Author

Now things get even more interesting.

When we pick up a book by Toni Morrison or even by Dr. Seuss, we know who the author is. We can use this information to help us understand the book and determine its meaning. We can speculate what the author's intentions in writing this book were. We can, or at least we think we can, get a fix on authorial intention by availing ourselves of information about the author. We can look into her biography, her artistic development, and try to identify the writers and books that influenced her.

With the Pentateuch this is not so easy. None of the five books comes with a visible by-line (though Deuteronomy invites us to see one). How do we speak of an author when each of the books we are dealing with is a composite of writings from several authors that has been redacted into a unified work? This potpourri effect is most pronounced in Numbers, where we see a textual salad of narrative, census data, and a catalogue of sacrifices, laws, poems, etc.

I'm getting ahead of myself here. The question of the authorship of the Torah is in fact a vexed one on which there are many views. Theologically it is the fault line that divides traditionalist and modernist Jews. The preceding paragraph shows my modernist perspective.[1] Within the framework of a modernist approach the Bible is the product of human hands. Within the traditionalist framework the question of authorship is a nonstarter: the five books were not edited or redacted; they were divinely revealed by God through Moses.

Theology is not a main preoccupation among most Jews today. But here we are willy-nilly immersed in a theological issue, a big one. At the root of this issue is the question of Revelation, of just how we are to understand the nature of how the two parties, God and the People of Israel, interact. Traditionalists slide the metaphorical lever over to the side of God. Revelation is top down: God supernaturally communicated His will to Moses and Israel at Sinai. Moses wrote down the revealed text at the divine behest (though some talmudic Rabbis move the lever slightly over to the human side and suggest that Joshua penned the closing verses about Moses' death). The source of the Torah text is in Heaven. We do not and cannot speak of any human author or authors of the *Humash* but of its Author. Nor need we speculate about that Author's intention; it is enshrined in the corpus of Rabbinic interpretation of the Torah that comprises the Talmud and the Midrash, and in the codes of Jewish law that resulted from that interpretation.

Modernists slide the lever over to the human side. Revelation was—and still is—bottom up: the People of Israel discover(ed) God's will through the processes of lived experience. The source of the Torah text is human. The people related their understanding (more precisely, their understandings) of God and God's will in their own words, at first orally and, later on, in writing.

I believe the place for the lever to be set is in the middle. To me the question of the authorship of the Pentateuch is not a matter of "either/or." In my view it is not fair to either side in the divine-human encounter to say that the *Humash* is either divine in nature because of its Author or that it is a strictly human document because we can discern its edited and redacted nature; that it has authority because it was revealed by God or that it is simply a construction of reality by certain human beings at a certain time in history and therefore has no special claim on how we are to live now.

Rather, I see the issue of authorship as a matter of "both/and." The Pentateuch was both written by human hands and its text contains the revealed will of God; the five books are both the Pentateuch and also the Torah. The *Humash* shows us the primal encounter of the Jewish people and God. They meet each other in its text. If the text does not have a supernaturally divine Author, a consciousness of the Divine informs it. And it has authority. It has authority because it enshrines an experience of God that led to a certain vision of the world, a certain vision of human nature and responsibility, and a certain way of living in this world; and because the Jewish people in its first days made an irrevocable commitment to this multidimensional vision and preserved it in writing as its Torah.

In sum, in the modernist view taken in these pages there is no one author of the Torah and its vision. The key figure who synthesized its various elements is the Redactor of the Pentateuch. It is to that Redactor or Redactors we should pay attention as we read the Torah portion each week.

# THE MAIN SOURCES
# OF THE PENTATEUCH

## As Contemporary Mainline Scholarship Understands Them

**J**—An early telling of the history of Israel from the Creation through the Patriarchs, Joseph, Moses, the Exodus, the Sinai Revelation, and the desert wanderings. This material circulated orally as far back as the second pre-Christian millennium and is believed to have been written in the Southern Kingdom of Judah sometime between 922 B.C.E. (when David's kingdom split in two) and 722 B.C.E. (when the Northern Kingdom of Israel fell). Hence its favoring of Judah over firstborn Reuben in its version of the stories of Jacob's sons. It was called "J" by 19th-century German scholars because its writer always refers to God as YHWH (Jahwe in German).

**E**—An account similar to J also derived from earlier oral traditions, though it begins not with the creation but with Abraham. It has material in it not found in J. It is believed to have possibly been written in the Northern Kingdom of Israel around the same time as J. It consistently favors Moses over Aaron, whose descendants held sway down in Jerusalem. It is called "E" because it consistently refers to God as "*Elohim*" or "*El*." Recent Bible scholarship has put this source in question as a separate text, now regarding it as possibly a variant of J.

**P**—An alternative version of what J and E relate plus more. It is believed to stem from the *Kohanim* in Jerusalem (hence its "priestly" origin and name "P") who understood the central event in the history of Israel to be not the Revelation of Torah to Moses at Sinai but the abiding presence of the glory of God in the Temple and in the sacrificial regimen run by Aaron and his descendants. The P source retells large parts of the stories in Genesis, Exodus, and Numbers in the light of this priestly perspective and comprises all of Leviticus, which makes it the biggest of the sources. It is believed to have been written sometime between the fall of the Northern Kingdom in 722 B.C.E. and the reforms of King Josiah around 621 B.C.E.

D—An attempt to present the full story of the People of Israel not so much as a project in holiness (as P would have it) but more as the living out of a covenant between them and God that was made at Sinai (which it calls Horeb) when Moses (who is the key player, not Aaron) received and wrote down a Torah book. D scripts the book of Deuteronomy as a series of farewell addresses by Moses in which he spells out the details of how the Torah of the Sinai covenant is to be actualized in biblical society. D thus extends past Deuteronomy into the books of Joshua, Judges, Samuel, and Kings. The books of D are believed to have been written in Jerusalem during the reign of King Josiah (640–609 B.C.E.).

Now what did the Redactor redact? Bible scholars have been studying this question for a long time. The investigation continues even in our day, principally in Israel, North America, and Europe. The conclusions and conjectures of this collective enterprise are complex and technical, and they are well beyond the scope of this discussion. What they boil down to is a consensus about what scholars as far back as the 17th and 18th centuries (the philosopher Baruch Spinoza being one of them) suspected and what 19th- and 20th-century scholars have upheld: that the Pentateuch is an artful stitching together of a number of texts. These texts are diverse. They relate to the history, the self-understanding, the rituals, and the moral values of the various Israelite tribes that emerged out of the ancient Near East and then around 1200 B.C.E. became the People of Israel, and then, after the Babylonian exile in 586 B.C.E., the Jewish people.

Like any family, a people wants to tell its story and preserve its most formative memories. It usually begins to do this orally, pass-

ing down from parent to child the exploits and foibles of the forebears. Those exploits and foibles may well have actually taken
place, but collective telling and retelling over time inevitably em-
bellishes the details and transforms the **history** of a people into
national **epic. It is the epic (sometimes called saga or chronicle),
not the historical details, that becomes important in a people's
collective memory,** for it is the epic that synthesizes all the stories
into The Story, the grand narrative that articulates the people's
deepest understanding of what it is about. Eventually the epic
gets written down and becomes a text, a text that is cherished and
revered, and, as it is lovingly read and reread, it is faithfully preserved and transmitted from generation to generation.

That is roughly the process that led to the production of the five
books of the *Humash* and later, at the end of the biblical period, the
39 books of the TANAKH anthology. There is general agreement
among biblical scholars today that the *Humash* represents a synthesis of four basic literary sources that had currency at various times
in ancient Israel. In biblical studies this understanding is known as
"the documentary hypothesis."[2] Each source comprises a document that puts forth its distinctive version or understanding of the
history and the meaning of the relationship between the People of
Israel and its God. These sources are listed on pp. 34–35.

Based on these sources, the books of the *Humash* look something
like this:

> **GENESIS**: basically J, with E's and P's versions spliced in
> at certain places.
>
> **EXODUS**: J, E, and P material intermingled.
>
> **LEVITICUS**: strictly P content.
>
> **NUMBERS**: mostly P, with J's and E's material at selected
> places.
>
> **DEUTERONOMY**: All D.[3]

In Part III I will consider how this identification of these sources
and an awareness of their presence in the text can sometimes
help, and sometimes hinder, us in our attempt to read a weekly
*parashah*. But now I want to say some things about the third par-
ticipant in the act of reading.

# The Reader

In the act of reading it is the reader who in many ways is the key figure. Without the reader there would be no reading. The author has done his thing; the text exists; it is the reader who, in opening the book, closes the interpretive circuit and turns on the interplay between the three parties.

But who is the reader? What can we say about him or her? How can we generalize? Just as every human face is different, so is every human mind. Each of us takes in and processes the world in a unique way. Each of us comes to the text, any text, whether it be a novel or a newspaper article or the *Humash*, with our own baggage, a considerable amount of baggage, in fact. We read in the first place with our own personal perspectives, with our own particular assumptions about life and the world, our own preferences and preconceived notions and hot buttons, and within the bounds and the limitations of our own knowledge. Second, we read from under the particular social and cultural and generational horizon in which we live and were formed, its values and its biases. We are not our parents or our grandparents, and we don't read as they did. Our world is different. We certainly don't read like the Rabbis of talmudic antiquity. In other words, the reader does not come to the text empty-handed.

I note all this because it has a bearing on how we will read a weekly Torah portion. Here's why.

I've described the act of reading as an interplay or an exchange among author, text, and reader. Actually, what transpires is more than an interplay. It's a tussle, a tussle over what the text **means**, and over **who decides** this meaning. The author is a party to this tussle because, after all, she wrote the text in the first place and surely had something in mind when she did that. The reader is involved because he is, after all, the one who is taking in the text at this moment, the author having checked out when she delivered her text to the printer. The text, for its part, sits there silently on the printed page, buffeted about by the creative energy of the author and the interpretive energy of the reader. The former says (putatively), "I wrote this thing and I think I know what I meant when I wrote it." The latter says (tacitly), "I'm the one holding this thing right now and I think I know what it means as I read it."

Who decides?

Many contemporary theorists of literature say that it's the reader. In the silent struggle to determine what a text means, it is the reader who ultimately holds the balance of power. The author (and to some readers of the Bible, the Author) is, for all intents and purposes, dead, out of the picture in any case.

This makes other theorists uneasy, for it turns reading into a totally subjective experience, and it regards interpretation, that is, the assignment of meaning, as totally subject to the particularities and vagaries of the reader that I noted above. That would make all interpretation relative and not absolute, and meaning contingent and not stable. One reader could say that *Macbeth* is a tragedy and another could say *Macbeth* is a comedy. Who would be right? Is there any way out of such subjectivity?

In the case of a text that hasn't been around a long time, like a newspaper article or an op-ed piece, there may not be. Different readers will come away from such texts with different understandings and interpretations. But with texts that have had staying power and have been read over many decades and centuries and millennia, there is a way to get beyond the inherent subjectivity of reading. Texts of this kind, whether secular ones like Dostoyevski's novels or Shakespeare's plays or religious ones like the Pentateuch or the Koran, are **canonical**. They have achieved this status because every generation that has read them has found in them artistic beauty, emotional power, intellectual brilliance, profound insight into human reality, and, above all, a relevance that is undiminished over the passing of time. With texts like these the inherent subjectivity of reading is checked by the fact that generations of readers have upheld the interpretation of their forebears. Such texts, we say, belong not only or merely to individual readers with all their particular quirks, but to **reading communities**.[4] Their meaning may have been and may still be relative and contingent, but it is stable. *Hamlet*, for example, has been deemed a definitive exploration of the vagaries and depths of the human heart regardless of whether it does or does not confirm the reality of Oedipal theory.

The Pentateuch, the entire TANAKH for that matter, is the ultimate canonical text. It is canonical to not one but two reading communities, a Jewish one and a Christian one. Over the centuries each of them has spilled an inordinate amount of ink—and blood—arguing and demonstrating that its reading of the text is the correct one. The meanings they have respectively assigned to individual verses and to the various books and to the Book as a whole have, to be sure, been subjectively determined. They are contingent on the assumptions (in this case theological assumptions about God and man) that each community has brought—and brings—to the text. But within each reading community, Jewish and Christian, these meanings have been, over time, more or less stable. To Jews the Bible is the TANAKH; to Christians it is the Old Testament.

What about those readers to whom it is neither of these? In their case a different kind of collective subjectivity will operate. Atheists, agnostics, and humanists will approach it much as they would works by Dante or Milton, as a document of a different canon, the secular canon of Western culture. Likewise, Muslims or Buddhists will read the Hebrew Bible within the premises of their particular faith communities. In any case reading the TANAKH is never an exercise in solipsism. There is always some reading community, its values and assumptions, that is the silent fourth player in the three-way encounter between author, text, and reader.

# 2.
# Reading the *Humash*

Generally, then, when we read a parashah, whether in the synagogue, at home, or in a library, the presence of the reading community within which we are situated is taken for granted. We are often not aware of it. That is why I have called it a silent player. But whichever one it is, Jewish or Christian or secular, it serves an important function: it qualifies the essential subjectivity of our engagement with the text. It impedes our advancing willful or idiosyncratic or even bizarre interpretations.

With the *Humash* there are other features that are not so subtle that not only qualify our subjectivity but actually subvert it. These are aspects of the text that call attention to themselves, things like the repetition of words and phrases and the juxtaposition of people and events. There are sometimes quirky observations by the narrator. It's hard to read the *Humash* for too long without realizing that we are in the hands of a writer or a redactor who seems to take delight in surprising us. We will examine these things more closely in Part IV when I'll go through the actual mechanics of reading a parashah. I note them here in order to bring this whole discussion full circle.

If it's fashionable in literary circles today to say that in the three-way exchange that goes on in the act of reading among author, text, and reader, it is the reader who holds the balance of power in determining meaning, in the case of the *Humash* the three agents are in equilibrium. The text is not nearly as pliable in the reader's hands as a modern text would be, and the redactor is by no means the passive secretary of an anthological committee. Text and redactor are almost as objectively present during the reading as the reader. So when we read the *Humash* and the text in question is the weekly Torah portion, we should not be too hasty to hand all the interpretive keys over to the reader.

In sum, here are some things to keep firmly in mind when we open a *Humash* and begin reading the weekly parashah:

- The text, though its meanings may be fresh and contemporary, is not from our time. Though we see it in modern typescript, it is suffused with antiquity. And if we are working from a translation, we are at an even further remove from the words and the syntax of the Hebrew original.

- The author is unknown and unknowable regardless of how we understand who this author is and when he wrote. We can believe that the author is God, or God through the medium of Moses. Or we can posit, as I do, that the hands of several authors are in evidence and what we're reading is a synthesis of their work into a unified whole, selected, compiled, and arranged by an anonymous redactor, a redactor with literary designs and a point of view.

- As readers we absorb the *Humash* through the prism of our individuality and our subjectivity. This prism need not be a prison if we are aware of the particular assumptions and biases that we bring to the text, and if we recognize that our subjectivity is not only individual but collective. For whether we know it or not, we read inside the cultural or theological premises of some social group, be it religious or secular. We may not always be conscious of these premises, but they are always vectors on how we read.

All this said, reading is not the only way in which we take in the Torah. There is another cognitive mode by which we do so, by which it invites us to do so: hearing.

# 3.

# On Hearing

One of the greatest transformations Judaism ever underwent was when it became a textual religion. Stories and laws that had been transmitted orally and received aurally were written down to be interpreted by reading. We don't know exactly when this metamorphosis of spoken word to written text occurred. Was it when the Judeans went into exile? Or during the exile? Or perhaps when Ezra brought a (the?) Torah document from Babylon to Judea (then called Yehud) in 458 B.C.E.? Perhaps the beginnings of this sea change in biblical religion predate the exile; the book of Deuteronomy (622 B.C.E.) already speaks of the Torah as a text, even though the will of God was still being proclaimed in mantic utterances by the prophets as God's appointed spokesmen (a few of whom were women). Whenever it was, by the end of the Babylonian exile the effect of the change was consequential. By then, even though there were still a few late prophets who would be heard from, God's will was securely installed in the written word to be explicated by God-inspired authorized interpreters. In time, the rabbi replaced the prophet, Judaism became a religion of reading, and the Jews became the People of the Book.

We should, therefore, always bear in mind that the Torah was spoken and heard before it was written and read. This observation accords with all the otherwise conflicting understandings of the Pentateuch; modern historical criticism, on the one hand, and the great medieval commentators and the Rabbinic tradition, on the other, agree with it. It is also how the Torah understands itself. The book of Exodus presents the Sinai event as a dialectic between hearing and seeing. In the passage just after the Ten Commandments we read, "All the people **witnessed the thunder** and lightning" . . . (Exod. 20:15). A few verses later God says to Moses: "Thus shall you say to the Israelites: You yourselves **saw that I spoke** to you from the very heavens" (20:19). Both senses, seeing and hearing, are in play here. But we get the idea that seeing is primary. This seems to be confirmed a bit later on. In the account of the miraculous deliverance at the Sea of Reeds, seeing is believing: "And when Israel saw the wondrous power which the LORD had wielded against the Egyptians . . . they had faith in the LORD and His servant Moses" (14:31).

Over against this is a strong strand of biblical thinking that regards hearing, not seeing, as the royal road to belief. The fundamental creedal affirmation of the Torah is couched in auditory terms: "*Shema Yisra'el*, Hear O Israel, The LORD is our God, the LORD alone" (Deut. 6:4). In fact, the opening words of each of the first two paragraphs of the *Shema* (6:4 and 11:13) stress the necessity of hearing. There are many other passages from all over the TANAKH that I could cite that make it clear that in biblical religion hearing is something far more than an auditory experience. It is an act of absorbing words and language and introjecting their import into our very being.

We are probably on firmer ground if we say that the Bible privileges both hearing and seeing.[5] If the first two paragraphs of the *Shema* foreground hearing, the third paragraph, which details the commandment to "see" the tzitzit (Num. 15:37–41), balances things off by holding up seeing as the pathway to awareness. Both cognitive modes lead in different ways to understanding, or at least to the beginning of an understanding, of what the world presents to us, what the world means, indeed what the nature of the reality into which we were cast when we were born means.

We have an interesting debate on this matter in the Midrash, between the two major schools of Rabbinic interpretation, that of Rabbi Ishmael and that of Rabbi Akiva. Rabbi Ishmael reads Exod. 19:15, "All the people **witnessed the thunder** and lightning," as an elliptical statement: "They [the Israelites] saw what was visible and heard what was audible." Rabbi Akiva parses the verse quite differently: it is telling us that the people "saw and heard what was visible."[6] For Rabbi Ishmael both cognitive modes functioned at Sinai in tandem, on an equal basis. For Rabbi Akiva the experience was beyond the cognitive. At Sinai the people experienced sensory overload; sound and sight were intermingled in a moment of what we call synesthesia.

It would be nice to think that the perspectives of both these architects of Judaism are honored when the Sinai event is reenacted by the public reading of the Torah in synagogues today. Rabbi Akiva's, I think, is not. In how many synagogues these days do the people stand and listen in silent, rapt attention, transfixed and transformed by the voice of the text? Rabbi Ishmael's view is presumably closer to our reality. The *baal korei* (the Torah reader) sees the text on the scroll and declaims it aloud, and the people in the congregation hear it and follow it on the printed page. Seeing and reading are in equilibrium with chanting and hearing.

At home, though, it all happens differently. There we have to do double duty. We have to read the text—to ourselves—and at the same time hear it.

# 4.
# Hearing the *Humash*

What does it mean to **hear** the Torah? How do we do this?

One way, of course, is to hear the text chanted by the Torah reader during the services on *Shabbat* morning and other designated times. Each word has its own distinctive melody or trope based on a chanting, or cantillation, system that goes back farther than any other aspect of reading the Torah.

> **The medieval Jewish sources ascribe a Divine origin to cantillation. They taught that Moses heard the voice of God chanting the Torah at Sinai, and Moses began the process of orally transmitting that tradition through the generations until it was finally put into writing.**[7]

More historically,

> **Avenary notes that in the practices of reading scripture in every Asiatic tradition, from Vedic recitation in India to Buddhist recitation in Japan, none is spoken, none is sung: all are cantillated in a system resembling that of the Jews.**[8]

The trope for each word, then, is very old, much older than the cantillation markings, called in Hebrew *te'amim*, that were in time devised to be placed over or under each word of the Pentateuch to denote the specific melody for that particular word. During the late Rabbinic period and in the early Middle Ages there were, apparently, several different ways in which the *te'amin* could be marked, just as there were several different ways in which an individual trope could be sung. The former were finally fixed by the

Masoretes (see p. 47), most particularly by Rabbi Aharon ben Asher and his school in the 10th century. Ben Asher developed a clear set of visual signifiers for the *te'amin* to indicate how each word would be chanted and accented. This is known as the Tiberian notation system. It became the standard for Jews the world over and is in use to this day.

In printed editions of the *Humash* these Masoretic *te'amim* symbols are visible over each and every word. The Masoretes placed them at the point of accentuation of the word, an important fact that many Torah readers seem to overlook. The symbols are absent from the script of the Torah scroll itself (as are all Masoretic notes) and have to be memorized by the *baal korei*. Such memorization constitutes the lion's share of what a bar or bat mitzvah must accomplish for the performative aspect of the big event.[9] Generally, the *te'amim* follow the sense of the words and the Hebrew syntax, and so if one is familiar with them and their patterns, they provide steady direction to the construction of each verse. But not always; sometimes, as the Rabbis in the Talmud already noticed, the trope is at variance with how we break up a verse.

Now while the trope sign for each word was fixed, the actual melodies by which they were chanted were not. The trope we hear in synagogues that follow Ashkenazic (north European) rite sounds different from trope we hear in Sephardic (Spanish-Mediterranean) congregations. Even within these broad categories there are regional variations. Polish and German trope are not quite same, though both are Ashkenazic, and Iraqi and Moroccan Torah chanting are unmistakably different, though both are Sephardic. And the trope of Yemenite communities is something else again.

But hearing the Bible is different from reading it in another way. To understand this way we must look to Martin Buber (1878–1965) and Franz Rosenzweig (1886–1929), two of the most eminent Jewish thinkers of the 20th century. In the great flowering of serious Jewish adult learning that took place in pre-Holocaust Germany, Buber and Rosenzweig wanted to bring to the fore the original oral/aural nature of the Bible. They did this by striving to craft a German translation of the Bible that they hoped would enable modern readers to experience the text auditorily and not only visually.[10] My discussion here follows their main ideas.

## WHO WERE THE MASORETES?

By the end of the 9th century the need was recognized to definitively fix the text of the TANAKH as it had come down from preceding centuries so that future generations would possess a correct and authoritative version. The Ben Asher family, working in Tiberias, on the shore of the Sea of Galilee, instituted a scribal school that, in the 10th century, accomplished these important tasks. They did several things that helped standardize how the Torah was written, read, and heard. They pointed the text, introducing a system of vowel signifiers and dots in certain letters so as to indicate exactly how each word should be pronounced (necessary since only consonants are written on the Torah scroll). They made notes in and around the text about where the paragraphs should break, spelling, and other textual anomalies. They did a verse count for each parashah and for each of the five books, a verse, word, and letter count for the entire *Humash*, and a verse count for each of the subsequent books in the TANAKH. And, most important for our purposes, they introduced a notation system for the cantillation (the *te'amim*).

Because they worked to safeguard the integrity of the received textual tradition (in Hebrew the *masorah*) of the TANAKH, this consortium of Rabbis came to be known as the *ba'alei masorah*, preservers of the tradition.

When we read the Bible we are engaged in an endeavor that is primarily visual. We see words on a page. We accumulate their individual meanings in our mind so as to make sense of how they all work together holistically to make a meaningful sentence. In reading we are processing language as a system of visual signs. Usually we do this rapidly, without being aware of the mental operations in which we are engaged. It is only when we hit a word we don't know or an unfamiliar idiom or a complex sentence that we are slowed down. Often the reading is halted as we consult a dictionary or review the whole verbal construction. Then we go on.

It is all very intellectual. We are working on the text, operating on it. We are subjecting it to our best critical analytical powers. The text is there for us as an object to decipher. It is in our hands. We are in control. Interpretation is the name of the game here and it is we the readers who run it.

And when we're done reading, we fancy that we know what the text on which we have operated means—if the interpretive challenge it has posed has not been too onerous. Though it may have been a tough read, we think we've figured it out. We come away from the text satisfied and proud that we have used our ingenuity and the critical and analytical tools at our disposal effectively. They have enabled us to penetrate the text, to advance a reading of it that we know is clever, original, sometimes even brilliant.

Admittedly I've overstated things a bit here. Most of us are not that smug when we read the Bible. But even so, the point I'm making is that in such reading we stand in a relation to the text that is one of subject to object. In Buberian terms it is the relation of an "I" to an "It."

Hearing involves a very different kind of relationship. With hearing we meet the text reciprocally, as equals, as an "I" meets a "You." The text is not (yet) an object in our hands, an object on which we can apply and demonstrate our analytical prowess. Nor is it "a totemic object sanctioned by rabbinic authority,"[11] which is how I fear all too many traditionalists relate to it. The text, inert as it may look on the page, is a living organism. It is a verbal organism. In fact, it speaks. Buber and Rosenzweig often noted that the Hebrew name for the TANAKH is *mikra* (מקרא), a Hebrew word that derives from a Hebrew verb stem (*q-r-a*) connoting both "to call out" and "to read" and which can be translated as "calling out" or "the calling" (i.e., "what is spoken").[12] The Koran derives its name from the same Arabic root.

How does the text call out to us? Here is how Dan Avnon, a keen elucidator of Buber's ideas, explains it:

> **Emphasis on the text's orality led Buber to pay attention to the repetition of Hebrew words and sounds. This attention accords with Jewish tradition, which considers that every letter and every word in the Bible**

> has been carefully chosen and that no word or sound
> is coincidental or unintentional, including instances
> in which the text may seem unnecessarily repetitive or
> obscure. Rosenzweig shared Buber's conviction that
> their translation should retain repetitions that abound
> in the original Hebrew.[13]

In other words, the biblical text speaks to us through its repetitions, through the different ways it uses repetition. It will repeat words; it will repeat sounds; it will repeat phrases; it will repeat motifs. In doing this it will often throw up permutations of the three (sometimes two) letters that make up the roots or the stems of verbs and nouns. Buber calls these repeated signifiers *Leitwörter* (German for "leading [or guiding] words").

> A *Leitwort* is a word or a word-root that recurs significantly in a text, in a continuum of texts, or in a configuration of texts: by following these repetitions, one is able to decipher or grasp a meaning of the text, or at any rate, the meaning will be revealed more strikingly. The repetition . . . need not be merely of the word itself but also of the word-root; in fact, the very difference of words can often intensify the dynamic action of the repetition. I call it "dynamic" because between combinations of sounds related to one another in this manner a kind of movement takes place: if one imagines the entire text deployed before him, one can sense waves moving back and forth between the words. The measured repetition that matches the inner rhythm of the text, or rather, that wells up from it, is one of the most powerful means for conveying meaning without expressing it.[14]

It is these repeated words and roots and patterns of meaning that attract the reader's attention. They are meant to flag us down. That is how the text speaks to us.

---

Here are some examples.

1. Toward the end of *parashat* Lekh Lekha in Genesis, God tells Abraham, "Walk in my ways [literally "walk before me"] and

be blameless," הִתְהַלֵּךְ לְפָנַי וֶהְיֵה תָמִים (Gen. 17:1). A reader who's been paying attention might notice that this sounds rather similar to what had been said earlier of Noah in the parashah of that name: "Noah was a righteous man; he was blameless in his age; Noah walked with God," נֹחַ אִישׁ צַדִּיק תָּמִים הָיָה בְּדֹרוֹתָיו; אֶת הָאֱלֹהִים הִתְהַלֶּךְ נֹחַ (6:9). We are thus invited to consider what kind of connection there might be between Noah and Abraham. If one knows Hebrew, he could further notice that while both men were "blameless," תָמִים, Noah walked **with** God (as did Enoch; see 5:24), whereas Abraham is told to "walk **before**" God. What might that mean?

2. In Numbers (*parashat* Balak) we learn that the Israelites, now on the threshhold of the Promised Land, sinned egregiously when they allowed the Moabite women to seduce them into participating in the rites for their god Ba'al. This was evidently a fertility cult and involved promiscuous sexual activity. The guilty parties were severely punished. The place where this occurred is named Pe'or, פְּעוֹר (Num. 25:1–3). We would probably forget this place and its name except that it is exactly where Israel is encamped before entering the Promised Land and where Moses gives the farewell speeches that Deuteronomy presents (Deut. 4:44–46). He reminds the people of what they did at Pe'or (4:3 and 9:7) and he recapitulates for them there the Sinai event by reviewing the Ten Commandments (chapter 5). And then, in the final passages of the Torah, where Moses' death is cryptically narrated, the text tells us: "He buried him in the valley in the land of Moab, near [lit. facing] Beth-peor," מוּל בֵּית פְּעוֹר . . . (34:6). We can wonder: Why do we get this nugget of detail that Moses was buried "facing Beth-peor,"? It seems extraneous. (If the surface of the text here is interesting, it is not because of this detail but because of something else: the pronoun "He" as the subject of the verb "buried." To whom does this pronoun refer? God? Did God himself bury Moses? That is what the context suggests. We can ponder that, too.)[15]

But still, we ask: Why are we told that Moses was buried "facing Beth-peor"? Is it simply because Pe'or was the Israelites' final stopping point before crossing the Jordan and we know that Moses did not accompany them? Or perhaps we hear something more here. The sin at Pe'or was, next to the Golden Calf, the most grievous regression the Israelites committed. It controverted everything Moses had been teaching. The text has led us to an important insight as we close the book on Moses. Though the exact location of his grave is unknown, his final resting place is "over against Pe'or"! In death as in life, Moses stands against the error of idolatry and its morality.[16]

3. These first two examples turn on the repetition of a single word. Sometimes, though, a recurring phrase begins to ring in our ears. Consider the opening verses of the book of Exodus. Joseph has died, the descendants of Jacob remain in Egypt, and a whole new and fateful series of events is about to unfold. We are told that "the Israelites were fertile and prolific; they multiplied and increased very greatly, so that the land was filled with them," ובני ישראל פרו וישרצו וירבו ויעצמו במאד מאד; ותמלא הארץ אתם (Exod. 1:7). Sound familiar? Yes: the opening verses of Genesis! On the fifth day of Creation, "God said: 'Let the waters bring forth swarms of living creatures . . . ,'" ישרצו המים (Gen. 1:20). On the sixth day God created man, "male and female He created them. God blessed them and God said to them: 'Be fertile and increase, fill the earth and master it . . . ,'" פרו ורבו ומלאו את הארץ (1:27).

The writer is clearly connecting this new book to what has come before and placing it in the perspective in which he wants us to see it.[17] Whereas Genesis gave us the creation of the world, this new book will tell of the creation of Israel. And lest we think that this people is a wholly new entity, it is not. Israel is the organic continuity of the Patriarchs. Of Abraham it was foretold that he would *"become a great and populous nation"* היו יהיה לגוי גדול ועצום (Gen. 18:18), and now the Israelites have *"increased"* ויעצמו (Exod. 1:7). And they have done so exactly as Jacob did. Of Jacob's sheep-breeding proficiency among the flocks of his father-in-law, Laban, and his procreative success with his two wives and two concubines, Genesis reports: "So the man [Jacob] grew exceedingly prosperous . . . ," ויפרוץ האיש מאד מאד (Gen. 30:43). Exodus 1 echoes this by noting: "The more they [the Israelites] were oppressed, the more they increased and spread out . . . ," וכאשר יענו אתו כן ירבה וכן יפרוץ . . . (Exod. 1:12).

4. Here is one final example of how verbal artifice works to communicate meaning in a more complex way. To see this we need

a "one-minute" Hebrew lesson. In Hebrew the three letters *k-b-d*, כבד, form a root from which a number of words stem. The three consonants can be vocalized and read as an adjective meaning "heavy." Or, if another consonant is added to them, you get the word כבוד, which means "honor." The same three letters can also be inflected as a verb. In one form, לכבד, it means "to honor." In another form, להכביד, it means "to make heavy."

In the story of the struggle between Moses and Pharaoh told in the first half of Exodus this word-root functions to set up a whole contrapuntal pattern of guiding words:

- During the plagues we learn that "Pharaoh's heart hardened" (literally, "became heavy," ויכבד לב פרעה [Exod. 9:7]).[18] And shortly thereafter: "God said to Moses, 'Go to Pharaoh. For I have hardened his heart . . . ,'" that is, "made his heart heavy," כי אני הכבדתי את לבו (10:1). (I will not here enter into the perennial question of whether Pharaoh had free will or not. Suffice it to note that at the outset, before any plagues had been called down, God made an objective statement to Moses about Pharaoh: "Pharaoh's heart is heavy," כבד לב פרעה [7:14]).[19]

- Deployed against this heaviness are the plagues: "heavy swarms of insects" (or "a heavy horde"), ערוב כבד (Exod. 8:20), "a very heavy pestilence," דבר כבד מאד (9:3),[20] "a very heavy hail," ברד כבד מאד (9:18), and "the locust went up over all the land of Egypt, and settled, very heavy . . . ," ויעל הארבה על כל ארץ מצרים . . . כבד מאד (10:14).

The game God is playing with Pharaoh is tit for tat, measure for measure. And God wins it in the same way. When the story reaches its denouement at the Sea of Reeds:

- God tells Moses: "I will stiffen Pharaoh's heart and he will pursue them [the Israelites], that I may gain glory [literally, "honor"] through Pharaoh . . . ," וחזקתי את לב פרעה ורדף אחריהם ואכבדה בפרעה (Exod. 14:4).

- And so it is. When the onrushing Egyptians pursued the Israelites into the sea bed, God "took off the wheels of their chariots so that they moved forward with difficulty" [literally, "heavily"], וַיְנַהֲגֵהוּ בִּכְבֵדֻת. "And the Egyptians said, 'Let us flee from the Israelites, for the LORD is fighting for them against Egypt' " (Exod. 14:25).[21]

I could cite many more instances of guiding words and how they work. Often they extend over different contexts that on the surface seem to have nothing to do with each other. Sometimes they are even sustained over different books in wonderfully subtle ways.[22]

The guiding word "technique" is unquestionably one of Buber's signal contributions to a modern understanding of the Bible. But it has its limitations:

- It is most visible and works best in the prose narrative parts of the *Humash*. It is less useful, if it is useful at all, when narrative gives way to poetry and when we read the many passages that detail laws, rituals, and sacrifices. Those kinds of text have their own formal and stylistic principles.[23]

- The words that do the guiding are in the Hebrew. Robert Alter writes that the guiding word effect

  will not be so evident in translation as in the original: Buber and Rosenzweig went to extreme lengths in their German version to preserve all the *Leitwörter;* unfortunately most modern English translations go to the opposite extreme, constantly translating the same word with different English equivalents for the sake of fluency and supposed precision. Nevertheless, the repetition of key words is so prominent in many biblical narratives that one can still follow it fairly well in translation, especially if one uses the King James Version.[24]

- Even so, the whole thing is mightily dependent upon the literary acumen of the reader. Buber's work with guided words has been critiqued on these grounds. It

  lacked any precisely defined instructions as to how his method could be transmitted from teacher to pupil,

> how anyone could learn his technique without having
> been blessed with Buber's masterly ability to attain to
> an instinctive understanding of the Bible text.[25]

Let us here call the proverbial baby by its name: it's not an abstract disembodied "text" that speaks, but the consummate verbal
genius of the anonymous redactor(s), to whom all these discussions seem to lead back. It is what Rosenzweig called the "unitary
consciousness" of the redactor(s) that informs the Pentateuch and
is so crucial to making it Torah. This is why Rosenzweig could fa-
mously write of the underlying premise of his work with Buber:

> We . . . translate the Torah as one book. For us . . . it is the
> work of a single mind. We do not know who the mind
> was; we cannot believe that it was Moses. We name that
> mind among ourselves . . . R. We, however, take this R
> to stand not for Redactor but for *rabbenu* [our rabbi]. For
> whoever he was, and whatever text lay before him, he is
> our teacher, and his theology is our teaching.[26]

But now we arrive at a truth more important to the whole idea of
hearing the Torah than the guiding word technique: **In order to
hear we have to listen**. And in order to listen we have to stop
talking. By "talking" I mean anything that we generate within
ourselves and with others that drowns out the voice that is coming to us from within the text. This means suspending our own
thoughts, however brilliant, parking outside the door all the assumptions and presumptions we bring to our reading. It means
putting ourselves not in a transmitting but in a receiving mode. In
short, it means opening ourselves to the text. For when we hear
the Torah it is not the reader who is in charge but the text. Or, we
can say, the Redactor.

Here is how Buber describes what it means for a modern or postmodern person to hear the Torah:

> People today have little access to sure belief, and can-
> not be given such access. When they are serious, they
> know this and do not let themselves be kidded. But an
> openness to belief is not denied them. They too can, if
> they are really serious, open themselves up to this
> book and let themselves be struck by its rays wher-

ever they may strike. They can, without anticipation and without reservation, yield themselves and let themselves come to the test. They can receive the text, receive it with all their strength and await what may happen to them, wait to see whether in connection with this or that passage in the book a new openness will develop in them.

For this [to happen] . . . they must take up Scripture as if they had never seen it, had never encountered it in [Hebrew] school or afterwards in the light of "religious" or "scientific" certainties. . . . They must place themselves anew before the renewed book, hold back nothing of themselves, let everything happen between themselves and it, whatever may happen. They do not know what speech, what image in the book will take hold of them and recast them, from what place the spirit will surge up and pass into them, so as to embody itself anew in their lives.

But they are open. They believe nothing *a priori;* they disbelieve nothing *a priori.* They read aloud what is there, they hear the word they speak, and it comes to them. Nothing has yet been judged, the river of time flows on, and the contemporaneity of these people becomes itself a receiving vessel.[27]

In this passage Buber is doing something extremely important: he is trying "to transform discourse to meet the needs of the day."[28] Buber had no illusions about the spiritual condition of modern man in general and of the secularized, acculturated, liberal Jews of Weimar Germany for whom he was writing. He was, after all, one of them. He understood well the profound disconnect between the past and the present and he knew that there was no way back. Neither Orthodoxy, Christianity, Marxism, psychoanalysis, or even Buddhism could restore the existential security that had evaporated. But the Judaism of the Bible—Torah in its pristine sense—could. If only it could be accessed or even glimpsed. To do this Buber had, in Dan Avnon's words, to

depart . . . from established . . . Jewish interpretive practices . . . in one significant way: traditional forms

> of Jewish renewal assume a theological basis, while
> Buber's interpretation of the "voice" required no prior
> theology. His work can be read as an increasingly fo-
> cused attempt to resensitize his and future genera-
> tions to the decisive experience that precedes any
> fixed, authoritative textual interpretation. As such, his
> work is anarchical and challenges Jewish orthodoxy.[29]

Avnon's comment makes it clear why I think Buber is important
to the overall objective of this book. He opens up an approach to
the *Humash* that is as relevant to our time and place as it was to
his. The "people today" that he talks about in the third person in
the passage above are you and me. The strangeness of the Bible
and the estrangement from it that Buber addresses in this passage
and in virtually all his writings on the subject are as great now as
they were then, if not greater.

What Buber gives us is a strategy, a strategy to overcome this
strangeness and estrangement. He asks of us, when we open the
*Humash*, to put away all our received notions about what we see
in it, to not get hung up on religious or theological issues that vex
us or on historical or literary issues that attract our attention, to
take off our spiritual clothes, so to speak, and stand, like primordial Adam and Eve, naked in the world. Then we are in the world
as the Bible presents it. Then we are ready to hear the word. The
German historian von Ranke said that "every generation is equi-
distant from eternity." It is likely that Buber had this in mind
when he wrote those words and these:

> The Jewish Bible has always approached and still
> does every generation with the claim that it must be
> recognized as a document of the true history of the
> world, that is to say, of the history according to which
> the world has an origin and a goal. The Jewish Bible
> demands that the individual fit his own life into this
> true history, so that "I" may find my own origin in the
> origin of the world, and my own goal in the goal of
> the world.
>
> But the Jewish Bible does not set a past event as a mid-
> point between origin and goal. It interposes a move-
> able, circling midpoint which cannot be pinned to any

> set time, for it is the moment when I, the reader, the hearer, the human person, catch through the words of the Bible the voice which from earliest beginnings has been speaking in the direction of the goal. The midpoint is this mortal yet immortal moment of mine.
>
> Creation is the origin, redemption the goal. But revelation is not a fixed, dated point poised between the two. The revelation at Sinai is not this midpoint itself, but the perceiving of it, and such perception is possible at any time.[30]

At any time?

At any time when we read/hear Torah. At any time when we open ourselves to looking for and discovering the guided word process that the Redactor has encoded into the text in order to communicate meaning and implication. Hearing the word of God was not a onetime event but is an ever-present possibility in our lives.

So we can take from Buber and Rosenzweig something that I think is even more crucial than an appreciation of and an openness to the guided word style. That is the idea that the Torah **addresses us** here and now; that it addresses us in our subjectivity, in our individual particularity; and that it addresses us, too, in our collectivity, as part of that people that, however imperfectly, are living out the covenant at Sinai in this still unredeemed world.

Buber sees this awareness as the starting point for any encounter with the Bible. As he notes in the seminal essay on which I have drawn for this discussion, it is "a way in. . . . [It is] still . . . not yet standing within biblical reality. But it is the way into it, and the beginning."[31]

From it we can go on to more objective ways of reading, such as the historical-critical approach. Or such awareness could be the end point, the existential destination at which we arrive after we will have analyzed the text in more empirical terms. Either way, this awareness is fundamental to our weekly encounter with the Torah portion.

# PART III

# Some Major Approaches to Reading a Parashah

**1.**
Modern Historical-Critical
Approaches

**2.**
Premodern Ahistorical
Approaches

**3.**
Existential Readings

There are any number of ways to read the Bible. (Note: In the following discussion I talk a lot about the Bible, but always with the purpose in mind of advancing the ultimate objective of this book: how to read a Torah portion.) Likewise, there are any number of ways of organizing and listing the various approaches.

What follows is hardly a definitive or an exhaustive presentation but simply my own way of selecting and detailing them.[1] I do so out of an awareness that how we read a parashah, how we read anything, will depend of how we **want** to read it, or how we **choose** to read it. And that will depend of what we are looking for in our reading. One of my teachers at the Jewish Theological Seminary, Abraham Joshua Heschel, used to say in class: "The Bible is an answer. Do we know what the question is?"[2]

When it comes to the Bible and the parashah, there are many possible questions. The ones we ask will shape the answers we look for in our reading. More often than not, our questions will be only implicit, below the surface of our conscious awareness as we read.

The great divide in approaches to the Bible is what I'll call historical consciousness. On one interpretive side is the premise that life is lived not only in space but in time, and that human events unfold sequentially, the process of which is called history. Such a premise predisposes anyone holding it to want to understand the Bible in historical terms. The modern, post-Enlightenment mind is hardwired this way.

Over against this is a point of departure that reads the Bible as a book that transcends history. This view is not necessarily antihistorical; it is ahistorical. This perspective prevailed in premodern eras. If it persists in our time, it is by no means to be equated with religious fundamentalism; in fact, it is increasingly prominent in the contemporary teaching of the humanities. As we shall see, modern ahistorical approaches do not deny the historical origins of any of the books but rather hold that the Bible is about much more than the merely historical.

These two perspectives are not mutually exclusive. The richness and depth of the text can accommodate—indeed requires—both. We can, and should, read a parashah out of both interpretive stances, though it will take time—many readings over many years—to be able to do this. That said, let me now outline what these different approaches entail.

There is one other point, though, before we begin: this discussion is not about commentaries. We must distinguish between **the way of reading** and **the reading itself**, between the principles and objectives that drive the reading and the actual practices and results of interpretation. Although I will show in the next few pages how the different approaches work by citing commentaries that exemplify them, I will discuss commentaries in Part V.

# 1.
# Modern Historical-Critical Approaches

Notice the fusion of two analytical methods in this commonly used label. The historical and the critical are certainly related, interrelated in fact. I separate them out so as to illuminate the spectrum of possibilities they offer.

## The Historical Approach

Were Adam and Eve real people? Abraham and Sarah? Did the Israelites really go out of Egypt? When? How? Is the account in Exodus historically accurate or reliable? What was the "leprosy" that Leviticus talks about?

Questions like these set up how we read the *Humash* and how we understand what we read. What's involved here is an appreciation of the difference between **myth and epic** on the one hand, and **history** on the other.

Myth in contemporary parlance has gotten a bad rap. The modern mind privileges the historical so much that anything that didn't actually happen is called a myth. In its own way this is a kind of intellectual fundamentalism for it distorts the nature and the significance of what myth really is. As any cultural anthropologist will tell you, myth, among other meanings, refers to the story a people or a nation tells about itself that encapsulates its deepest values and aspirations. In academic discourse myth denotes the narrative of a collective entity (and in this sense "narrative" denotes something different from the literary technique of storytelling).

Consider how the American people relate to Abraham Lincoln. Here is a person whose existence was never in question and about whose life we know a great deal. We know how tall he was and what he looked like. We have many biographies of him that detail not only his achievements but his foibles, his depressions, his shortcomings. Is that the Lincoln we revere? There is the historical Lincoln and the mythic Lincoln. Which one do you think is enshrined in the American national memory? And so with George Washington, Martin Luther King Jr., and other iconic figures. In the long run myth may be more important than history.

Epic (or saga) is closely related to myth. Sometimes the two get confused. Myth is the core story, the grand narrative of a people or a culture; epic is the telling of that story, the lore, the legends, the literature that a people or a culture collects about its core or founding myth and passes down to its successive generations. Generally both myth and epic have their origins in an event or events that (may have) actually happened, but which get embellished as the tellings and retellings multiply over time.

An historical approach to the Bible understands that what the biblical text reflects is epic. It seeks to cut through the layers of epic so as to uncover and identify the historical kernel that lies at the bottom. If you read the *Humash* this way you will need to know something about the ancient Near East. The *parshiyot* in Genesis will require your having an inkling about Mesopotamia in the second millennium before the Common Era. Similarly with Exodus and the history, culture, and mores of ancient Egypt. Knowledge about the Merneptah stele, for example, the stone monument erected by Pharaoh Merneptah around 1207 B.C.E. to commemorate a military victory in Canaan, documents the presence of Israel as a collective entity there at that time. If history is the lens through which you want to read the *Humash*, Rabbinic midrash and the great medieval commentators will not be so interesting or relevant. Biblical archaeology will. Most of the Leviticus portions will only make sense if you have some grasp of the rudiments of Israelite religion and the centrality in it of animal sacrifice. The learnings of cultural anthropology are valuable here.[3]

# Critical Approaches

The historical approach can be applied in several ways so as to yield a more precise account of the historical context of the *Humash*. We call such applications "critical," not because they take a dismissive attitude to the text but because they simply believe that the Bible can be subjected to literary and textual analysis no less than any other literary artifact from any period or place—ancient, medieval, or modern. Whereas fundamentalism in both its Jewish and Christian varieties and nonfundamentalist Jewish Orthodoxy hold the Torah text to be "perfect," and any apparent contradictions or anomalies in it are always reconcilable or explainable through correct **textual** interpretation, biblical criticism "de-privileges" the text and accounts for contradictions and anomalies in **contextual** terms, that is, within the literary, linguistic, and cultural contexts in which the text was written. I have already noted the philosophical or theological underpinning that underlies these antithetical approaches: the debate over the relationship between the divine and the human in the production of the books that make up the Pentateuch.[4]

Two major critical approaches are linguistic criticism and source criticism.

## Linguistic Criticism

Careful analysis of the Hebrew shows that the language of the Pentateuch, and of the whole TANAKH, changes as we move from book to book. Different books, and parts of different books, reflect different stages in the development of Hebrew. Scholars have noted the borrowings in biblical Hebrew from Ugaritic and other northwest Semitic languages from which Hebrew descends. They have come to distinguish between "Judahite" Hebrew of the Southern Kingdom and "Israelian" Hebrew of the Northern Kingdom; between the Hebrew of biblical prose and that used in biblical poetry; and between oral and scribal usages. These differences show up in nouns, verb forms, terminology, and other grammatical and syntactic features. They have led scholars to advance more precise conjectures about just when the different books were written.

Obviously you have to be deeply rooted in biblical Hebrew for such an approach to have any utility. Even if you do know some Hebrew, linguistic criticism will be too specialized. But knowing about it and reading modern commentaries where its contributions are noted can be helpful at times.

## Source Criticism

Source criticism is the central method of the historical-critical approach. It seeks to identify the different hands and voices that are visible and audible in the text. Source criticism builds on linguistic analysis but looks at larger literary issues such as style and point of view. The 19th-century Documentary Hypothesis is at the root of this approach. Its elaborations in the 20th century have produced a consensus that the Pentateuch is a stitching together and an integration into one book of four main sources—J, E, P, and D by an anonymous Redactor. I've noted the rudiments of this approach in Part II.

Source criticism is also quite technical in its methods, but its achievements are now more accessible to the general reader thanks in large part to the work of Richard Elliot Friedman. Friedman is a scholar who has worked hard to present to the nonspecialist the results of modern source criticism, and to show how they can impinge on how we read the Pentateuch.[5] His book *The Bible with Sources Revealed*[6] displays the full text of the *Humash* in his own English translation in a polychromatic manner and with different typefaces. The reader can instantly see in different colors and different fonts the four different strands that the Redactor wove together.

Not all biblicists agree with Friedman's assignment of sources and the assumptions on which he bases it. They quibble over whether certain parts belong to, say, E and not to P. Moreover, in recent decades the whole notion of there being four discrete sources has come under attack. It's been suggested, for example, that J is not an unalloyed source but is itself an amalgam of different traditions and documents. In recent decades E's existence as an independent source has been challenged; many scholars now think it may be simply a variant of J. I will have more to say about these critiques of source criticism below, but for now let's set them aside and try to see what the documentary hypothesis, however it is revised, can achieve for an attentive reader. Friedman's typographical performance allows us to see that there are things going on in the text that were hitherto invisible. We grasp immediately the various strands out of which the Pentateuch is woven. We come to appreciate their individual voices and viewpoints. We come to understand that each one wants to tell the story of Israel in its particular way, with its own particular ax to grind. Suddenly hitherto the invisible and inaudible becomes visible and audible.

To show this polyphonic aspect, let's take one story in the book of Numbers. Numbers is essentially a P document. It continues the material and the point of view of Leviticus, which is totally a "priestly" book, that the *Kohanim* were the chief agents by which the Israelite God was accessed and the sacrificial rites the means of this access. But at various points in the middle of Numbers we get a few narratives that present a very different perspective. One such narrative comes at the end of parasahat Be-ha'alotekha, a parashah that, up to that point, is written, to use a musical idiom, in the key of P. But then, in chapter 12, we have a story about Miriam and Aaron talking against their younger brother, Moses.

> **When they were in Hazeroth, Miriam and Aaron spoke against Moses because of the Cushite woman he had married: "He married a Cushite woman!"**
>
> **They said, "Has the LORD spoken only through Moses? Has He not spoken through us as well?" The LORD heard it. Now Moses was a very humble man, more so than any other man on earth.**
>
> **Suddenly the LORD called to Moses, Aaron, and Miriam, "Come out, you three, to the Tent of Meeting." So the three of them went out. The LORD came down in a pillar of cloud, stopped at the entrance of the Tent, and called out, "Aaron and Miriam!" The two of them came forward; and He said, "Hear these my words:**
>
> *When a prophet of the LORD arises among you,*
> *I make Myself known to him in a vision;*
> *I shall speak with him in a dream.*

*Not so with my servant Moses;*
*he is trusted throughout My household.*
*With him I speak mouth to mouth,*
*Plainly and not in riddles,*
*and he beholds the likeness of the LORD.*
*How then did you not shrink from speaking against My*
*servant Moses?"*

**Still incensed with them, the LORD departed.**

**As the cloud withdrew from the Tent, there was Miriam stricken with snow-white scales! When Aaron turned toward Miriam, he saw that she was stricken with scales. And Aaron said to Moses, "O my lord, account not to us the sin which we committed in our folly. Let her not be as one dead, who emerges from his mother's womb with half his flesh eaten away."**

**So Moses cried out to the LORD, saying, "Oh God, pray heal her!" (Num. 12:1–13)**

Friedman identifies this passage as coming from the E source.[7] He follows the view that E is a separate source and that the E writer(s) lived and wrote sometime between about 900 and 722 B.C.E. when the Israelite kingdom was divided into two: a northern one, called Israel, and a southern one, called Judah. E, he believes, was written by a priest or a group of priests (*Kohanim* who came out of the tribe of Levi) who lived in the Northern Kingdom and traced their descent back to Moses himself. There was, he surmises, a kind of sibling rivalry between them and another group of *Kohanim* who lived in the Southern Kingdom, almost certainly in Jerusalem, and who believed themselves to be descended from Aaron. E tells its stories in a way that makes Moses look good and Aaron bad. The Golden Calf narrative in Exodus, chapters 32 and 33, for example (*parashat* Ki Tissa') makes Aaron out to be the key figure in the fashioning of the idolatrous fetish and glorifies the role of Moses in cleaning up the mess.[8]

In the same way, this Numbers narrative is a ringing defense of Moses. God figuratively takes Miriam and Aaron to the woodshed and dresses them down for their attempt to usurp Moses' place as God's exclusive interlocutor. After such an admonishment Aaron grovels before his brother and Miriam, for her part, is stricken with leprosy. Friedman observes in a note that "Aaron suffers no punishment, even when [he has] committed the same offense [as Miriam]. This may be because E could not picture Israel's first high priest as suffering leprosy or any other direct punishment from God."[9]

By interpolating this story and a few others like it into the middle parts of Numbers, stories that hold up Moses and prophesy and not Aaron and sacrifice as the prime avenue to the Israelite God, the Redactor has done something more than serve as a faithful collector of Israel's heritage. He has shown us that the *Humash* is not monophonic but stereophonic, that the religion of our biblical forebears was already a two-track system in which the way to God was through both the *Kohen* (ritual functionary) and animal sacrifice, and the *navi* (prophet) and the proclamation of God's word. The dialectic that is created here between E and P, between Moses and Aaron, anticipates a thread—and a tension—that will run through Judaism in all the stages through which it would evolve and, indeed is still evolving: the tension between ritual and ethics, between rite and right, between an affirmation and a celebration of the status quo and a critique of the flawed present that the prophetic vision of the future demands. The Redactor, Rabbenu, is signaling to us that in the total economy of human life in this world, the Torah requires both.[10]

Source criticism is helpful in another way, too. It enables us to understand a feature of the *Humash* that baffles many readers. I refer to the many instances where a story or a law is told, and then, at some later point, we hear it again. (This is something quite different from *Leitwörter*, which play on individual words and their permutations.) Here the repetition is not always verbatim, but it's close enough to make us wonder why the text is repeating this material. Scholars are clear that the high number of twice-told tales in the Pentateuch is not a coincidence or an aspect of the literary style of the ancient Near East. They call such repetitions doublets. Doublets are the surest indication that more than one version of an event or a teaching is being recorded in the text. They are the result of the Redactor's wish to preserve and present all the sources that tell the story of the People of Israel.

Here are some examples of doublets.[11] I choose here only a few of the more familiar ones:

- the wife-sister story, in which a Patriarch passes his wife off to the locals as his sister. In Gen. 12:10–20 this is told about Abraham and Sarah with respect to Pharaoh (J); in Gen. 20:1–18 the two run into a problem with Abimelech (E). (There's a third version, too, in Gen. 26:6–14, this one about Isaac and Rebekah vis-à-vis Abimelech, and this one again assigned to J.) This last one shows us that doublets do not necessarily indicate the presence of two different sources but rather can be variants within a single source.

- the commandment not to cook a kid in its mother's milk. This occurs three times: Exod. 23:19 (in the Covenant Code attributed to E), Exod. 34:26 (J), and in Deut. 14:21 (D).

- the story of God providing manna and quail in the wilderness. The P version is in Exod. 16:2–3 and 6:35; E's is in Num. 11:4–9 and in the rest of that chapter.

- the sin at Beit Pe'or. Numbers 25 gives the J version in verses 1–5; P's follows immediately in verses 6–19.

- the most familiar doublet in the *Humash*, and possibly the most significant one, is the Creation story. The first version in Gen. 1:1–2:3 and is ascribed to P. The second version is 2:4b–25 and is seen as the work of the J writer. Friedman's note on this doublet is worth citing:

  > The P story begins with "the skies and the earth" (1:1) whereas the J story begins . . . with "earth and skies" (2:4), reversing the order. This is . . . notable because, from their very first words, the sources each reflect their perspectives. P is more heaven-centered, almost a picture from the sky looking down, while J is more human-centered (and certainly more anthropomorphic), more like a picture from the earth looking up.
  >
  > This is also an example of the way in which the combining of the sources produced a work that is greater than the sum of its parts. The more transcendent con-

> ception of God in P merges with the more immanent
> and personal conception in J, and the result is: the Five
> Books of Moses in its final form now conveys a picture
> of God who is both the cosmic God and the "God of
> your father." And that combined conception of the de-
> ity who is both transcendent and personal has been a
> central element of Judaism and Christianity ever since.[12]

Like any interpretive tool, source criticism has its limitations.
Before it can enrich our reading, we must acquire some familiarity with J, E, P, and D and have an awareness of their biases
and agendas. Realistically, not every reader, especially those
just beginning to make their way with the weekly portions, is
going to be equipped with this knowledge. Nor is every reader
going to have Friedman's multicolored text in front of him
while reading, which would seem to be a precondition for anyone who is not in the field of biblical studies for this kind of understanding to take place.

In his comment on the two Creation stories, Friedman captures
the essence of what source criticism can contribute to our understanding of how the *Humash* works as a book. As the Miriam and
Aaron story illustrates, source criticism helps us hear the Pentateuch as a polyphony and not as a flat, one-dimensional work.[13]

Yet it is on these grounds that the source approach has been as-
sailed, especially by critics who take a literary approach to the
TANAKH. They have attacked source criticism for undermining the
literary integrity of the Pentateuch. Its emphasis on the different
strands has been seen as obscuring the overall unity and esthetic
coherence of the *Humash* as a holistic anthology, and of the individual books, too. I think such concern is misplaced. For at the
same time as it separates out the sources and enables us to hear
different voices in the text, source criticism, paradoxically, serves
to highlight the presence of the Redactor and to appreciate how
he, as anthologist, has pulled the whole thing together. After all,
it was the Redactor who spliced the story of Miriam and Aaron
into the P narrative that forms the bulk of Numbers.

Source criticism and literary criticism, then, need not be seen as
antagonistic to each other but as complementary ways of reading
the *Humash*.[14] If the former is the ideational foundation on which

modern Bible study rests, the latter has great currency today. So let us now turn to it and see what an approach to the Pentateuch as a unified redacted literary work entails and accomplishes.

## Literary Criticism

Whatever else it is—and by now we know that it is many things—the Bible is universally held to be a great work of literary art, one of the masterworks of human creativity. Literary criticism comes to the Bible—in our case, the *Humash*—with just that presupposition. It approaches the text with a readiness to discover how language and words and form work poetically together to create meaning. Robert Alter, one of the major figures in developing this approach to the Bible, likes to call the verbal and esthetic brilliance of the biblical text its "literary artifice."[15] His attention to this artifice has prompted him to question the value of source criticism: "What . . . are we to do with our literary notions of intricate design in reading these texts that the experts have invited us to view, at least in the more extreme instances, as a crazy quilt of ancient traditions?"[16]

Alter belongs to the way of handling literature known in academic English departments as New Criticism. In our time this method is not so new, but when it came into vogue in the 1940s it was, for it was a reaction against an earlier kind of literary criticism that looked to the author for the key to a work's meaning. New Criticism looks to the text. It reads the text independently of anything the author may have said about what she meant when she wrote it, and independent of the details of the author's life and situation at the time she wrote it.

New Criticism focuses on how the work is made, the different techniques the text uses to create meaning. This necessitates what the New Critics called close reading. Here again New Criticism is not new. Source critics read no less closely, even if they are looking for different things in the text. And, as our examination of midrash will show, the Rabbis were close readers, too; Rabbinic midrash is very often the result of a microscopic analysis of the Torah's language and form. Where the modern literary approach to the Bible differs from source criticism is in its insistence on looking at the text and on paying attention to its structure, genre, style, and narrative point of view, the elements that make up its "intricate design." In its original manifestation New Criticism was decidedly ahistorical. Source criticism, as its name implies, is ultimately concerned with the author, and midrash with the Author. Literary criticism of the Tanakh is attuned to its esthetic dimension. It analyzes the text, and the work as a whole, as an esthetic object, as, in the words of one New Critic, a "verbal icon." It seeks to illuminate the internal coherence of an individual narrative, of a poem, of a book, of the Pentateuch as a whole, even of the Tanakh as a whole. Here is how one literary scholar puts it:

> **It is not that the documentary hypothesis is necessarily wrong in substance; Genesis is clearly made up of a number of traditions which have been combined at different stages. But is not the task of the critic to try and come to grips with the final form as we have it, and to give the final editor or redactor the benefit of the doubt, rather than to delve behind his work to what was there before?**[17]

Notice that this scholar does not repudiate historical data or source criticism. He accepts them as a given. In this respect the literary approach to the Tanakh in our time is much more conscious and accepting of the historical dimension than New Criticism originally was. It is just that to those who take a literary approach, historical criticism will not be adequate to receive all that the biblical text can deliver. To do that the text needs to be read for its literariness.

Let me give one example where such reading explains the text more satisfactorily than source criticism. Genesis 37 relates how it came about that Joseph wound up in Egypt. His brothers had wanted to kill him but Reuben prevailed upon them to throw Joseph into a pit—presumably to allow the brothers to vent their enmity that way and to enable him (Reuben) to return Joseph to his father (vv. 21–22). This is done. A few verses later, however, we are told that the brothers see "a caravan of **Ishmaelites** coming from Gilead" (v. 25). Judah advises that Joseph be sold to them, thus sparing his life and " . . . his brothers agreed" (v. 27). But then, in the very next verse, we read: "When **Midianite** traders passed by, they pulled Joseph up out of the pit. They sold Joseph for twenty pieces of silver to the **Ishmaelites**, who brought Joseph to Egypt" (v. 28). And if all this isn't sufficiently confusing, the final verse of the chapter tells us: "The **Medanites** . . . sold him in Egypt to Potiphar, a courtier of Pharaoh and his chief steward" (v. 36).[18]

What is going on here? Who attempts to save Joseph: Reuben or Judah? Who pulls Joseph out of the pit: the brothers or the Midianites? And who brought Joseph to Egypt: Ishmaelites, Midianites, or Medanites?

Source criticism attempts to explain the passage as a doublet. There are two different versions of the events intertwined here, one from the E source and one from the J. The E account is about Reuben and the Midianites/Medanites. The J version is about Judah and the Ishmaelites.

Maybe so. But in commenting on the whole episode Alter writes:

> **This is the one signal moment when the two literary strands out of which the story is woven seem awkwardly spliced. . . . Elsewhere, Midianites and Ishmaelites appear to be terms from different periods designating the selfsame people . . . so the selling of Joseph to the Ishmaelites looks like a strained attempt to blend two versions that respectively used the two different terms. And the Midianite intervention contradicts the . . . stated intention of the brothers to pull Joseph out of the pit themselves and sell Joseph to the Ishmaelites for profit.[19]**

But now let's look at this narrative as it presents itself to us: as one holistic story. And let's look at it through a literary screen. The third-person point of view of an omniscient narrator who conflates both versions need not fool or confuse us; it may be the Redactor's way of recounting the events from the perspective in which Joseph experienced them. A modernist narrator might have done it differently. What is really being expressed here, **what holds the narrative together, is Joseph's consciousness of what is happening to him.** And what is happening is all a fast-moving blur. Here he is, arriving in Dotan where he finally finds his brothers. And then—he's in the pit. It is dark and dank. He surely hears the brothers talking. Something about Ishmaelites. He hears noises of passersby. Then, suddenly, he is being pulled out of the pit. By whom? Does he know? Are these Ishmaelites? He hears

they are Midianites. Or are they Medanites? Does it make a difference? The next thing he knows he is in Egypt.

Read this way, the events are indeed confusing, not only to the
reader, but indeed—and this is the important point here—to
Joseph himself. Our hero is unsure how and under what circumstances he was pulled from the pit and taken to Egypt, and the
prose of the narrative reflects this confusion through its use of in-
tentionally confusing and ambiguous language.[20]

A literary approach helps us see the linguistic and formal principles that underlie the construction of many narrative units in the
*Humash*. A fine example of this is Joel Rosenberg's treatment of the
Garden of Eden story. He shows how specific guiding words
(*Leitwörter*) work together with explanations of names (etiologies)
and repeated patterns of events that complement and refract one
another as the story progresses to produce a tightly crafted text in
which all the parts are organically related.[21] Alter has similarly uncovered the underlying artistic and thematic unity of the whole
Joseph story cycle. He sees it as a grand "fictional experiment in
knowledge . . . for in it the central actions turn on the axis of true
knowledge versus false, from the seventeen-year-old Joseph's
dreams of grandeur to his climactic confrontation with his brothers
in Egypt twenty-two years later."[22] This is true not only of the characters in the story; the reader, too, is implicated in the experiment.

Literary critics come to the Bible after long experience with such
modern writers as James Joyce, Marcel Proust, and Franz Kafka,
and with such theorists of narrative, genre, and signification as
Mikhail Bakhtin, Northrop Frye, and Roland Barthes, among others. Irony is a touchstone of modern literature and scholars like
Robert Alter and Meir Sternberg are especially helpful in enabling
us to see and appreciate the subtle ironies that well up from many
narratives in the *Humash*.

The same is true for biblical poetry. Literary critics, who read the
*Humash* after having been trained to handle secular poetry, open
up this less accessible material. Modern literary criticism did not
discover the essential principle of biblical poetry—parallelism—
but it certainly has been useful in explicating how the parallelism
works.[23] Consider the following passage in Gen. 4:17–19 and
23–24:

> Cain knew his wife, and she conceived and bore
> Enoch. . . . To Enoch was born Irad, and Irad begot
> Mehujael, and Mehujael begot Methusael, and
> Methusael begot Lamech. Lamech took to himself two
> wives: the name of the one was Adah, and the name of
> the other was Zillah. . . . And Lamech said to his wives:

*Adah and Zillah, hear my voice; O wives of Lamech, give
ear to my speech. I have slain a man for wounding me, and
a lad for bruising me. If Cain is avenged sevenfold, then
Lamech seventy-sevenfold.*

Here we have, in the middle of one of the "begot" lists that we see
in the early chapters of Genesis, a snippet of poetry—two verses
(Gen. 4:23–24)—that come upon us quite suddenly. We know this
is poetry because these verses scan differently than the surrounding narrative. The verses are constructed with two parallel or balanced parts. The first half of each line (called a "stich"), which I
will designate "a," presents a thought, and then the second half,
"b," repeats it in different words.

But look carefully and you will see that there is more to the parallelism than saying (a) and then mechanically restating it in different words in (b). While the "b" stichs seem to display an almost
literal equivalence to the "a" stichs, each "b" subtly builds on and
expands what has been stated in "a." Thus:

**4:23: "a": Adah and Zillah, hear my voice; "b": O wives
of Lamech, give ear to my speech.**

"Hear my voice" (שמען קולי) is common and weak; "give ear to
my speech" (האזנה אמרתי) is rarer and stronger. And so it is in
the rest of the passage:

**"a": I have slain a man for wounding me, "b": and a
lad for bruising me.**

**4:24: "a": If Cain is avenged sevenfold, "b": then
Lamech seventy-sevenfold.**

This tiny poem serves to show us the essential technique of parallelism: "a," and what's more, "b." The pattern, repeated in

every line, generates the energy that propels biblical poetry forward. Of course, once we've seen how it works, we have to ask what this wild bragging poem of Lamech is doing here at all. This question and the insights that lead up to it are what we get from this kind of close reading.[24]

There is one more historical approach to the TANAKH that I would mention, but it is one that will not be readily accessible to the non-specialist. I include it here because I believe the reader should at least know about it and how it works.

## Form Criticism

Form criticism builds on what source criticism has achieved. It, too, throws the words on the page into relief and it, too, raises questions about them. It asks not where that text came from but what **kind** of a text it is: a poem, a law, a ceremony, or a story. The basis on which it distinguishes between different passages is, as its name implies, form and not source. It is interested in knowing not when a given text was written or who wrote it but in recognizing its form. Once that has been identified, inquiry can proceed into how such a text functioned in the social context in which it was formulated. Form criticism looks for the life situation, what scholars call the *"sitz im leben,"* in which the law or poem or ritual in question took place.

So if the form we are looking at is a law, then the investigative trail leads to an inquiry into how that particular law was understood and applied in ancient Israel and how it evolved from and compares with legal systems or codes that prevailed in Mesopotamian or Egyptian or Canaanite cultures. If it is a poem, then the agenda is to see if there are comparable poems in those literatures and if so, who they were written for and how they were used or performed. The main thing is to see the text for what it is and understand it in its own terms.

Such an approach is particularly helpful in reading the *parshiyot* of Leviticus and Deuteronomy, the two books of the Pentateuch that do not present themselves in the same relatively straightforward terms of historical narrative as do Genesis (chapters 12–50), Exodus (chapters 1–24), and parts of Numbers. Leviticus is almost entirely bereft of narrative material that might furnish some clues as to its historical context. Deuteronomy is confusing because it fudges the issue: it puts material that clearly comes from a later stage of Israelite life (because it presupposes an already functioning society) into the mouth of Moses. By looking at specific and arcane rituals (such as the ones involving purification after childbirth or skin afflictions) in Leviticus or some of the laws that we find only in Deuteronomy (such as laws about a king, an army, and courts of justice), form criticism can connect them to what we know about ancient Israel from other books of the Bible and what we know about the social institutions and practices of other parts of the ancient Near East.

To work through a specific example of how form criticism works would require a longer and more technical discussion than our purposes here warrant. I will note briefly one attempt by one scholar to do so. The text on which he focuses as a proper subject for form criticism is not a law or a poem or a story but a whole book, namely the book of Deuteronomy.

The operative question here is: What kind of a book is this? Given that it originated in a time later than Moses, what might have been the social context in which three farewell addresses that summarize the Israelites' experience of the Exodus and the Sinai covenant are put into Moses' mouth? "How are we to account for the mixing of genres within it [Deuteronomy]: historical surveys, moral exhortation, ceremonial laws, curses, poems, and descriptions of solemn rituals?"[25] Was the occasion some "covenant renewal" ceremony that took place during the First Temple period or during the Babylonian exile? Or is the book a kind of very early commentary or midrash—maybe even the first one—on an existing Tetrateuch that came into existence after the return from the Exile in the late biblical period, that is, after about 525 B.C.E.? Barton writes:

> **This exposition of possible form-critical approaches to Deuteronomy may well make the reader feel that the ground is shifting under his feet. We do not know how to read Deuteronomy until we know which genre to assign it to; yet there seems no unambiguous way of deciding on its genre. To some extent this certainly does mean that form criticism can never be an exact method.**[26]

## Feminist Criticism

In the popular mind feminism is often identified as a political movement. It is that, but it is much more than that. Feminism has been and is a major force in advancing our still evolving understanding of what a human being is. As such it has brought to the forefront of contemporary life the recognition that gender and gender issues are crucial factors in shaping how we understand the past and how we will use that understanding in the future. In short, feminism has uncovered a vast array of questions and issues that have implications for both men and women.

Since the Bible is a cornerstone of the entire cultural tradition of the West, reading it through the lens of gender opens up powerful new ways of seeing it not only in its historical but in its social context. Like no other interpretive approach, feminist biblical scholarship foregrounds in its reading the relationship between the sexes and seeks to inject into our ongoing study of the Bible an issue that until relatively recently has been under the cultural radar: the issue of power and how it has been leveraged in Western societies. In that respect the feminist approach is political—but then much of what the Bible is about is political.

Feminist criticism of the Bible is not monolithic. It goes in several directions. Some of its practitioners use some of the other approaches I note here to show how women's voices have been suppressed or erased and, at the same time, how they can be recovered and rendered audible. Though the biblical text was undoubtedly written by men living in a patriarchal culture, there are plenty of female characters in the *Humash*, not to mention the rest of the Tanakh, to consider: the four foremothers (Sarah, Rebekah, Leah, and Rachel), Hagar, Dinah, Tamar, Miriam, Zipporah (Moses' wife), and the five daughters of Zelophehad, to name some of the main ones. And there are many women who make only brief, but telling, cameo appearances: Lot's daughters, Mrs. Potiphar (who tried to seduce Joseph), the Cushite woman Moses married (who may or may not have been Zipporah), Cozbi (the Moabite princess in the Beit Pe'or story), Serah (Jacob's granddaughter and Asher's daughter, who gets all of one verse, Num. 26:46, and about whom all we learn is her name; see also Gen. 46:17). And let us not forget Eve.[27]

Two examples of how feminist criticism proceeds will suffice, one from narrative, one from law. A feminist reading of the challenge that Miriam and Aaron hurl at Moses in Numbers 12 raises questions quite different from those of source criticism. It would focus not on what this narrative is doing here but on the details of the narrative itself. What does Miriam want in her complaint? Why is she even here as a claimant to receiving God's word if the issue of whom God speaks with is between Aaron the priest and Moses the prophet? Why is she punished more severely than Aaron? Was there more to Miriam than meets the eye? After all, in the great deliverance at the Sea of Reeds, she is named as a prophetess (Exod. 15:20). So maybe her claim here is not without foundation.[28]

A legal example—and considering how much material there is in the *Humash* about the regulation of sexual relations, marriage, rape, and divorce, there are many from which to choose—is from what is taught in Deuteronomy:

> **If two men get into a fight with each other, and the wife of one comes up to save her husband from his antagonist and puts out her hand, and seizes him by his genitals, you shall cut off her hand; show no pity. (Deut. 25:11–12)**

Here again the same questions arise: Does the punishment fit the crime? What is the crime? The woman is defending her husband and her future progeny, motives that accord well with the values of biblical law. Are we being told here that male genitals are more important than female hands? More important than marriage and the family? Is this a case of measure for measure, the displacement of castration onto amputation? Feminist reading forces these questions.[29]

Questions of sexuality, gender, and power are not confined to feminists or to Jews. The feminist perspective opens up onto a broad horizon of approaches to the Bible that read and analyze it in even larger social, political, economic, and ethnic contexts. Some of this kind of cultural reading has developed within a Christian context, some within the postcolonial approach to both contemporary and classical texts. A detailed treatment of these kinds of readings is beyond the scope of this discussion. I mention them because in any account of contemporary approaches to the Bible, these types of readings, diverse as they are, are certainly worth noting.

# 2.
# Premodern Ahistorical Approaches

## Midrash

When people quote the Rabbis with the words "the Midrash says
. . . ," chances are they are referring to midrash as a collection of
interpretations of the Torah that circulated orally in the Rabbinic
period (from as early perhaps as 200 B.C.E. to as late as 800 C.E.)
and were later collected and written down; they are not themselves engaging in such midrashic interpretation. In the context of
this discussion midrash is an **activity**, not a body of material.
Midrash as I discuss it here is an interpretive process, a way of
reading the *Humash* that goes back to Rabbinic times.

The Rabbis read the Torah text very, very closely. In doing so they
left a legacy that is significant in telling us not only what the text
means but **how** it means it. Rabbinic midrash is a rich repository
of techniques to extract meaning from the words of the *Humash*.
These techniques still stand us in good stead today and, in fact,
they anticipate insights into how literary texts produce meaning
that modern understandings of language and systems of signification have discovered.

When the Rabbis read the Torah they had one objective: to know
what the text meant. After all, to them the words were—and remain—unequivocally God's words, and every single one of them
carries within it a content or a meaning that has to be extracted. It
is interesting that the Rabbinic word for "word" is *teivah*, which is
the same term Genesis uses for the ark that bore Noah and his
passengers. We may say that in the Rabbinic mind, just as Noah's

ark carried cargo that embodied the living material out of which God would rebuild His world and on which He pinned His hopes, so, too, do the living words of the Torah hold freight that is critical to the ultimate success of the creation.

In extracting content from the Torah's words, that is, in doing midrash, the Rabbis follow a double agenda. When their objective is to determine what the text meant with regard to how the commandments (mitzvot) are to be performed, they are engaged in *midrash halakhah*. This requires certain specific interpretive methods appropriate to determining legal norms and Jewish practice. When their objective is to explore what the text means in nonlegal terms, that is, when its implications are not binding and do not concern observance or any performative act, they are engaged in *midrash aggadah*. This involves using interpretive techniques sometimes similar to those of halakhic midrash, sometimes not. Whereas halakhic midrash is almost scientific in the rigor with which it parses a given verse or word to extract its meaning, in aggadic midrash the Rabbinic imagination is unfettered and often treats the text loosely and playfully so as to make it yield its insight. That is the kind of midrashic reading that I shall be talking about here. It is the one most relevant for parashah readers. In this discussion I call it simply "midrash."

Midrashic reading works in a variety of ways. Many of them focus on the intricacies of the Hebrew text and involve wordplay with it or on it that is often extremely clever. Puns are a favorite tactic. What I did above with the Hebrew word for "word" gives you an idea of what this involves. Such wordplay will not advance our purposes here unless one is grounded in Hebrew. So I will focus on those midrashic methods that can help shape our reading of a parashah even in translation.

## Gaps in the Text

Biblical narrative is laconic. It minces words. J and E will tell you what individual characters do; they will rarely tell you what they are thinking about what they are doing or how they feel about it. A good case in point is the *Akedah* story in Genesis, chapter 22. Abraham is told to take his son Isaac and offer him up as a sacrifice. We are given no inkling of what Abraham said at hearing

God's command or how he felt about it. He is silent here as he is not when God earlier told him that God had marked out the wicked cities of Sodom and Gomorrah for destruction (Gen. 18:18–33). Then Abraham challenged God; here he does not. So now, as father and son walk along in pregnant silence to the appointed place for the fateful offering, some scant dialogue between the two is reported (22:7–8). But this dialogue conceals more than it reveals. Was Isaac scared? Did he have an idea of what this expedition was about? Is his question—"Where is the sheep for the burnt offering?"—a naive one or a rhetorical ploy to get his father to talk? Is Abraham's reply—"God will see to the sheep for His burnt offering, my son"—bitterly sarcastic, or does it reflect the purity of Abraham's trust in God? Further, as many have wondered, where is Sarah here? And at the end, where is Isaac? On the way to Moriah father and son **"walked together"** (vv. 6 and 8); on the way back **"Abraham returned . . ."** (v. 19). Was Abraham now alone? What happened to Isaac?

Midrash comes to fill in such textual gaps. The Rabbis supply the emotions and motivations about which the text is silent. They do so out of their own powers of what we can only call poetic imagination.

Here's another example: The end of Deuteronomy tells of the death of Moses but it tells it quickly and sparingly, in all of three verses (Deut. 34:5–7). Again, we are not told how Moses felt, or God, for that matter. The Rabbis surely felt this glaring lack of detail. They develop midrashically an extensive and wonderfully poignant exchange between Moses and God. They imagine Moses doing everything he can to convince God to let him live on a bit longer so he can enter the land. God, having once had His mind changed by Moses (at the Golden Calf episode when God was ready to wipe out all the people, Exod. 32:9–14), almost relents here. But, the midrash makes clear, God does not. Moses, too, is a mortal being and, in the end, a part of the generation that was fated to die in the wilderness, outside the land.[30]

Midrash, then, invites us and helps us, when we read the *Humash*, to see the gaps in the text and to look into how the Rabbis and the great commentators (most importantly Rashi), who draw and build on their insights, suggest how they might be filled. Midrash challenges us to use our own imaginations in supplying context or motivation we feel is missing. The gaps the rabbis saw may not be the same gaps we see. As a process, as a way of reading, midrash continues in our time—and not always in books; films like *The Ten Commandments* and *The Prince of Egypt* are in their own way modern midrashim.

## Juxtapositions of Episodes

Sometimes two stories or passages are contiguous and the second one seems to have nothing to do with the first. It does not follow logically from it and no reason is given for the linkage. The Rabbis saw such juxtapositions as an interpretive challenge. Though they did not read the *Humash* as a text that had undergone redaction by human hand, they intuitively understood that the units of the text were not haphazardly arranged. Some explanation was in order.

Consider as an example of midrashic thinking Genesis 38, the story of Judah and Tamar. This comes right in the middle of the story of Joseph and his brothers and seemingly interrupts the narrative flow in a jarring way. What is it doing here?

Midrashic thinking suggests some interesting possibilities. One is to read the story as a parallel to the one that is about to be told (in Genesis 39) about Joseph and Mrs. Potiphar. Placing the two stories side by side enables us to compare and contrast the behavior of the two women, Tamar and Mrs. Potiphar, or the behavior of the two men, Judah and Joseph, when they encounter available women. Both stories are introduced linguistically with variations of the verb "to go down" (Hebrew *y-r-d*, ירד). Compare "About that time Judah left [lit., "went down from"; Heb. וירד] his brothers and camped near a certain Adullamite . . ." (Gen. 38:1) with "And Joseph was taken down [Heb. הורד] to Egypt . . ." (39:1). Both men "descend" and, in their respective ways, rise again.[31]

In fact, the interpolation of the story of Judah and Tamar into the story of Joseph may suggest that we read chapter 38 as the first installment of an unfolding story about **Judah** and his growth over time to moral awareness. The episode with Tamar in chapter 38 is only the point of departure. In it Judah initially looks rather shabby. But at the end, when Tamar exposes him, he shows the courage to acknowledge, "She is more in the right than I . . ." [Heb. צדקה ממני] (Gen. 38:26). If the story of Judah and Tamar antedates the events of chapter 37, where Joseph is sold into slavery, then that story shows that Judah's moral intelligence has by then increased even more. For it is Judah who advocates that Joseph be sold and not killed. As he says: "What do we gain by killing our brother and covering up his blood? Come, let us sell him to the Ishmaelites. . . . After all, he is our brother, our own flesh" (37:26–27). Judah now has grown in virtue: he saves Joseph from death and he recognizes a fraternal tie. But he still falls short in important ways, for he is not uncomfortable consigning his brother to an unknown fate. And he is oblivious to what all this might mean and do to Jacob. But later, at the climactic point of the story, Judah evinces a keen awareness of this. It is his impassioned speech to Joseph (44:18–34), the longest speech in Genesis at 17 verses, that triggers Joseph's disclosure to his brothers (45:1ff.). The whole speech turns on Judah's deep understanding of what the entire tragedy of the brothers has done and might still do to their father. Judah, *Yehudah*, now has emerged as a moral being, the ancestor of the *"Yehudim"* (the Jews).

Notice that in considering these two stories in Genesis I have described the midrashic approach as "suggesting" what their juxtaposition might imply. Midrash of the kind with which we are dealing here never purports to present the only or the exact meaning of a passage or a verse or a word. It offers it as a possibility. That is why when one reads midrash one frequently sees, after a certain interpretation has been given, the words *"davar aher,"* דבר אחר, "another interpretation," so as to make clear that all the various midrashic readings that have been put forth can be held up and considered. This is an important and refreshing perspective to take when we read a parashah. It is not that in midrash anything goes, or that there can be so many interpretations of a text that we may ultimately conclude that it has no meaning at all! David Stern notes that "multiple interpretation as found in midrash is actually . . . the guarantee of a belief in Scripture as an inexhaustible fount of meaningfulness."[32]

Our discussion of the two stories illustrates another important principle of midrashic thinking as a way of looking at the *Hu-*

*mash.* One of the postulates from which Rabbinic midrash operates is that "there is no earlier or later in the Torah," אֵין מוּקְדָם
וּמְאֻחָר בַּתּוֹרָה. To the modern Western reader such an idea is
counterintuitive. We don't need to be instructed as Alice in
Wonderland was: "'Begin at the beginning,' said the King of
Hearts, very gravely, 'and go on to the end: then stop.'"
Midrash holds that the Torah need not necessarily be read that
way; it can be read in any order—backward, a bit here and a bit
there, sideways. I think that is part of what Rabbi Levi saw
when he looked at a Torah scroll and saw the paragraphs
aligned as they are and said what he said about them. This perspective is undoubtedly rooted in the Rabbis' belief that the divine nature of the Torah allows its words to transcend the
finitude of linear time. It accords well with the "guiding word"
method whereby a passage or a word in one book anticipates or
harks back to one that was heard in another. And it is also compatible with postmodern ways of reading in which the reader,
not the author or the text, sets the interpretive agenda and con-
structs meaning.

The contiguity of the Judah–Joseph stories is only one instance of
a meaningful juxtaposition of two passages. There are several others in other parts of the *Humash*. But we have to be careful. It is
not juxtaposition in itself that generates interesting interpretations; it is the juxtaposition of two seemingly disparate passages
that we need to look for. In the case we have considered it is the
interruption of one story by another, the contiguity of two different narratives. More often than not it is the interruption of a narrative by a law. This kind of juxtaposition forces us to inquire into
a possible connection between what has just been told and what
is now being taught. Examples of this are

- the story in Leviticus 10:1–5 (*parashat* Shemini) of the untimely
  death of Aaron's two sons Nadab and Abihu and the laws that
  follow directly afterward (and maybe also the ones that pre-
  cede it in chapter 9).

- the story in Numbers 15:32–36 (*parashat* Shelaḥ-Lekha) of the
  man who gathered wood on *Shabbat* that interrupts (was inserted between) laws of inadvertent and flagrant transgression
  by an individual and by a community (vv. 22–31) and the law
  of fringes, tzitzit (vv. 37–41).

## Textual Oddities

Sprinkled throughout the Hebrew text of the *Humash* are a number of curious markings and visual anomalies. Occasionally we see one letter written larger than all the others or one written smaller. Here and there we see dots over a letter in a word or dots over all the letters of a word. All this, as I say, is only in the Hebrew.

What are these? Why are they there? Are they of any significance?

The historical answer is that they are of the same order as the "open" and "closed" *parshiyot* I described in Part I: part and parcel of scribal tradition. A long time ago, in the Rabbinic period if not earlier, the laws of how a Torah scroll must be written included the insertion of these markings.[33] Where or when or how these markings originated we can only speculate. Perhaps scribal copying in its earliest stages may have allowed for individual styles and spellings and at some point the process was tightened up in order to protect the integrity of the holy text: the words had to be written exactly as the scribe saw them in the manuscript from which he copied. Perhaps there were ancient oral traditions about the hidden meaning of certain words and these were preserved by encoding them into the text by means of these devices so as to draw attention to those words.

Whatever the reason, by the Rabbinic period these markings were in the text and integral to it. They fairly clamored for midrashic interpretation, and they still do.

A famous example is in *parashat* Va-yishlaḥ in Genesis. The scene is the tense moment when Jacob is about to meet Esau after 20 years of separation and estrangement. Remember that Jacob, with the help of his mother, Rebekah, had maneuvered to receive the birthright blessing from Isaac and then had to flee his older brother's wrath. Now, as he is returning to the land from Paddan-aram, he learns that Esau is advancing toward him with 400 men. It doesn't look good. Jacob splits his camp in two so that at least some can escape if Esau attacks. He sends generous gifts ahead to his oncoming brother, hoping that this gesture will foster some goodwill. He prays. During the night he wrestles with a mysterious being. Then, in the morning, comes the confrontation. Brother advances toward brother. And we read:

וירץ עשו לקראתו ויחבקהו ויפל על צוארו וַיִּשָּׁקֵהוּ
ויבכו

**Esau ran to greet him. He embraced him and, falling
on his neck, he kissed him, and they wept. (Gen. 33:4)**

Scribal tradition mandated that dots be placed over the letter of
the word וַיִּשָּׁקֵהוּ, "and he kissed him." Why? Did a scribe somewhere back in time doodle while writing these words and the
doodlings later were regarded as part of the text? Or maybe a few
ink drops fell onto the parchment and they got preserved? Or are
the dots there to call our attention to the word itself and to ponder what it is saying: What kind of kiss is this? Is it a formality, the
ancient Near Eastern equivalent of a handshake between men,
something we still see today? Or was Esau genuinely overcome
by emotion at the sight of his brother, whom he hadn't seen for 20
years? The midrash holds up all these possibilities. It even records
the view of one close reader who noted that the kiss comes after
Esau has fallen on Jacob's neck, that the dots tell us that Esau was
literally going for Jacob's jugular vein, that the kiss was a bite,
and that Jacob's neck turned to ivory![34] I said the Rabbinic imagination was fertile.

There are nine other places in the Torah where words or individual letters are dotted like this.[35] I have held up the one in
*parashat* Va-yishlaḥ to indicate the midrashic possibilities such
markings offer.

There are other kinds of anomalies, too. The enlarged letter *bet* ב
with which the Torah begins is a justly famous one. Less known
but equally fascinating are the two inverted letter *nun*s that en-
close two verses in *parashat* Be-ha'alotekha (Num. 10:35–36).
When we read a parashah we should always be on the lookout
for these textual oddities and follow up on how they have been
interpreted.

As a way of reading, midrash may not be to everyone's taste. It
may not be to yours. There is a definite strand in the Jewish exegetical tradition that regards midrash as playing so fast and
loose with the text as to obscure the basic plain sense of what it
is saying, the *peshat*. Abraham Joshua Heschel finds the question

of the limits of midrash in the long-standing debate between Rabbi Akiva and Rabbi Ishmael over how the Torah is to be read and interpreted.[36] We got an inkling of this argument in Part II when we saw how the two differed over just what transpired at the Sinai experience. On the large question of interpretation Rabbi Akiva holds that since the words of the Torah originated in the divine mind and are verbal concretizations of what God thought and revealed, no piece of Torah text is without meaning—every verse, every word, every letter—indeed even the filigreed crowns that scribal tradition says must embellish the tops of some letters.

Over against him stands Rabbi Ishmael, who holds that "the Torah speaks in human language," that is, what you see is what you get—and what you get is plenty! (Rabbi Yishma'el might have agreed with a certain modern Jew, namely Sigmund Freud, who founded a whole system of interpretation with its own midrashic principles and yet [reputedly] cautioned that "sometimes a cigar is just a cigar.")

Heschel thinks that the debate between Akiva and Yishma'el is more than just an ongoing disagreement between two venerable figures of Rabbinic antiquity. Rather, he believes, the two positions they embody represent paradigms of two fundamentally different ways of extracting meaning from the Torah text: looking for the plain meaning, *peshat*, or going beneath the surface of the words, *derash*. Throughout the ages commentators have lined up on either side of this debate, though there are some major ones, notably Rashi and Ramban (Nachmanides), who take a pluralistic approach.[37] They employ both *peshat* and *derash* as they think the text warrants. This makes sense. Midrash is an important tool in enabling us to read Torah. It not only connects us to our Rabbinic forebears, it teaches us **how to think midrashically** even now, in our time. It reminds us of the truth expressed by the French-Jewish writer Edmond Jabès (1912–91) that when it comes to Torah—and not only Torah—"in each word there burns a wick."[38] Midrash, as I said at the outset of this discussion, is an activity, an ongoing activity, not restricted to the hoary past. Contemporary midrash is being created and written all the time, particularly by women midrashists for whom the *Humash* is a fertile textual field.

# Medieval Commentaries

One of the glories of the Jewish textual tradition is the corpus of commentary on the Torah that accrued between the end of the Rabbinic period (around the 7th century) and the beginning of the modern era, that is, in what we call the Middle Ages (which for the Jews lasted until the end of the 18th century, longer than they did for the Christian West). During that time a twofold project unfolded. One part was to apply the emerging understanding and articulation of how Hebrew grammar works to the biblical text. This was the Jewish parallel to what Muslim grammarians were doing at the same time with Arabic as they sought to exposit the language of the Koran.[39] The idea was that to know what either language was saying (how it was saying it grammatically and syntactically and what the words meant) would be the way to define objectively what the text meant, that is, its *peshat*. The other task that many leading medieval rabbis undertook was to cull the vast body of interpretation that the Rabbis had generated in the Talmud and the midrash and to weave the relevant material into a running commentary on each verse. Thus if the former commentators were *pashtanim* (focused on the *peshat*), the latter carried on the midrashic tradition as *darshanim* (focused on the *derash*).

## Four Major Commentators

Of the many commentators who flourished in the medieval period, I would identify the following four as the major ones. To read them in the original one must, of course, have the requisite textual facility with Hebrew and Aramaic as they are used in biblical, talmudic, and midrashic sources. One must also be able to recognize those sources when these commentators cite them because medieval style, alas, does not know of quotation marks or, for that matter, other such modern punctuational conveniences as commas, semicolons, periods, and question marks. The good news is that these commentators all exist in serviceable, annotated English translations. In Part V I will indicate the relevant bibliographic information on them.

- **Rashi** (Franco-Germany 1040–1105). RaSHI is an acronym for Rabbi Shlomo ben Yitzhak. He is unquestionably the most important and influential commentator on the *Humash* (not to speak of his work on much of the rest of the TANAKH and on most of the Babylonian Talmud). This is so because of what he writes and how he writes. Rashi formulates concise notelike comments on the verses, and sometimes on individual words he thinks need explanation and interpretation. He writes them in a crystalline Rabbinic Hebrew and you will not find one superfluous word. Yet after you have read a comment by Rashi, you will understand the verse or the word it deals with in a way you did not before. Rashi's goal, as he himself formulates it, is to elucidate the *peshat*, but in fact he will bring in midrash when he thinks it serves this purpose. (This mixed agenda tells us that in the Middle Ages the boundaries between *peshat* and *derash*, between the plain sense of a verse and its midrashic interpretation, were not objectively definable and impermeable. Postmodern reading strategies, which question whether there can ever be one objective meaning to a text, have again made it unclear where *peshat* ends and *derash* begins.)

- **Rashbam** (Franco-Germany, ca. 1085–ca. 1174). RaSHbaM is an acronym for Rabbi SHemu'el ben Meir. He is Rashi's grandson. Rashbam takes issue with his venerable grandfather for resorting to midrashic material too often. Midrash, he feels, perverts the plain meaning of text. Rashbam is interested in expositing "the *peshat* and only the *peshat*." He comments generally on verses where he thinks Rashi got it wrong, and he is not shy about saying so.

- **Ibn Ezra** (Spain, 1089–1164). Rabbi Abraham ibn Ezra injects a distinctive voice into the colloquy of medieval commentary. While he is a *pashtan* in the best tradition of the Spanish grammarians—many of his comments are miniature Hebrew lessons—he is not deaf to the overtones midrashic interpretation sounds out in the text. What makes his commentary particularly interesting are his acumen as a close reader and his intuitive sense that the text of the *Humash* can, and maybe should, be read in a specific historical context. Both these qualities give Ibn Ezra's commentary a modern feel. He anticipates the historical and literary approaches I outlined earlier in this part.

- **Ramban** (Spain and Palestine, 1194–ca. 1270). RaMBaN is an acronym for Rabbi Moses ben Nachman (Nachmanides). Coming after the above three, Ramban is able to build on their work, principally on that of Rashi and Ibn Ezra. He does this by writing a magisterial commentary (in a less than fluid and elegant Hebrew) that sometimes develops what they said about a particular verse, sometimes takes issue with and (in his view) corrects it, and sometimes goes beyond it. Ramban was a master talmudist as well as a distinguished kabbalist, and so he reads the text on many levels: *peshat*, *derash*, the allegorical, and the mystical. He regards the latter as yielding the ultimate meaning but since that meaning is esoteric, he never articulates it but only points to it cryptically. Ramban's multiple agendas are what make his commentary so rich and important.

Let's see these four major commentators in action in a rudimentary way. The verse on which they will each comment is Exod. 17:11. The Israelites are in the wilderness. Having crossed the Sea of Reeds, they are making their way to the Promised Land. But their tempers are growing short, and they clamor for food and water. To quiet them down God arranges for the manna and Moses strikes the rock to bring forth water. Then a desert tribe, Amalek, launches an attack and a fierce battle ensues. Joshua leads the troops, and Moses, staff in hand, together with his brother Aaron and Aaron's son Hur, go to a hilltop overlooking the battlefield.

והיה כאשר ירים משה ידו וגבר ישראל וכאשר יניח ידו
וגבר עמלק

**Then, whenever Moses held up his hand, Israel prevailed; but whenever he let down his hand, Amalek prevailed.**

**RASHI: "Did the hands of Moses bring victory in battle? No, it means that as long as Israel looked upward and subjected their hearts to their Father in heaven they prevailed. When they did not, they fell."**

**IBN EZRA: "Some say that this [Moses raising his hand] was a signal, like the one who holds a flag in battle. But if this had been the case, Aaron or Hur could have done it, or they could simply have**

propped it up on the mountain high enough for everyone to be able to see it. Others think he spread out his hands in prayer. But what our predecessors the Sages have said about this is correct. It was done by divine command. . . ."

RASHBAM: "'Whenever Moses held up his hand with the rod, Israel prevailed.' For when military units see their banner held high—their *gonfalon,* as we call it—they prevail. And when it is cast down, they generally flee and are defeated."

RAMBAN: "The straightforward explanation is that whenever his hands were too heavy to hold up, he saw that Amalek was winning, so he ordered Aaron and Hur not to let his hands down. A midrash says, 'Do you think Moses would let Amalek win? But it is forbidden to hold one's hands up for three hours straight.' "[40]

Now as we can see, there is a clear disagreement among the four on how the verse is to be understood. The problem is how to explain the remarkable phenomenon that the verse reports: the correlation between the position of Moses' arm or arms and the fortunes of the Israelite troops.

Rashi's comment is actually a direct citation from the Mishnah (*Rosh Hashanah* 3:8). He evidently thinks that this moralistic explanation most adequately communicates what the verse is telling us.

Ibn Ezra holds up a more prosaic, naturalistic reading, but he comes to reject it in favor of Rashi's approach or something approximating it.

Rashbam, however, puts forth the military explanation, presumably because it conforms most closely to the surface *peshat* of the verse. In his desire to make this clear he associates what Moses does to what his medieval readers would likely have seen: the ensigns horsemen carried into battle. To make his point Rashbam provides the Old French term for these banners.[41] (Rashi frequently also provides Old French.)

In his comment Ramban is explicit about the dichotomy between the *peshat* of the verse and the *derash* possibilities it offers. But the *peshat* he gives is even more literal than Rashbam's: the verse is not about military procedure but about the simple matter of muscle fatigue! And the "midrash" he cites is not from the Mishnah but from a kabbalistic source, *Sefer ha-Bahir* (The Book of Illumination), one of the fundamental works of medieval Jewish mysticism.[42] Ramban does not explain why it is forbidden to hold one's hands up for three hours straight, but then in his commentary he is always laconic about esoteric kabbalistic ideas.

This brief example should serve to show how the exegetical conversation between the great medieval commentators runs and how lively it can be.

# The Zohar

The previous sections make it sound as if midrashic interpretation of the Torah ended with the Rabbis of the talmudic period. Not so. The impulse to create midrash continued unabated into the Middle Ages, when the midrashic enterprise was wedded to the Jewish mystical tradition of theosophical and cosmological speculation. That tradition was always present in Judaism, flowing in subterranean channels from the Bible (e.g., the vision of the elders of Israel in Exodus 24 and the book of Ezekiel) into the Rabbinic period (e.g., the *merkavah* [chariot] mystics, many of whom were the same rabbis who populate the halakhic discourse of the Talmud), and from there into the Kabbalah of the Middle Ages.

The zenith of mystical midrash is the Zohar (The Book of Radiance), a work that is sometimes considered as foundational to Judaism as the *Humash* and the Talmud. Like the TANAKH, the Zohar is a collection of texts. It is written in Aramaic and Hebrew. Though it reads a lot like Rabbinic midrash (it incorporates a vast amount of that material in its discussions) and presents itself as the work of the legendary 2nd-century rabbi Shimon bar Yohai, the Zohar is a product of medieval Spain. It was composed in the late 13th century, possibly by a kabbalist named Moses de Leon.

The core of the Zohar is a comprehensive parashah-by-parashah commentary on the *Humash*. It is not easy to read. It is filled with arcane language, esoteric ideas, and Kabbalistic doctrines (many of which are found already in the earlier *Sefer ha-Bahir)* that challenge even the most advanced parashah reader. But in its understanding of how God and the cosmos operate and the interrelationship between God, the Jewish people, and the Torah, the Zohar offers profound, often thrilling, insight and furnishes the religious seeker with the inner plenitude of ultimate meaning.

I include the Zohar in this discussion only because at this writing it is in the process of being rendered into an excellent English translation by Daniel Matt. Matt's translation, along with his superb commentary, now makes this complex work accessible to the nonspecialist. The Zohar is certainly not a starting point but rather a destination to which one can aspire after several years of parashah study.[43]

Let me give an example of how the Zohar reads and spawns a series of significant interpretations. I cite here selected passages from its commentary on two *parshiyot* in Genesis—Lekh Lekha and Va-'era.' The Zohar is focusing on Abraham, trying to understand why **he** was chosen to be the progenitor of the Jewish people. A cautionary note: to understand what is being said here one must have some knowledge of three concepts that are fundamental to kabbalistic thinking:

1. an idea of God not so much as a noun but as a verb, not a static entity but an eternal and inexhaustible energy field beyond the universe that flows from a completely unknowable Source of Being down into the cosmos;

2. the notion that among the various worlds into which divinity flows there is an upper world that is unavailable to mortal men and a "lower world" that mankind inhabits;

3. the idea that in this upper world, divinity is manifest in 10 *sefirot* (plural; singular *sefirah*). The *sefirot* (literally, "countings" or "numbers" or "numerical entities") are 10 aspects or attributes of God expressed in Hebrew words, for example, *Din*, *Hesed*, *Tiferet*, etc. Each of the *sefirot* represents symbolically a

nodal point of ideas about God and Divine energy. *Hesed*, for example, is the fourth *sefirah* and represents God's lovingkindness and graciousness. *Din* is the fifth *sefirah* and connotes God's judgment and power. These two forces are seen as polar opposites and are balanced by or in the sixth *sefirah*, *Tiferet*, which comprises God's beauty and harmony. And so on.

This is all complicated, to be sure. Such metaphysics or theosophy is admittedly not everyone's cup of tea. If it's yours, or could be, read on. If not, you can safely skip the next several paragraphs and go on to the next section.

Now we turn to the context and the text.

*Parashat* Lekh Lekha begins with God abruptly breaking His long silence. His last communication with any human being was with Noah 10 generations previous. Now God calls to Abraham: "Go forth [lit. "get yourself"] from your native land and from your father's house to the land that I will show you." לֶךְ-לְךָ מֵאַרְצְךָ (Gen. 12:1).

The Zohar responds:

> **Rabbi El'azar said, "*Lekh lekha, Go for yourself*, to refine yourself, to perfect your rung.**
> **. . . *Lekh lekha, Go to yourself*, to know yourself, to refine yourself.**[44]

Daniel Matt explains that in his first reading "Rabbi El'azar interprets the phrase *Go for yourself*—for your own benefit." (He notes that Rashi and Ramban both give this interpretation. Since these two major commentators both antedate the composition of the Zohar, we have to say that in this case the author of the Zohar, presumed to be Moses de Leon, is tweaking an older source kabbalistically.)

On Rabbi El'azar's second reading, Matt writes:

> **Here he adopts another hyperliteral reading: *Go to yourself*, know yourself. Consider the comment of Moses Zacuto . . . [who cites the kabbalist] Hayyim Vital: "Every person must search and discover the root of**

> his soul, so he can fulfill it and restore it to its source,
> its essence. The more one fulfills himself, the closer
> he approaches his authentic self."[45]

A modern therapist should say it so well.

(A contemporary of Vital, Rabbi Shlomo Ephraim of Luntshitz [1550–1619] gives this idea a twist that is no less suggestive. He reads the opening words of Gen. 12:1, "Go forth from your native land," לֶךְ-לְךָ מֵאַרְצֶךָ, not as an isolated phrase but as it relates to the end of the verse, "to the land that I will show you." The apparently superfluous word לְךָ teaches that "whoever goes up to the Land of Israel ascends to his deepest self and returns to his root."[46] I have heard many friends and colleagues who live in or have visited Israel describe their experience there in just these terms.)

So far the Zohar's reading of Abraham doesn't sound much different from what one could find in earlier Rabbinic midrash. But there is more to it that this. God's call to Abraham to leave his ancestral home and go to a new place is only the first step in Abraham's evolution as a human being. This is made clear as the Zohar unpacks Abraham's subsequent deeds in the Land of Israel and in his brief sojourn in Egypt. Those deeds serve to set in motion developments in the upper world that Matt will call "the sefirotic drama." The climax of this drama comes in *parashat* Va-'era' with the binding of Isaac (the *Akedah*, Genesis 22). There we are told: "Some time afterward, God [Hebrew: "Elohim"] put Abraham to the test" (Gen. 22:1). On this the Zohar, "quoting" Rabbi Shimon bar Yohai, comments:

> Here we should contemplate [the phrase] *Elohim
> tested Abraham.* The verse should read: *tested Isaac,*
> since Isaac was [as established by the Midrash] already
> 37 years old and his father was no longer responsible
> for him. If Isaac had said, "I refuse," his father would
> not have been punished. So why is it written *Elohim
> tested Abraham,* and not *Elohim tested Isaac*?

> But *Abraham* precisely! For he had to be encompassed
> by judgment, since previously Abraham had contained
> no judgment at all. Now water was embraced by fire.

> Abraham had been incomplete until now, when he was
> crowned to execute judgment, arraying it in its realm.
> His whole life long he had been incomplete until now
> when water was completed by fire, fire by water.

> So *Elohim tested Abraham*—not *Isaac*—calling him to
> be embraced by judgment. . . . One was judged, one
> executed judgment—encompassing one another.[47]

Matt's notes on these opaque sentences give us the keys to what
the Zohar is doing here: it is linking the *Akedah* as an event that
took place in this lower world with its effects in the cosmic realm
of the *sefirot*. Before the *Akedah*, Matt writes,

> Abraham had attained the rung of *Hesed* ("Love"), but
> he was devoid of its complementary opposite: *Din*
> ("Judgment"). Being too one-sided, he now had to bal-
> ance love with rigor in order to round out his person-
> ality and become a complete human being in the
> image of God.[48]

The Zohar's locution "water was embraced by fire," Matt explains, is a way of saying that

> the free-flowing love of *Hesed* was encompassed by
> the fervid power of *Din*. . . . By binding Isaac on the al-
> tar, Abraham manifested the quality of *Din* both on
> earth and in the sefirotic realm. . . . Father and son
> completed each other: Abraham by manifesting severe
> judgment, Isaac by submitting lovingly. Their interac-
> tion balanced the corresponding *sefirot* above. . . . Isaac
> submitted to Abraham and together they enacted the
> sefirotic drama.[49]

We have here a reading of the *Akedah* that sees it not in ethical
terms but as an event that had a transformational effect on Abraham and, as we shall discover, on God as well. With respect to
Abraham we see this in the later verse (Gen. 22:11) that narrates
the climactic moment: "Then an angel of the LORD called to him
from heaven: Abraham! Abraham!" The Zohar remarks that the
words "Abraham Abraham" are "separated by a punctuation
mark, for the latter Abraham was unlike the former: the latter,

complete; the former, incomplete." As Matt explains, the Zohar here is noticing that

> in the Masoretic text, the two occurences of the name are separated by a vertical line [ | , called a *p'sik*]. Rabbi Shim'on takes this to mean that now, having undergone this ordeal, Abraham was a new, fulfilled person."[50]

But the *Akedah* affected the Godhead, too.

Zohar:

> Who would have created a compassionate father who turned cruel? It was only so that division would manifest: water versus fire, crowned in their realms, until Jacob appeared and everything harmonized—triad of patriarchs completed, above and below arrayed.[51]

Matt:

> Having undergone severe judgment, Isaac manifests *Din* alongside Abraham, who manifests *Hesed*. . . . The two patriarchs and their respective *sefirot* have completed one another, but they are not yet harmonized. Their dialectical relationship awaits synthesis. . . . Jacob, the third and decisive patriarch, symbolizes the *sefirah* of *Tif'eret*, who balances the polar qualities of *Hesed* and *Din*, symbolized by Abraham and Isaac.[52]

The *Akedah*, then, is a paradigm for a key idea in Kabbalah, one that has great resonance and relevance for our time: that everything in the universe is connected. All being is interrelated and in balance. As Abraham's actions show, what we do here is critical, for it affects and has consequences not only for us but for God as well. The onus is on man to act, not on God to perform.

# 3.
# Existential Readings

Of all the ways to read the *Humash* these are the most subjective. I use the plural because there are many approaches that could fall under this rubric. When we read existentially we come to the text to discover how it addresses us—you and me—in the life situation in which we are at the moment. Or if it addresses us at all. The perspective is personal.

As we have seen, Martin Buber would have us read the *Humash* this way, though he is not inattentive to or unappreciative of the contribution more objective approaches make to our understanding of the biblical text.[53] Buber, a thoroughly Western Jew, was much influenced in his religious thinking by his encounter with the Hasidism of eastern Europe, and many of his ideas of how we should read the Bible are grounded in Hasidic thought. So we may hold up Hasidic reading as a good model of what it might mean to read the *Humash* existentially.

Hasidism descends from the kabbalistic tradition. But as an expression of—or perhaps a response to—the Enlightenment, the winds of which were blowing through Europe in the 18th century and figuratively rustled the curtains as far east as Czarist Russia, Hasidism focuses on the individual in a way Jewish mysticism in the Middle Ages, for example, the Zohar, did not. This is probably one of the factors that accounts for its appeal to many Jews today who are otherwise marginal to Jewish communal institutions.

Hasidism has generated a rich literature on the *Humash*, most of it in Hebrew, that works in an essentially midrashic way to yield insights that I can only call existential.[54] Here is an example where one verse—indeed one word—can be abstracted from the biblical narrative to be read in the context of the personal life of the reader.

> In 1798, Rabbi Schneur Zalman of Liadi [the founder of Lubavitch Hasidism] was imprisoned on charges, put forth by the opponents of Hasidism, that his teachings undermined the imperial authority of the czar. For 52 days he was held in the Peter-Paul Fortress in Petersburg.
>
> Among the Rebbe's interrogators was a government minister who possessed broad knowledge of the Bible and Jewish studies. On one occasion, he asked the Rebbe to explain the verse (Genesis 3:9): "The Lord God called out to the man and said to him, "Where are you?" Did God not know where Adam was?
>
> Rabbi Schneur Zalman presented the explanation offered by several of the commentaries: the question "Where are you?" was merely a "conversation opener" on the part of God, who did not wish to unnerve Adam by immediately confronting him with his wrongdoing.
>
> "What Rashi says, I know," said the minister. "I wish to hear how the Rebbe understands the verse."
>
> "Do you believe that the Torah is eternal?" asked the Rebbe. "Do you believe that its every word applies to every individual, under all conditions, at all times?"
>
> "Yes," replied the minister.
>
> Rabbi Schneur Zalman was extremely gratified to hear this. The czar's minister had affirmed a principle which lies at the basis of the teachings of Rabbi Israel Baal Shem Tov, the very teachings and ideology for which he was standing trial!
>
> "'Where are you?'" explained the Rebbe, "is God's perpetual call to every man. Where are you in the world?

> What have you accomplished? You have been allotted a
> certain number of days, hours, and minutes in which to
> fulfill your mission in life. You have lived so many
> years and so many days (Rabbi Schneur Zalman
> spelled out the exact age of the minister). Where are
> you? What have you achieved?"[55]

But the *Humash* is more than a screen on which we can project the
particular concerns of our individual attempts to find meaning in
our journey through this world. However else we read it, we also
read it in our collectivity, as Jews, and it addresses us in that context as well. The story the 54 *parshiyot* tell is our story. Abraham
and Sarah, Jacob and Rachel and Leah, Joseph and his brothers are
our family. They may be a "dysfunctional family," as Aviva Zornberg has trenchantly observed, but at some level don't we feel that
we know these people? I think of Tolstoy's opening to his novel
*Anna Karenina:* "Happy families are all alike; every unhappy family is unhappy in its own way." We read Genesis and we intuitively understand this family's problems and foibles. We read
Exodus and its trajectory from slavery to redemption as a paradigm for the Jewish people's perennial struggle for a world of free-
dom and justice. We don't confine our awareness of this struggle
to the Passover seder. Leviticus may originally have been a guide
book for *Kohanim* to attain holiness; we try to read it out of our attempt to understand ourselves as contemporary members of "a
kingdom of priests and a holy nation." The shortcomings of the
people told in Numbers, their dissent and backbiting, are not unknown to Jewish communal and political life in our time. And the
whole iteration of the Israelite experience in Deuteronomy and its
spelling out of the terms of the covenant is as much for our ears today as it was for those who first heard it, whenever that was.

In addressing us in our collectivity as Jews, the *Humash* presents
us with a whole network of ideas that it invites us to consider:
about this beautiful blue ball we live on as a divine project, as a
work in progress, about the joint responsibilities in it of man and
God, about the tangled relationship between the People of Israel
and God, and about how this relationship was and is to be lived
out in time. Such ideas constitute a theology, a word that I daresay is outside the discourse of much of Jewish life today. No matter. We can disregard, even jettison, the word. It is the ideas on
which we should focus. They are the bedrock on which the rest of

the TANAKH and the totality of what would later become Judaism and Jewish tradition rests. Part of the adventure—I should say the challenge—of reading the *Humash* is to pick up what it might be saying to us about the purpose and meaning and content of our existence as Jews living in the 21st century.[56]

I do not wish to suggest that reading the *Humash* from under this collective or communal horizon can be accomplished easily or facilely. There is much material in many a parashah that serves to widen the distance between us and the biblical past. We should not hesitate to own up to the fact that from a contemporary perspective many things in the *Humash* are problematical. Years ago I had a colleague in the campus rabbinate who created, together with his Protestant counterpart, a lunch-time study series titled "The 10 Most Obnoxious Passages in the Bible." They each had no shortage of material to work with.

Acknowledging such problems can be salutary. It can help us move to an understanding of the *Humash* on its own terms and an appreciation of it that is clear-eyed and intellectually honest. It can allow us to forge a commitment to Torah in "the smithy of our own soul," one that is indisputably and authentically ours. The Torah was never meant to be a souvenir.

In the end, reading the *Humash* reduces itself to an encounter between two parties: the words on the page and the needs and expectations and aspirations of the heart and mind and soul of the individual reader. A simple and fundamental question drives the encounter: What is this piece of *Humash* saying to me? The question has several permutations:

- What does this text tell me about how I should look at the world—at its order and its disorder?
- About how I should look at my society?
- About how I should look at other people?
- About how I should look at (my fellow) Jews?
- About how I should look at my family—my parents, my children, my spouse or my partner?
- What does this text tell me, however subtly, about how I should live?
- About how I should act?
- About how I should use my time here in this world?

- What does this text tell me about God?
- About how I can relate to God?
- If I can relate to God?

We do not necessarily have to ask just these questions or all of them. Nor do we have to ask them all together; one at a time may be quite sufficient. We can ask them after reading a parashah or, sometimes, beforehand. The point is that when we read with these kinds of questions before us, we are most closely in touch with the *Humash* as Torah, as Torah in its original meaning as "teaching" or "instruction."

When we read *Humash* this way there are no preconceived answers to such questions. Chances are that when they come, they will come to us as a surprise.

# PART IV

# How to Read a Weekly Torah Portion

We are now ready to get down to business and focus specifically on the weekly Torah portion, the *parashat ha-shavua,* and how to go about reading it.

Actually, I've already said a great deal about this. Knowing what a parashah is and how it fits into the larger scheme of the Five Books prepares us to get into the specifics of a weekly reading routine. Knowing what the act of reading involves and the issues it presents in assigning meaning to a text lays the groundwork for engaging with the weekly parashah in real time. But as we now move from theory to practice, here are three things to keep in mind:

1. There is no one definitive reading of any parashah, no ultimate "mother of all interpretations" that contains the essence of what a given parashah is saying. How can there be an "essence" to a piece of text that is really nothing more than one of 54 slices of the *Humash,* cut out of the whole simply to fit the scale of the calendar year?

2. There is no one single way to read a parashah. No one lens alone will allow us to see a parashah in all its many dimensions, and no one reading technique will render audible all its multiple implications. There are many approaches, as the previous section has hopefully shown.

3. It doesn't matter if one is reading a parashah for the first time or the 20th. A parashah can yield up something interesting and worthwhile to both. Certainly these will be very different experiences and kinds of reading. A beginning reader will relate to a parashah as a single unit. Someone who has gone through the cycle of all 54 for decades will have a more synoptic perspective and will be able to have some sense of how a given parashah is connected to the composite work that is the *Humash.* Both kinds of reading are valid. Bible reading is like sudoku or chess: there are strategies for beginners, intermediates, and advanced players.

An awareness of these points will help dispel some commonly held misconceptions, will keep frustration and disappointment at bay, and will keep the pathway into a given parashah open to all who would follow it.

# 1.
# Which *Humash* to Use?

A serious runner or walker would give careful consideration to which shoe he would choose. So, too, a tennis player with her racket and a golfer with his clubs. Equipment is a factor in the comfort and success of many a worthwhile endeavor.

We should, therefore, not be too casual in deciding which *Humash* we want to use for the regimen of weekly parashah reading. We want a version that displays the Hebrew in clear characters and provides an English translation that is readable, accurate, and does not drip with the unctuousness that we often associate with biblical text. Am I thus disparaging the vaunted King James Version? To some extent, yes. King James is unrivaled in the beauty and cadence of its English and reading it aloud gives one an intimation of how gorgeous the Hebrew original is. But King James was done in 1611 and its English locutions, elegant and eloquent as they are, are not those of 21st-century England, much less of the United States. They are the product of a multifaceted Anglican agenda that involved using both the original Hebrew and Greek translations.[1] Besides, the knowledge of Hebrew of the divines who did the King James Version, admirable as it was for that time and place, does not compare with that of contemporary linguistic scholarship of biblical Hebrew.

## Translations

In the last two decades or so there has been an explosion of attempts to render the *Humash* into an English that is not only of our time but also incorporates what Semitic linguistics and biblical archaeology have achieved in the 20th century. The following are the editions that will be most useful to you. Many of them come with commentary, the discussion of which I defer to Part V.

## The NJPS Translation

The English translation that has become the standard one is that of the Jewish Publication Society. It is known as *The New JPS Translation* (NJPS). It is actually not so new; it came out in 1962 and has since been recognized as the most authoritative English version of the *Humash*. The JPS translation project continued with the appearance of *The Prophets (Nevi'im)* in 1978, and *The Writings (Kethuvim)* in 1982. The "new" nomenclature derives from the fact that this translation of the Tanakh updates and replaces the "old" one that JPS did in 1917 (OJPS). Like the former, it was done by a consortium of the best Bible scholars of the time. It is a very readable translation.

The NJPS is available both in a single volume, *The Torah*, and as part of the NJPS translation of the complete Tanakh.[2] It is also available in the five volumes of the *JPS Torah Commentary*, an important resource that I will discuss in Part V.

In line with heightened interest in gender issues in the Bible, the NJPS has recently undergone a major revision so as to make it reflect more clearly how the Torah's language expresses gender.[3] Careful thought was given to the rendering of every verse in which God, angels, and people are gendered.

The NJPS serves as the English version in three editions of the *Humash* that are widely used today in synagogues, temples, and study groups. One is *The Jewish Study Bible* (JSB). This volume presents the complete Tanakh with an excellent, wide-ranging commentary in the margins.[4] The others are the Plaut *Humash* and *Etz Hayim*, both discussed below.

## Everett Fox's *The Five Books of Moses*

The NJPS version has been criticized by some Bible scholars as being *too* readable, that is, too accommodating to English style and syntax and thus too far from the rhythm of the Hebrew original.

In its effort to sound fresh, it also tends to lose *Leitwörter*. Fox endeavored to address this problem by creating a translation of the *Humash* that would make its English replicate the cadence and feel of the Hebrew. That is what Buber and Rosenzweig were after when they made their German version, and it is Fox's model. To some degree he succeeds. But as can be expected, the English now is strained, at times eccentric and even tortured. Fox is worth consulting if only to be reminded of the linguistic differential that the more comfortable NJPS version obscures.[5]

## Robert Alter's *The Five Books of Moses*

Alter has the same agenda as Fox except that he works harder at revealing Hebrew wordplay. The result is a version that reads better than Fox and at the same time is more ornate than the NJPS. At times the renderings are ingenious, at times a bit too precious. Alter's notes, though, are superb; they illuminate the no-man's-land that the translator had to traverse as he shuttled between two linguistic systems on his dangerous mission.[6]

## Richard Elliot Friedman's
### *The Bible with Sources Revealed*

As an accomplished scholar of the Bible, Friedman is beholden to no one in his mastery of the linguistic matrix from which the Bible sprang. He has striven here for a fresh English version that falls easily on the ear of an American reader yet is consistent with Hebrew style and the best of current scholarship. Friedman's translation is available in two forms: in the English alone and with the Hebrew and a commentary.[7]

## Other Recent Translations

Two other relatively recent translations are worth mentioning here. They both present a more traditional perspective, that is, they are based solely on classical Jewish sources for their readings. One is *The Living Torah*, translated by Rabbi Aryeh Kaplan.[8] The other is *The Chumash: The Stone Edition*, done by a consortium of Orthodox rabbis and published in the ArtScroll series.[9] Of the two, Kaplan's is preferable. His approach is similar to Friedman's; the text flows naturally and idiomatically. It is a wonderful antidote to King James. The Stone *Chumash* version is more ponderous and it follows only Rashi in its rendering of problematical passages, an approach that to many a reader is unnecessarily restrictive. Stone commends itself for reasons other than its translation, as I shall presently explain.

The Fox and Alter translations give us the *Humash* in English only, as does Friedman's *The Bible with Sources Revealed*. These three volumes also have another drawback: they do not divide the text according to the weekly Torah portions. It can be annoying to have to determine for yourself where each one begins and ends. All the other volumes mentioned in this section, including all that use the NJPS translation, do show the parashah divisions.

If you do not read Hebrew, any of these will certainly suffice. Ideally, though, and in principle, it seems to me that one should have the Hebrew text always in view if only as a visual reminder of the difference between the original and the translation. Those who do know biblical Hebrew will, of course, be going back and forth between the two regularly.

## Humashim

Here are some editions of the *Humash* that stand the best chance of being helpful to you. Each of them presents both the Hebrew original and an English translation. All of them are configured according to the weekly portions. Each one includes a commentary or commentaries that I will describe briefly here and treat more fully in Part V (because the whole subject of commentary deserves a separate discussion).

### W. Gunther Plaut's *The Torah: A Modern Commentary*

Plaut's *Humash* is the product of the Reform movement, but its utility extends far beyond denominational boundaries. Its original version, published in 1981, was intended for use in adult study groups and not for use in the synagogue. For that reason it was organized, book by book, into sequential thematic sections and not by the weekly portions. In spite of that fact the Plaut *Humash* established itself over the years not only as an excellent tool for *Humash* study but for synagogue use as well. The need was seen to make it conform to the Torah reading cycle. This was done in a revised edition that came out in 2005. The English is an updated version of the NJPS and takes care to be "gender-accurate" and use gender-neutral God language. The commentary is a marvel of intellectual and verbal lucidity and is punctuated by the interpolation of short but substantial essays that are unfailingly thoughtful. All this, together with its new clear arrangement, make Plaut a prime *Humash* to own and to use.[10]

## Kaplan's *The Living Torah*

The Living Torah has a feature that no other *Humash* has: it breaks up the text into the original paragraph (*parashiyah*) units exactly the way the Torah scroll does (see above, Part I, for discussion of this). Kaplan has numbered each of the paragraphs within each of the five books and captioned them. On top of this arrangement he superimposes the chapter divisions and verse numbers and also marks off each weekly portion. This setup generates an excellent table of contents at the front that lists each weekly portion with its constituent *parshiyot* numbered and captioned. The reader can thus instantly get a bird's-eye view of any given weekly portion and of the whole *Humash*, for that matter. The commentary is concise and always informative, though only Rabbinic and medieval sources are cited. The various maps, pictures, and diagrams scattered throughout the text add to the utility of this very fine edition of the *Humash*.

## *Etz Hayim: Torah and Commentary*

Etz Hayim was produced by the Conservative movement for use in its synagogues.[11] It was designed to replace the well-worn Hertz *Humash*, which first appeared in England in 1936 and has gone through several printings. (Hertz is Rabbi Joseph H. Hertz, who was the chief rabbi of the British Empire from 1913 to 1946.) Etz Hayim uses the NJPS translation. The commentary is bifurcated. There are notes on the *peshat* of the text drawn from *The JPS*

*Torah Commentary*. Beneath those notes are snippets of ideas and nuggets from the midrashic literature. *Etz Hayim* contains at the back some good maps and a collection of 41 essays covering a wide array of topics relating to biblical society, religion and law, how the *Humash* fits into the totality of Jewish life, and the different modes of biblical interpretation.

### The Chumash: The Stone Edition

The Stone *Chumash*, noted above, is a treasure-trove for those who want to see the midrashic approach in its fullness, that is, in both its aggadic and halakhic modes. The copious commentary, written by rabbis with deep talmudic learning, synthesizes a vast range of Rabbinic interpretation.

There are, to be sure, many other versions of the *Humash* available. In time you may discover some others not mentioned here that you particularly like. But these four collectively encompass the range of approaches to the text that I have highlighted. No serious parashah reader should, however, restrict him- or herself to one *Humash* only.

# 2.
# Reading a Parashah:
# A Four-Step Process

I do not need to invent or devise a method of reading a weekly Torah portion. There is already one on the books. As I mentioned in Part I, the Talmud records the following dictum of Rabbi Ammi:

> **One should always complete one's [private] reading of the weekly Torah portion . . . twice in Hebrew and once in an Aramaic translation [lit. *Targum*] by the time that it is read publicly by the congregation in the synagogue. . . . (Babylonian Talmud, *Berachot* 8a)**

Look how much is packed into this short statement:

- Hearing the parashah read in the synagogue on *Shabbat* morning is—or should be—the culmination of a weeklong encounter with it.

- During the week, presumably at home, one should read the parashah not once but twice. R. Ammi does not explain why two readings are necessary and not one or three. Perhaps it is obvious to him that one will not be enough, that a second reading will reveal new things, since no two readings are ever alike, and that it is not realistic that most people will find time for three or more readings.

- One should also read the parashah in translation. (At that time Aramaic was the vernacular, and *"Targum"* refers to the Aramaic version, of which there were three, just as there are multiple English versions today.) In recommending this, R.

Ammi may have had in mind that the individual reader at home should mimic the way the Torah was read in the synagogue in talmudic times: the *baal korei* (the public reader) would read a verse from the scroll in Hebrew and the *meturgeman* (translator) would recite that verse from the Aramaic version (actually, not a bad idea for synagogues today to consider). But another reason for R. Ammi's specification is likely: the reading should not be superficial or perfunctory; one must have some comprehension of the text. That is probably why, when Jewish law began to be codified in the Middle Ages and Aramaic was no longer the vernacular, the authorities amended this third step to a reading of the commentary of Rashi.[12]

R. Ammi, then, envisions a Jew's encounter with the weekly Torah portion as a four-step process: the first three at home during the week and the fourth on *Shabbat* in the synagogue. With a little tweaking, this routine can serve our purposes today quite well. If we adjust for linguistic and cultural differences we can preserve in our time the spirit of what he is advocating. It is still a four-step process.

1. We still prepare at home during the week for the public reading of the parashah on *Shabbat*.

2. We still do two readings, though they may not be in Hebrew.

3. The third reading is still done so as to enhance our understanding, but now it involves not merely looking at a translation—if we've read the parashah in English we've already done that twice—but also looking into commentaries.

4. We come to synagogue on *Shabbat* morning ready to listen and to hear.

Do the first three steps all have to be done in privacy? Can they be done with a study partner (*havruta*) or in a group? My answer is a qualified yes. Steps two and three can certainly be done with another person or with a few people. Many of my colleagues would say they should be done that way, especially if you are just starting out in your parashah study. But my recommendation is that the first reading be done on your own. That way the intimacy of the one-on-one dialogue between you and the text is preserved. It doesn't matter what this dialogue does or does not contain, whether it's active and noisy or a dud. What's crucial is that there be nothing between you and the text and that this meeting be the starting point of your encounter with the parashah. Neither of these things can happen if your parashah reading already begins in a group setting.[13]

The four steps thus revised might look something like this.

## Step 1: At Home—A First Reading

Early in the week block out some dedicated parashah time, as you might for a yoga or meditation session. Find a comfortable and quiet place where there are no distractions or interruptions (telephone, pager, e-mail). Arrange for child care if possible. For this first step you shouldn't need more than an hour.

As you sit down and begin reading, you may want to keep a notebook handy, a kind of parashah journal. As you read you can use it to jot down your answers to some questions I will invite you to think about and to note anything else that strikes you.

So here you go:

1. **Survey the textual terrain**: Scan the parashah and get a sense of what kinds of texts you see. Narrative? Poetry? Laws? Genealogies? A mixture? (Use the box on p. 17 in Part I.) Knowing this will help you anticipate the kinds of things you will need to look for as you read.

2. **Get the context.** Find out where you are in the book or in the story. If you haven't been following the previous *parshiyot,* you will have some work to do in getting the background. Is the parashah continuing directly from where the previous one left off? Or does it open with new material?

   These two operations need not be performed in this order. The sequence you follow will depend on the particular parashah you are reading, how your mind and your eye work, and how much you already know about the *Humash.*

3. **Now read through the entire parashah** or as much of it as you can. But **read only the text**, no commentaries or explanatory material. Let this first reading just be a one-on-one encounter between you and the text. Try reading the parashah or a part of it aloud. You will experience the text differently that way. You may hear or feel things in it that you don't get from silent reading.

When you have finished, consider the following questions:

- What is happening here? What is this parashah about—at least on the surface?

- Did you see any words or details or ideas or themes that kept recurring? These could be the guiding words I discussed in Part II. If you are an experienced parashah reader, did you notice any thematic patterns emerging or other kinds of connections to other parts of the *Humash* or to other works of literature?

- Did you see in the parashah any strange markings over the Hebrew words or other oddities that I talked about in Part III?

- Did the text contradict itself at any point? Did you get any sense of different scribal hands at work here? Did you see any differing points of view or emphases?

- Are there things you didn't understand, or that confuse you, or that you want to know more about, or particular details in the text that pique your curiosity or attract your attention?

These are all intellectual and cognitive matters. Make a note of them. They will shape your second reading.

Sometimes objective features of the text will trigger affective responses:

- things that impress you or move you;
- conversely, things that disturb or even anger you.

Only you can know or say what these will be. They are important because they originate with you. Knowing what they are will also help you in your second reading. Mark them down, too.

## Step 2: At Home or with a Study Partner or Study Group—A Second Reading

Later in the week sit down again. What you do now in this second reading will depend on how the first one went. You may want to reread the entire parashah. Or if you couldn't finish it in the first session, do so now. If you got a good idea of what is in the parashah the first time around, you may now want to reread more closely those parts or features that attracted your attention and that you marked down as noteworthy.

This second stage of reading allows you to define your agenda with the particular parashah with which you are working. Take your cue from the notes you made in your first reading. Ponder them in the light of this second reading.

As you do this, ask yourself:

- Why does this particular story or event or detail or law grab me? Why am I interested in it? What is it I want to know about it?

- Are the issues or questions I want to explore informational and intellectual, that is, ones that point me toward looking at historical or archaeological or anthropological commentary?

- Are they literary, that is, ones that can be illuminated by reading literary analysis of this material?

- Are the issue(s) that have pushed my buttons spiritual and existential? Do they relate to where I am in my life right now? Or to where my congregation or my community or the Jewish people are right now, at this particular point in the cycle of weekly Torah readings for this particular year? The energy generated by the intersection or conjunction of these two placeholders can produce the existential meaning that reading Torah can provide.

## Step 3: At Home or with a Study Partner or Study Group—Commentaries

Your search for understanding and meaning, whether intellectual or emotional, now takes you to commentaries. You want to find out if others have addressed the questions or concerns that you have identified as yours and if they have, how they have done so. Considering how long our people have been reading the *Humash* and how many Rabbis and teachers and scholars have written about it over the centuries, it is likely that someone at some time dealt with the issues you want to look into.

Here I must qualify the course of inquiry I am laying out. It need not be as mechanically schematic as I am making it sound. Sometimes it is only by seeing what others have said about a passage or an event or a detail that we are stimulated to see things that eluded us in our reading. Often the questions a commentator asks will give us new insight into the text that enables us to think about it in a new way. And then there will be *parshiyot* where we simply cannot understand the text without consulting a commentary.

This is because commentary, or exegesis, actually has two separate functions and involves two different activities: explanation and interpretation. (The differences between them may be more apparent than real for at bottom every explanation is an interpretation and vice versa.) Nevertheless, I would propose the following rule of thumb when you need to decide when to consult commentary:

**When reading narrative**, it is likely that what you are looking for is interpretation—and that usually can—I believe should—wait until you have worked through the step 2 questions on your own.

**When reading law or poetry**, you are probably in need of explanation without which you cannot proceed—and so you should go ahead and delve into commentary.

In either case, at some point during or after the second reading you will be ready to check out classical Rabbinic midrash, or some of the great medievals like Rashi and Ramban, or some of the moderns and contemporaries. There is a vast array from which to choose. In Part V I'll offer a road map to the magnificent world of Torah commentary. Your research into the commentaries will move you along in your understanding of whatever it was you wanted to investigate.

Then again, it may not. It's possible that the commentaries will not address the issues that sent you to them in the first place, or, if they do, they do so in a way that doesn't satisfy you. It's not inconceivable that the net result of all your reading and thinking is a deeper confusion or concern about what you found in the parashah than when you first read it.

Do not let this discourage you. This is what it means to be in dialogue with the Torah. There are times when the Torah challenges us and there are times when we challenge the Torah. The dialogue is ongoing. **Reading and studying the Torah portion each week have to be seen as part of a lifetime project.** What is unclear or problematic this year may become understandable in another. I think this is what the prayer book means when it says of the words of Torah: "For they are our life and the length of our days, and we will meditate upon them day and night."

Sometimes we just have to live with our questions. Sometimes questions are stronger than any answers that could be given. There is a surfeit of certainty in the world today both religious and secular, and skepticism and cynicism, which are also forms of certainty, are not lacking either; what is in shorter supply is the uncertainty that comes from honest struggle.

# 3.
# What to Look for in a Parashah

Some readers will open themselves and the *Humash* they are working from to the parashah of the week and simply start reading. They choose to let the text take them where it will. You may be such a reader, and if that approach works for you— good!

The approach I recommend, especially for beginners, is to survey the textual landscape in advance. You want not only to get an idea of the story line or the content but, more important, to scope out the kind of material the parashah will present: narrative, poetry, laws, lists, etc. You want to know what kind of terrain you will be navigating in this particular parashah. A parashah in Genesis, for example, is a very different textual entity than one in Leviticus. In general I think it is very important when reading any parashah always to know and be aware of what book it is a part of. We focus each week on an individual parashah, but we should never forget that whatever is in it is there to advance the larger agenda of that particular book.

It is a good idea, therefore, to know the following in advance.

- Which of the five books are you reading? If you want a quick sense of that book, go to the introduction to it that most *Humashim* have.

- Where in the book is the parashah you are reading situated? Is it the opening one that initiates the textual flow? The final one that effects closure on the book? Or one in the middle? Location can have a bearing on what's going in a parashah.

- What kinds of text—genres—are in the parashah? The answer will allow you to calibrate your expectations and attune your perceptions. When you know what you are **looking at** you will have a better idea of what to **look for.**

Here are some basic tips to help guide your reading.

## When Reading Narrative

One tip is to watch for repetitions and repetitive patterns of words, actions, themes, or ideas. Take, for example, the issue of brothers and brotherhood and fratricidal conflict that runs like a thread though the *parshiyot* of Genesis: Cain and Abel, Isaac and Ishmael, Jacob and Esau, Joseph and his brothers, Judah and Reuben.

Or consider the whole matter of dreams and pits in the Joseph story. Early on (Gen. 37:5–11) we read of Joseph's dreams and his brothers' dismissal of them. When they conspire against him they say, "Here comes that **dreamer!** Come now, let us kill him and throw him into one of the **pits;** and we can say, 'A savage beast devoured him.' We shall see what comes of his **dreams**" (37:19–20). Later on we read of the dreams of Pharaoh's royal cup-bearer and baker in prison (Genesis 40) and, not long after that, of the dreams of Pharaoh himself (41:1–46), the interpretations of which get Joseph out of **the dungeon** (see 41:14)—and we come to see the irony of what the brothers said. Genesis concludes with Joseph, the dreamer and the interpreter of dreams, dead, entombed **in a box in Egypt** (50:26), an ending that prefigures the descent of his descendants into slavery there and setting the stage for their eventual liberation, and with it, the redemption of his bones from the pit of exile.

Do you see the pattern? Articulating the depths of his unconscious lands Joseph in the physical depths of the pit; illuminating the depths of the unconscious (through interpretation of the dreams of the cupbearer, the baker, and Pharaoh) elevates Joseph from the dark dungeon out into the bright Egyptian sunlight. Biblical narrative has a way of suggesting that the disparate and apparently random events of human reality are really parts of a larger, coherent, transcendental one.

A second tip is to observe how the narrative tells us the actions of the characters but seldom lets us know how they feel or what they are thinking or what their motivations are. We saw this in our discussion of the *Akedah* story (Genesis 22) in Part III. These are the gaps that the spare nature of biblical narrative creates. We should see them as invitations to exploration and interpretation.

Also, don't be surprised to find two accounts of the same story. These are the "doublets" I pointed out in my discussion of source criticism in Part III. The *Humash* is filled with them. Don't take such seeming redundancy at face value. Ask yourself: Why am I hearing this story or event twice? What possessed the Redactor to include both tellings? A key example is the two versions of the Creation story in the opening of Genesis (Gen. 1:1–2:3 and 2:4b–25). See if you can discover the differences in details and emphases between them. Then you may want to consult commentaries that report how source criticism accounts for such narrative duplication as well those that provide more midrashic explanations for them. And so it goes with any of the doublets.[14]

## When Reading Biblical Poetry

In many English translations of the *Humash* poetic verses are marked off in the text differently from narrative material. They are not set in solid columns of print like narrative but are indented, with large spaces between the verses and the parts of a verse. When you see that kind of typographical arrangement you will know that you are reading poetry and not prose.

As you read the verses, try to discern the parallelism that is the structural principle of biblical poetry (discussed in Part III). Try to discover if the translation you are using gives you a sense of how the two, and occasionally three, stichs of each verse relate to each other. Does the second half merely reiterate in different words what the first half said, or does it in some way complement it? Does the second half of the verse go beyond the idea expressed in the first half and add something that was not in it? (You may want to review the close reading of the short poem of Lamech in Part III.)

When you come upon a poetic passage, consider how it relates to the context in which it comes. Often the poetry will depict events differently from what has just been told in the narrative. The Song of the Sea in Exod. 15:1–19 is a prime example of this. It recounts poetically (some of) the events of the escape from the pursuing Pharaoh told in Exod. 14:21–31. A poem inserted into the text sometimes offers a vision of the future suggested by the preceding narrative. A case in point is Jacob's almost incantational blessing of his sons on his deathbed (Genesis 49). If we compare his utterances about each of his sons with what we have already seen of them in the preceding chapters and with what we learn later on about their descendants, we see how Israelite reality is formed and transformed in the crucible of poetic vision. Other such poems that comment on Israel's past and prefigure its future are Moses' swan song in Deut. 32:1–43, and his final blessing of the 12 tribes in Deuteronomy 33.[15]

## When Reading Biblical Law

Throughout the *Humash* (except for Genesis) there is a great deal of legal material. We find this both in individual verses and in long passages. There are three major collections of law that span whole chapters and read like legal codes

- The mini-code that runs from Exod. 21:2–23:19, often called the Book of the Covenant;

- The Holiness Code in Levit. 17:1–26:2;

- The Deuteronomic Code that makes up the heart of the book of Deuteronomy: Deut. 12:1–26:15.

These are actually not formal codes but at best legal compendia. Edward Greenstein has noted that "the Torah does not encompass a complete code of law. It is selective, illustrative, paradigmatic. Its arrangement is imbalanced. Some laws are repeated twice or more; laws we would expect to find are often absent."[16]

Reading this material is challenging, for, as with biblical poetry, it has connections in both style and content to the legal traditions, norms, and codes of the ancient Near East, most notably the code of Hammurabi, the Babylonian king of the 18th century B.C.E. So if you want to understand what is behind this material you will need to study it comparatively.[17] But when you will have done so you will be only halfway there. For as Greenstein notes, "The Torah's laws . . . seem to have served less as a book for the judiciary than as a vehicle for religious instruction."[18]

This is our cue for how to read the legal material. Try to discover how it reflects the larger concerns of the Torah and the context in which it operates.

For example, the laws of slavery given in Exod. 21:2–11 are the very first laws set forth in that series. They come directly after the Mount Sinai revelation (chapter 20). As many commentators point out, the experience of slavery in Egypt and the liberation from it are fresh in the minds of the Israelites—more important, in the mind of the reader—and so the Torah, in detailing these laws, is teaching: here is how you treat your slaves.

Or take the various laws about blood in Lev. 17:1–14 and in Deut. 12:23–25, which revolve around the principle that "the life of the [living] flesh is in the blood" (Lev. 17:11). To understand what lies behind this we have to connect these laws and the prohibition of eating blood to the fundamental teachings about blood laid down in Genesis. Cain sheds his brother's blood in the first murder, an act that after the Flood is explicitly forbidden because blood is equated with life itself (9:6). The very name for primordial man, Adam, אדם, contains within it the Hebrew word for blood, dam דם, and this sets up the idea that blood is life and that every murder is an effacing of the divine image.

Ultimately, if you want to know what the laws in the Torah came to mean in Judaism and how they were applied, you have to see how the Oral Tradition, that is, the Rabbis and Rabbinic tradition, interpreted them. The commentary in the *The Chumash: The Stone Edition* is particularly valuable for showing this.

## When Noticing Visible Quirks in the Text

Even if you are reading the parashah only in the English translation, it pays to look at the Hebrew original. This is because scattered here and there throughout the *Humash* are various markings and other curious features that attract attention. These are the textual oddities I discussed in Part III, such as occasional enlarged or diminutive letters and dots over certain words. Scribal tradition has left us no explanations for these anomalies. Nor did the Masoretes when they fixed the Bible's text for all time. They noted only that the text had to be written with all those markings. So when you spot them, regard them as openings for investigation and contemplation.

# 4.

# The Fourth Step

The good work you've done at home, the first three steps, are prologue. Now you are ready for the fourth and culminative step: to
hear the parashah read aloud in the synagogue. The first three
steps were done privately or, in the case of the second and/or
third ones, perhaps with a study partner or partners; the fourth
step is communal. We do well to appreciate R. Ammi's depiction
of this step as a "completion." It is a completion because in Judaism fulfillment is attained communally and not, as in Western
post-Enlightenment thinking, individually. The music of Torah is
scored as a symphony and not as a solo.

The communal experience of hearing the Torah read aloud in the
synagogue has both horizontal and vertical dimensions. Horizon-
ally, it connects us with the whole house of Israel all over the
world who are reading the same parashah on that same *Shabbat*.[19]
Vertically, that is, in time, it connects us with a long tradition of
reading the Torah in public that goes back to Moses. At the end of
his life, as he has handed the leadership over to Joshua:

> **Moses wrote down this Teaching and gave it to the
> priests [*Kohanim*], sons of Levi, who carried the Ark
> of the LORD's Covenant, and to all the elders of Israel.**
>
> **And Moses instructed them as follows: Every seventh
> year, the year set for remission, at the Feast of Booths
> [Sukkot], when all Israel comes to appear before the
> LORD your God in the place that He will choose, you
> shall read this Teaching [Torah] aloud in the presence
> of all Israel. Gather the people—men, women, chil-
> dren, and the strangers in your communities—that**

they may hear and so learn to revere the LORD your
God and to observe faithfully every word of this
Teaching. (Deut. 31:9–12)

It's not clear that what Moses prescribes here was done with any
regularity, partly because it's not clear just what book or text
Moses is referring to. Joshua conducted such a covenant renewal
ceremony during the conquest of Canaan (1200 B.C.E.?), but again
we don't know exactly what he read. The book of Joshua tells us
only that he read "a copy of the Teaching that Moses has written
for Israel" (Josh. 8: 30–35) that he had inscribed on the stones of
the altar he had built. Later on, in the last years of the First Temple period (622 B.C.E.?), King Josiah did the same, but in this case
we have a good idea of what was read out to the people. A mysterious hidden *sefer Torah* had been discovered in the Temple and
its contents motivated Josiah to convene the kind of assembly prescribed by Moses. At that convocation *"the entire text of the
covenant scroll"* was read (2 Kings 22:8 and 23:1–3). There is consensus among Bible scholars that the scroll in question was the
book of Deuteronomy.

The only other public Torah reading the TANAKH reports is the
one done by Ezra in the early years of the Second Temple, about
440 B.C.E.—and this is a significant one. It is significant because of
how it was done and what was read. Whereas the public readings
noted in the preceding paragraph are pre-Exilic and vague in
terms of their content, this one took place one Rosh Hashanah in
Jerusalem after the return from Babylonia, when the Pentateuch
as we know it, had come or was coming into existence.[20] The book
of Nehemiah records the event:

> The entire people assembled as one man in the square
> before the Water Gate, and they asked Ezra the scribe
> to bring the scroll of the Teaching of Moses [*sefer torat
> Moshe*, ‏ספר תורת משה‎] with which the LORD had
> charged Israel.

> On the first day of the seventh month, Ezra the priest
> [*kohen*] brought the Teaching [Torah] before the con-
> gregation, men and women and all who could listen
> with understanding. He read from it, facing the
> square before the Water Gate, from the first light un-

> til midday, to the men and the women and those who
> could understand; the ears of all the people were
> given to the scroll of the Teaching.
>
> Ezra the scribe stood upon a wooden tower made for
> the purpose, and . . . Ezra opened the scroll in the sight
> of all the people, for he was above all the people; as he
> opened it, all the people stood up. Ezra blessed the
> LORD, the great God, and all the people answered,
> "Amen, Amen," with hands upraised. Then they
> bowed their heads and prostrated themselves before
> the LORD with their faces to the ground.
>
> [Thirteen men] and the Levites explained the Teach-
> ing to the people, while the people stood in their
> places. They read from the scroll of the teaching of
> God, translating it and giving the sense; so they un-
> derstood the reading. (Neh. 8:1–8)

This sounds very much like a covenant renewal ceremony mod-
eled after the one mandated by Moses. But it is also sounds a bit
like the way Torah was read in Rabbinic times and even like the
way we read it in synagogues today: from a *bimah* (platform), un-
rolling and holding aloft the scroll in full view of the congregation, with a pronounced blessing, and a concerted attempt to
render the text comprehensible. Ezra, who may have been the
first rabbi, officiated at what became the performative paradigm
of how the Torah has been read publicly on *Shabbat* since the 1st
and 2nd centuries, when the Rabbis developed the synagogue
service, and which continues even today.

All this is very historical—and that is fine. History for Jews is a
gateway to sanctity. But there is more to sanctity—and to this
fourth step—than history. Hearing the Torah read in the synagogue on *Shabbat* morning is meant to be a numinous experience
that transports us beyond the particularities of time and space.
That is how the Jewish mystical tradition understands it. The Zohar regards the public reading of the Torah as a virtual reenactment of the Sinai revelation.

> Rabbi Shimon said: When the scroll of the Torah is
> taken out [of the ark] to be read to the congregation,

the heavenly gates of mercy are opened and love is aroused in the world above. . . . The scroll of the Torah should be read by only one person, and everyone must listen to him in silence, so that they may hear the words from his mouth, just as if they were receiving [the Torah] at that moment on Mount Sinai.[21]

# 5.
# Navigating the *Parshiyot*

The fair neck of Israel is adorned by five golden necklaces on which a total of 54 pearls are strung.[22] We will now consider these necklaces in turn, selecting as we go one pearl on each to hold up to the light.

From a distance the necklaces all look quite similar. Collectively they and their jewels dazzle. When we looked at them up close, we see that while they all hang together quite nicely, they are different from one another. Each of the five books of the anthology that is the *Humash* has its own character, structure, and function. A parashah in one will look and read very different from a parashah in another. And this is true even for *parshiyot* within one book.

In the pages that follow I want to treat each of the five books in a way that will help you read their respective *parshiyot*. This will entail three operations for each of the five books:

1. I will first note some basic features of the book's content and sources and lay out the rudiments of its structure. These notes do not replace the general introductions to the books that every one of the *Humashim* noted above and in Part V provides. Those introductions supply, each in its own way, more detailed background, historical or otherwise, to the books. Some of them also have fuller synopses of the *parshiyot*. My purpose here is to flag salient issues in or about the book that will enable you to be a better reader of a parashah in that particular book.

2. For each book there will be a guide to its textual landscape parashah by parashah. This is a bullet-point listing of each

parashah's contents; it is not a detailed synopsis. The map is designed to help you see the book as a whole at one glance and thus to locate quickly the general context of each parashah.

3. Then I will select one parashah as a specimen for a guided reading. No one parashah is ever representative of the book in which it occurs, but the one I choose will have enough salient features that will be relevant for many, if not all, the other *parshiyot* in that book.

---

# On Reading Genesis and Its 12 *Parshiyot*

Compared to the other four books, Genesis is relatively easy to negotiate. It is less diverse in content and in form, even though it is the longest of the five.

- Source-wise Genesis is preponderantly the J writer's book with important additions of E material and interpolations from P.

- Structure-wise it consists of two big units, as the guide on the accompanying pages shows:

  - **a prologue** that lays down the mythic substructure on which not only Genesis and the Pentateuch rest but the entire TANAKH.

  - **narratives** that tell stories of the three Patriarchs, the four Matriarchs, and their descendants.

Each of these large sections as well as the subsections within them concludes with a genealogical list. So when you see such a list you will know you are about to transition to another part of the book.

### The Prologue (Chapters 1–11)

The Prologue presents what the Bible understands as prehistory. It covers the first two *parshiyot*, B'reishit and Noaḥ. Most of the material is derived from the mythology of the pre-Hebraic ancient

Near East. But these are not mere transcriptions into Hebrew of stories originally written in Sumerian, Akkadian, or Ugaritic, the languages of Mesopotamia and Canaan of the second and third millennia B.C.E.; they are transmutations of that material. What had been told of contending gods created in the image of men was now recast in monotheistic terms as the will and actions of a God who transcends the world, nature, and humanity. The ideas and the language of these two *parshiyot* are fundamental to the biblical view of God, man, and the world, and to the values and worldview of Rabbinic Judaism and its subsequent development in the medieval and modern periods. In short, the first assumptions of what will become Torah are found in these 11 chapters. These are the things for the reader to discover. It is a pity that the annual cycle gives us only two weeks to work closely with this material. These *parshiyot* fairly require some investigation of sources and the midrashic material on them is equally indispensable.

## The Narratives (Chapters 12–50)

Here we have the foundational stories of the progenitors of the human family that in time became the Jewish people. Literarily these stories are widely regarded as among the most consummate works of narrative art in human culture. We should not be deceived by the fluidity of the narratives as they rush along. Underneath them lie deep pools of implication for us to fathom and unseen channels of connection for us to discern and follow.

There is no legal material to contend with here; everything is pre-Sinai. But we should not fail to note two core ideas that thread their way through Genesis: **covenant** and **land**, that is, the Promised Land. They are cornerstones of the TANAKH and they underwrite what will later become Judaism.

Genesis has a clear trajectory: from the cosmic and the universal to the territorial and the particular. A book that begins in the dark lifeless void ends with the mummified body of Joseph entombed in a box outside the ancestral land. What happens in between prefigures the reality not only of the Jewish project but of the human project on this planet, both of which, Genesis tells us, are God's project.

## A LIST OF THE 12 PARSHIYOT
## OF GENESIS

**The prologue** covers the first two *parshiyot*:

1. B'reshit (Gen. 1:1–6:8)
   - the Creation (two versions)
   - the Garden of Eden
   - Cain and Abel
   - the genealogy of Adam until Noah

2. Noah (Gen. 6:9–11:32)
   - Noah and the Flood
   - the genealogy of the nations of the world
   - the Tower of Babel
   - the genealogy of Shem to Abram

**The narratives** cover 10 *parshiyot:*

3. Lekh Lekha (Gen. 12:1–17:27)
   - the call to Abram and his journeys
   - the war of the four kings against the five
   - the covenant "between the pieces"
   - the birth of Ishmael
   - the covenant of circumcision

4 Va-'era' (Gen. 18:1–22:24)
   - Abraham's three guests and their promise
   - Abraham bargains with God over Sodom
   - the destruction of the cities of the plain
   - Lot and his two daughters
   - the wife-sister episode (Sarah and Abimelech)
   - the birth of Isaac and the expulsion of Hagar
   - the treaty with Abimelech
   - the binding of Isaac (the *Akedah*)

5. Ḥayyei Sarah (Gen. 23:1–25:18)
   - the death and burial of Sarah
   - the search for a wife for Isaac
   - Rebekah
   - the deaths of Abraham and Ishmael
   - the genealogy of Ishmael

*(continued)*

**A LIST OF THE 12 PARSHIYOT OF GENESIS,**
*continued*

6. Toledot (Gen. 25:19–28:9)
   - Jacob and Esau and the selling of the birthright
   - another wife-sister episode (Rebekah and Abimelech)
   - quarrels over wells
   - Jacob tricks Esau over Isaac's blessing

7. Va-yetse' (Gen. 28:10–32:3)
   - Jacob flees from Esau . . . and has a dream on the way
   - Jacob's stay with Laban in Haran
   - Leah and Rachel
   - the births of Jacob's sons and daughter
   - Jacob tricks Laban over his wages
   - the departure from Haran
   - the pact with Laban

8. Va-yishlaḥ (Gen. 32:4–36:43)
   - Jacob prepares to reencounter Esau
   - the nighttime struggle with the mysterious being
   - the meet-up with Esau
   - the Dinah incident
   - the deaths of Rachel and Isaac
   - the genealogy of Esau and the Edomites

9. Va-yeshev (Gen. 37:1–40:23)
   - Joseph and his brothers—part 1
     - the dreams and the selling of Joseph
     - the story of Judah and Tamar
     - Joseph in Egypt: Mrs. Potiphar
     - Joseph imprisoned

10. Mikkets (Gen. 41:1–44:17)
    - Pharaoh's dreams and the elevation of Joseph
    - the famine in Egypt
    - Joseph and his brothers—part 2
      - the brothers' first visit to Joseph
      - the brothers' second visit to Joseph

11. Va-yiggash (Gen. 44:18–47:27)
   - Joseph and his brothers—part 3
     - Judah's speech
     - Joseph reveals himself
     - Jacob in Egypt: the family reunited
   - the genealogy of Jacob
   - Jacob comes before Pharaoh
   - Joseph as viceroy of Egypt

12. Va-yeḥi (Gen. 47:28–50:26)
   - Jacob blesses his grandsons Ephraim and Manasseh
   - the poem of Jacob's blessing of his 12 sons
   - Jacob's death in Egypt and burial in Canaan
   - Joseph's death and embalmment in Egypt

## A Guided Reading of *Parashat* Va-yetse'

Let's now read closely one parashah in Genesis. I choose Va-yetse' (Gen. 28:10–32:3) because it presents a good array of features that are fairly typical of the narratives of Genesis. We'll follow the first two steps I suggested above. For best results I encourage you to review the parashah before continuing here and then have it open before you so you can see more clearly what I do. Since this is a "practice" reading, I will give you my answers to the questions I posed above for each step. They will give you an idea of the items a reading of the parashah might harvest. The ones I note here will by no means encompass everything that could or should be observed. You may find others. A specialist in biblical literature would surely find more. Nor is what follows meant to be an interpretation of the parashah. My concern here is the "how" of reading.

### Step 1: The First Reading

1. **The textual terrain:** A quick scan of Va-yetse' shows that it is all narrative. This parashah will not require me to change gears during the reading to accommodate generic shifts. I can proceed knowing that the issues here will be those presented by biblical narrative style.

2. **The context:** The narrative opens with Jacob leaving Beer-sheba for Haran. He is leaving because we learned at the end of the previous parashah, Toledot, that each of his parents has told him to do so, but for different reasons. Rebekah, who had been Jacob's "handler" all along, warned him to flee from Esau. She knew that the older twin was furious at how his younger brother had filched him out of the birthright—and she knew that Esau was a violent man. (See Gen. 27:41–45.) Isaac, however, other hand, urged him to leave for a different reason: he didn't want Jacob to intermarry with the Canaanites. He directed him northeastward, to Paddan-aram, where Rebekah had come from, to the house of her brother, Jacob's uncle Laban. A wife from there would preserve the line of Abraham and its attendant promise. (See 28:1–5.)

I see, then, two versions of the reason for Jacob's departure from Beer-sheba. Although they occur at the end of the previous parashah, they have a bearing on how I am to understand the one I am reading now, Va-yetse.' I'd jot this point down in my notebook for further investigation.

3. **The parashah:** After I read the parashah, here's what I write in my notebook.

- **Dreams:** Three dreams are reported, two by Jacob and one by Laban. Jacob dreams about the ladder to heaven at Gen. 28:12ff., and about animal husbandry at Gen. 31:10–13. Laban dreams about how he should talk to Jacob at Gen.31:24 and 29. I want to think about this. God communicates in dreams. Interesting.

- **The land:** Jacob is leaving *Eretz Yisra'el*. His dream indicates that he is deeply aware of this. Later on he is told to go back to the land and he does so. There is a circular movement to this parashah: out of the land and back to it. Interesting.

- **Stones:** Stones seem to be a big thing here. Stone is a *Leitwort*. Jacob falls asleep on some stones he finds and, when he wakes up the next morning, he takes one of them and sets it up as a monument (Gen. 28:18). When he gets to Haran he sees a heavy stone covering the well from which Rachel wants to water her flocks. The shepherds are not there to roll it away for her. Jacob does this by himself (29:1–10). At the end of the parashah, when Jacob is on his way back to the land, Laban catches up with him and they patch things up between them by way of a stone monument (31:44–52). Again there is a circular movement: stone monument at the beginning, stone monument at the end.

- **Deception:** There is definitely a pattern of deception here. Laban deceives Jacob when he promises him Rachel and gives him Leah instead (Gen. 29:18–28). Jacob in turn deceives Laban when he doesn't tell him he's leaving (31:20). Rachel deceives Laban in the alibi she concocts to prevent her from dismounting from her camel, thus preventing Laban from searching for his stolen gods (31:33–35).

- **Terafim:** What are the "gods" that Rachel steals anyway (Gen. 31:19)?

- **Measure for measure:** At two points in the parashah Laban asks Jacob, "What shall I pay you?": at Gen. 29:15 when Jacob starts working for him, and later on, at Gen. 30:28 and 31, when he has fulfilled the terms of his first employment and is negotiating a second contract with Laban. Laban had reneged on his promise in the first one, giving Jacob Leah instead of Rachel. Jacob gets back at him by forcing him to make good what he had agreed to in his second promise: that Jacob could have all the dark-colored sheep and all the spotted and speckled goats. He manipulates the breeding of the animals at Laban's expense. Tit for tat.

- **Jacob:** The central figure here is clearly Jacob. We are shown so many different sides of him: his unconscious, his reaction to his dream, his insecurity, his craftiness, his fertility. What kind of person is he? I want to think about this.

## Step 2: The Second Reading

My second reading prompts the following ruminations:

- **The context:** The contradiction between Rebekah's and Isaac's reasons for advising Jacob to leave continues to bother me. It looks like a biblical instance of a perennial problem: that of two parents giving different messages to their children, a recipe for confusing them. Is a look into source criticism indicated here? Source criticism could help account for the different motivations of each parent. Or maybe both versions (i.e., the two parents) are not in contradiction and what they each say can be reconciled? The *Humashim* I am using don't give me much to go on. My next step will be to look at Friedman's polychromatic version, *The Bible with Sources Revealed*. But I'll also want to look at what a literary critic like Alter says. He regards source criticism as the first but not the last word in illuminating a passage.

(Psst: Rebekah's concern is how the J writer presents the reasons for Jacob's departure. It follows logically from the whole story of this affair as J has been telling it. What Isaac advises reflects the more theological perspective of the P source.[23])

- **Dreams and reality:** I want to think more about Jacob's dream and what he sees in it. Actually, what really stirs me is what he says when he wakes up: "Surely the LORD is present in this place, and I did not know it. . . . How awesome is this place! This is none other than the abode of God, and that is the gateway to heaven" (Gen. 28:16–17). These words jump out from the page. They open to me the possibility that everywhere I go in this world is such a place. They also remind me of a book that I now know I have to read.[24]

- **Stones:** Does Jacob's rolling away the stone from the mouth of the well for Rachel (Gen. 29:10) presage the "opening [of] her womb" (30:22)?

- **Deception, measure for measure:** I see that in this parashah when Laban gives Jacob his firstborn daughter in place of his younger one, he is giving Jacob a taste of his own medicine. He is respecting birth order as Jacob did not when he maneuvered to get the birthright from Esau.

- **Jacob:** The human dimension of Jacob's situation at the parashah's opening haunts me. It prompts a meditation. I see Jacob here not as a mythical figure but as a real human being. He has to leave home, he is on his way to an unknown place, he has to fend for himself, he is alone. He has no support system. Isn't this what it comes down to for everyone? Isn't this the bottom line of the human situation? I made the passage into this world by myself. I will have to make the passage out of it on my own, too. True, I had, and may have, others with me at both these transitional moments. I certainly have them in between. I can't live without them. But I can't use them as an escape from myself. I can't get out of my skin, and there is no one else inside it. I had better get to know the person inside it, then, know him well, because I have to learn to live with him.

I wonder if the *Humashim* and the commentaries available to me will speak about these matters and what they will say.

---

## On Reading Exodus and Its 11 *Parshiyot*

Exodus initially presents itself as a direct continuation of Genesis. It is that—for a while. Then it veers off and becomes a very different kind of book. Its 40 chapters can be seen to comprise three large units:

- **A narrative** that tells what befell the descendants of Joseph in Egypt, their enslavement, their struggle against Pharaoh, and their liberation, culminating in the theophany at Mount Sinai (Exodus 1–20).

- **A mini-code of law** that accompanies and amplifies the 10 Commandments (Exodus 21–23).

- **A vision and detailed plans for the building of the** *mishkan*, the portable Tabernacle housing the sanctuary that the Israelites carried with them in their wanderings (Exodus 25–31), and **an account of its assembly** (Exodus 35–40). In between the vision and its realization is a narrative that relates the Golden Calf episode, the great falling-out between God and Israel, and their reconciliation (Exodus 32–34).

This content and structure present two central questions about the book of Exodus, the answers to which will influence how we understand its import:

1. Why is the Golden Calf narrative placed where it is: smack in the middle of the *mishkan* section? Why doesn't it come where it presumably belongs: right after the Sinai revelation (i.e., after Exodus, 20)? Or is this its proper place?

2. Where does the book of Exodus climax? In the center, with the Revelation at Sinai (chapter 20)? Or at the end, with the completion of the *mishkan* and the investment of God's presence in the sanctuary (at the very end of Exodus, 40)? Is Exodus shaped like a Shakspearean play, with a rising action and then a falling action? Or is it more like a musical crescendo, gradually building to a mighty conclusion?

The real issue here is the *mishkan*—its function and meaning. Over a third of the book is taken up with its details. Compared to those details, everything else in the book is relatively straightforward; the details themselves feel tedious and arcane. A main problem in reading Exodus is whether we can afford to rest content with this feeling and regard the *mishkan* section as an antiquated superfluity or whether we must rise to the challenge of engaging with it.

Source criticism sheds some light on these matters. In laying bare the various sources (and their biases and outlooks) from which the book was assembled by the Redactor, we begin to see how and why Exodus is constructed as it is. Source criticism views Exodus more or less like this:

- the narratives in Exodus, chapters 1–20, are mostly E and J, with P adding its version or emphasis here and there;

- the law code in Exod. 21–23:19 is E,

- the *mishkan* material is all P.

Now we know that P is later than J and E. It comments on the combined work of those two received versions of Israel's history. In doing this with Exodus, the *Kohanim* who were the P writers put their definitive stamp on the book. The great medieval commentator Rabbi Moses ben Nachman (Nachmanides or Ramban, 1194–1270) understands what this stamp is. In his introduction to Exodus he states better than anyone else I know the logic of how the book works:

> The Book of [Exodus] was set apart for the story of the first exile, which had been clearly decreed,[25] and the redemption therefrom. That is why He [God] reverted and began [this second book of the Torah] with the names of those persons who went down to Egypt. . . . It is because their descent thereto constituted the beginning of the exile, which began from that moment on.
>
> Now the exile was not completed until the day they returned to their place and were restored to the status of their fathers. When they left Egypt, even though they came forth from the house of bondage, they were still considered exiles because they were *in a land not theirs* [Gen. 15:13], entangled in the desert. When they came to Mount Sinai and made the Tabernacle, and the Holy One, blessed be He, caused his Divine Presence to dwell again among them, they returned to the status of their fathers *"when the Divine counsel was upon [their] tent"* [Job 29:4]. . . . Then they were considered redeemed. It was for this reason that this second book of the Torah is concluded with the consummation of the building of the Tabernacle, and the glory of the Eternal filling it always.[26]

Nachmanides thus accepts the agenda of the P school (though he certainly wouldn't have put it that way). In this agenda the real subject of Exodus is not the birth of the Jewish people and their epic struggle for liberation from oppression, and their acceptance of the Torah at Sinai. That is the outlook of the book of Deuteronomy. The real subject of Exodus is God and God's presence among the people, of which the *mishkan* is the permanent locus.

This view of Exodus rings true. But that is not how it is usually taught. Most of us, when we think of Exodus, think of the first 20 chapters. The *mishkan* section is peripheral, almost a curiosity. Which, if we think about it, is quite understandable. We have been without a Temple for two millennia now, and so the kohanic idea of God's presence as in-dwelling in a particular structure does not resonate in our daily lives. It is relegated to the traditional liturgy, to the prayer in the *Amidah* (the silent prayer said standing that is one of the staples of every synagogue service) for the return of the *Shekhinah* (God's presence) to Zion.

# A LIST OF THE 11 *PARSHIYOT* OF EXODUS

The **narratives** cover the first five *parshiyot:*

1. Shemot (Exod. 1:1–6:1)
   - the new Pharaoh and his decrees
   - the birth of Moses and his early years
   - Moses' flight to Midian
   - the burning bush and Moses' empowerment
   - the return to Egypt
   - the mysterious nighttime circumcision
   - Moses confronts Pharaoh

2. Va-'era' (Exod. 6:2–9:35)
   - the call to Moses reinforced
   - the genealogies of Reuven, Shimon, and Levi
   - the first seven plagues

3. Bo' (Exod. 10:1–13:16)
   - plagues eight and nine
   - instructions for Passover: the lamb and the matzo
   - the 10th plague
   - the Exodus
   - consecration of the firstborn

4. Be-shallaḥ (Exod. 13:17–17:16)
   - the deliverance at the Sea of Reeds
   - the Song of the Sea
   - the first complaints
   - water, quail, and manna
   - the battle with Amalek

5. Yitro (Exod. 18:1–20:23)
   - Yitro joins Moses . . . and gives him good advice
   - the arrival at Sinai: instructions and preparations
   - the Ten Commandments
   - the people's response

The **mini-law code** is in

6. Mishpatim (Exod. 21:1–24:18)
   • the Book of the Covenant
   • laws concerning slaves
   • criminal, civil, and judicial rulings
   • capital crimes
   • the three festivals
   • the Covenant ceremony

The **vision of the *mishkan*** is in

7. Terumah (Exod. 25:1–27:19)
   • the materials needed
   • the purpose of the *mishkan*
   • the Ark and its dimensions
   • the golden cover and the cherubim
   • the table
   • the menorah
   • the curtains
   • the sacrificial altar and the courtyard

8. Tetsavveh (Exod. 27:20–30:10)
   • the eternal Light
   • Aaron's wardrobe: ephod, breastplate (with the two oracles), robe (with bells), golden head-plate, linen coat and headdress, sash
   • *Kohanim*'s wardrobe: coats, sashes, turbans, linen shorts
   • consecration of the *Kohanim*
   • the incense altar

9. Ki Tissa' (Exod. 30:11–34:35)
   • the "half-shekel" tax
   • the bronze sink
   • the oil for anointing
   • the incense
   • the artisans: Bezalel and Oholiab
   • the injunction of the *Shabbat*

*(continued)*

A LIST OF THE 11 *PARSHIYOT* OF EXODUS
*continued*

the **Golden Calf episode**

- Apostasy and punishment
- Moses and God in dialogue
- God's attributes
- the second tablets and the renewal of the Covenant

the **assembly of the *mishkan*** is in

10. Va-yak'hel (Exod. 35:1–38:20)
    • the convening of the people
    • the *Shabbat* injunction repeated
    • the generosity and involvement of the people
    • the work of the artisans
    • Bezalel's artistry

11. Pekudei (Exod. 38:21–40:38)
    • the tally of the people's gifts and what was made from them
    • the completion of the construction
    • the activation of the Tabernacle
    • the fulfillment: the Divine Presence enters the *mishkan*

Which parashah in Exodus, then, commends itself for a guided reading? In the light of what I've just noted, I don't think any of the first five (Exodus 1–20) will do. They are mainly narrative, as is *parashat* Ki Tissa,' which tells the Golden Calf story. The stylistic issues these *parshiyot* present will not be too different from those in the Genesis narratives. The laws in *parashat* Mishpatim (Exodus 21–23) are specific to that parashah; they won't furnish keys to how to read the rest of Exodus. That leaves the four *parshiyot* that relate to the *mishkan*. If we follow Ramban, these are basic to Exodus. So let's look at the first of them, *parashat* Terumah.

# A Guided Reading of *Parashat* Terumah

As with Genesis, I'll share my notes—but only after you promise that you will first have looked at the text on your own.

## Step 1: The First Reading

1. **The textual terrain:** A quick scan indicates that this parashah is terra incognita. There's been nothing like this in the *Humash* so far. This parashah looks like an instruction manual or an architect's notes.

2. **The context:** Getting the context here is no simple matter. Unlike many other *parshiyot*, this one seems to have no connection to the one preceding it. Why is it here? Why am I being told these details? Where do they fit in to the larger story of the Exodus? What is this sanctuary that is commanded here?

3. **The parashah: After I read the parashah, here's what I write in my notebook.**

   • **What kind of structure is being described here?** I can follow some of the details; others are quite unclear. Is this a temple? A tent?

   • **Dolphin skins? Acacia wood? Gold?** Where did they get all those materials from if they were in the desert?

   • **The purpose of the sanctuary** was so that God may dwell among the people. Was He not already among them? I want to think about this.

   • **"There I will meet with you . . . from above the cover, from between the two cherubim that are on top of the Ark . . .** (Exod. 25:22). God meets with the people? A very interesting idea. More to think about.

## Step 2: The Second Reading

• **The structure that is being described:** A glance at the comments in the *Humash* I am using reveals a drawing of the floor plan of the Tabernacle. This helps a lot. Further investigation of other *Humashim* yields even more: drawings of what the various items may have looked like.

- **The context:** It is now clear that I'm not going to get too far with this parashah without consulting commentaries. Literary analysis may work with narrative but not with this kind of material. There's no narrative here. Nothing is "happening." There are no people. The parashah requires me to learn more about the religion of ancient Israel. Maybe that will help me understand the *mishkan* material, why it was put into Exodus, and why it shows up at just this point. A look into Friedman's *Who Wrote the Bible?* confirms this hunch. He has a whole chapter on "The Sacred Tent" with detailed drawings.[27] It looks to be a gold mine.

- **The sanctuary, meeting God:** More and more I am intrigued at this idea that God "meets" us. That we "meet" God. That we can arrange appointments with Him. The implications of this excite me. The Torah seems to be suggesting that God is not an idea or an intellectual construct but a **presence** we **encounter**, and that the sanctuary is the place where this happens.

- **The real and the symbolic:** I now wonder: Is this sanctuary or Tabernacle that is being described real or symbolic? Was it really built? Or is it something we should better imagine, a paradigm of how and where we meet God? Is the synagogue the modern functional equivalent of the *mishkan*? Does the Divine Presence dwell within the Ark? Has this fact been publicized? I recall now that passage in Kafka's *Letter to His Father* where he describes his childhood experience in the shul to which his father dragged him:

> And so I yawned and dozed through the many hours (I don't think I was ever again so bored, except later at dancing lessons) and did my best to enjoy the few little bits of variety there were, as for instance when the Ark of the Covenant was opened, which always reminded me of the shooting galleries where a cupboard door would open in the same way whenever one hit a bull's eye; except that there something interesting always came out and here it was always just the same old dolls without heads.[28]

"Dolls without heads": Is that how children see the Torah scrolls? In any case, I am ready for commentaries.

---

## On Reading Leviticus and Its 10 *Parshiyot*

With Leviticus we enter into a book that is, literally and figuratively, forbidding and at times impenetrable. The focus is on animals, sacrifices, purity, skin disease, leakage of bodily fluids, moldy houses, incestuous relationships, and real estate regulations, among other matters. There are also, in the penultimate chapter, some hair-curling warnings. There is little if any narrative here, no personalities, no dialogue. The voice in the text is monophonically flat and almost always prescriptive.[29]

I think it is fair to ask whether we moderns can ever understand Leviticus. A contemporary Christian (Mennonite) scholar speaks for many when he opines:

> I do not think . . . that we have reason to be overly optimistic in this regard. Often the gulf between ancient experience and modern experience is underappreciated. People who read Leviticus 1–7 [and I would add, most of the rest of the book] too easily bring their own responses to the text, especially in the visceral reactions to killing, flaying, and manipulating blood. There is no way to know how various people in ancient Israelite society felt about killing an animal. This becomes clearer when keeping in mind the illusion in the phrase "ancient Israelite society," as if all people in all times of Israel's history would have reacted in similar ways. Any claim to understand all of these possible physical and mental responses is overstated.[30]

These are humbling words.

But now, along comes Leon Wieseltier with a notion of how to get beyond this interpretational roadblock. He sees a way for us living here and now to get into Leviticus: "But suddenly the historical consciousness of the Jew plays a prank upon its own distance. Irrelevance is transformed into incitement. . . . Leviticus may seem strange, but it is the origin. It holds lessons."[31]

Let me elaborate on how I understand what Wieseltier is saying. First, what are the lessons that Leviticus holds? I would suggest that they derive from the placement of the book at the very center of the Torah. After all, it could have come after Numbers, when the rest of the story of the children of Israel would have been told (except for the death of Moses). But no: the decision was made (by whom?) to stop the narrative flow in the middle, just after the construction of the Tabernacle, and confront the reader with this material—as if to say: let's showcase even now, before the story is over, what the ultimate point and content of this people's existence is. Consider: In Egypt the 12 tribes coalesced into a people. The people were liberated from their bondage. They went to Sinai and received a Torah, the document of their covenant with God. After a brief adulterous affair with another god (a sacred cow that wasn't sacred), which affair threatened the sacred marriage, they renewed their covenant with the One to whom they were betrothed. Moses' role in repairing the breach was crucial. The people then built a *mishkan* in which God could dwell and in which they could commune with him. Now, in Leviticus, come the details of their life together. The details are crucial because **holiness** is in the details.

That's the big teaching of Leviticus: holiness. "Holy" (Hebrew *kadosh*, קדוש) is the word God used about Israel when their relationship was consummated in the Sinai experience:

> **"You shall be to Me a kingdom of priests and a holy nation." (Exod. 19:6)** ואתם תהיו לי ממלכת כהנים וגוי קדוש

Holiness is the point of Israel's existence and Leviticus is a prime source for the explication of this idea. It is an explication formulated legally and fostered performatively by those whose stock in trade is the holy—the *Kohanim*. Leviticus is their book. Source critics regard Leviticus as wholly the product of the P school, kohanic descendants of Aaron in the 7th or maybe 6th century B.C.E. They put this book together not only for their own instruction but also for the edification of those who figuratively and collectively embody the holy: the People of Israel. On this view Leviticus is seen to comprise two main documents:

- **A Kohanic ("Priestly") Handbook—P**: A compendium of procedures and practices for *Kohanim* that reflects a variety of "priestly" concerns. It is located in Leviticus 1–16.

- **The "Holiness" Code—H**: A book for all Israel detailing the laws and moral standards that lead to holiness. It is located in Leviticus 17–26.

Chapter 27 of Leviticus, the final one, is understood as an appendix, a miscellany of laws that come from the P school that may have been collected and added after the two documents had been combined.

In this whole book there are only two purely narrative passages:

- the story of the deaths of Nadab and Abihu (Lev. 10:1–7).

- the story of the blasphemer who is stoned for his crime (Lev. 24:10–23).

In both these cases narrative functions not as the expression of the storyteller's art but in the service of the priestly point that is being made. Nadab and Abihu die because they offer the sacrifices in an improper way. The blasphemer is killed because he pronounces aloud the divine name. Both are transgressive infringements on the realm of the sacred.

As a totality, then, Leviticus encompasses a wide range of material. Wieseltier deftly sums up the book when he writes that "Leviticus is the classical text of what might be called hard-core Judaism."[32]

But what is the incitement that Wieseltier speaks of? To what does Leviticus incite us? This will require some close reading, specifically of the book's opening words: "The LORD called to Moses and spoke to him from the Tent of Meeting saying: 'Speak to the Israelite people and say to them: . . .'"(Lev. 1:1–2)

ויקרא אל משה וידבר יהוה אליו באהל מועד לאמר:
דבר אל בני ישראל ואמרת אליהם . . .

Although these verses come at the beginning of a new book, they can only be understood as the direct continuation of what was told at the very end of Exodus:

> **When Moses had finished the work [of the Tabernacle], the cloud covered the Tent of Meeting, and the Presence of the LORD filled the Tabernacle. Moses [therefore] could not enter the Tent of Meeting, because the cloud had settled upon it and the Presence of the LORD filled the Tabernacle. (Exod. 40:33–35)**

Thus God calls Moses "from [inside] the Tent of Meeting."

We might have thought upon closing the book of Exodus and opening up this new one that we were done with the whole business of the Tabernacle. But Lev. 1:1–2 tells us no—we are still within the context that began back at Exodus 25, when the first commandments concerning the erection of the Tabernacle were given. So when Leviticus opens, Moses is outside the Tent and can't go in because of the cloud of glory. The force of the opening verse is that God calls to him—invites him in—and, though we are not explicitly told this, he enters, there to receive the teachings. A supplementary comment attributed to Rashi, not found in his main commentary, explains the linkage between the end of Exodus and the beginning of Leviticus to mean that **all the laws and teachings that this new book contains were given from inside the Tabernacle**.[33] In other words, the whole book of Leviticus, all the details of the sacrifices, the purifications, the ethical commands—all of it—was the product of a direct and deep communication between God and Moses in the Tent.

We know this from the fact that the opening verses contain no less than three verbs of communication: **calling [קְרָא], speaking [דַּבֵּר], and saying [אָמַר].** These are not synonyms or tautologies but three very different verbal activities that are not simultaneous. They occur in sequence. "Calling" means summoning someone, trying to attract her attention. "Speaking" takes place after the person's attention has been attracted. "Saying" takes place when the conversation is already under way and involves imparting something. This whole sequence goes on here in the short space of these first determinative verses with its three verbs. God "calls" to Moses, inviting him into the *mishkan*. (We have to infer that Moses goes inside.) God there "speaks to" him and "says," imparting to him what He imparts. Moses then does the same with the people: he "speaks to" them and "says," imparting to them what we will now read in the book.

Look what has happened here. There was an experience of God (the call) and then, very quickly, the report of the experience. The content of the call is, **within one verse**, already reduced to teachings. Wieseltier writes: "It was precisely when the report of the voice did the work of the voice that tradition was born. . . . [But] tradition was never all there was. There was experience, too."[34]

That is what Leviticus, in its opening words, incites us to see. Lev. 1:1 captures for us that instant when tradition was not yet, and text was not yet. There was only experience. But then comes verse 2 and immediately the directness of Moses' experience is transmuted into—and vitiated by—the verbiage of text. Wieseltier calls this "the reduction of divinity by textuality."[35] As this process continues the verbiage of text begets the verbiage of commentary. The verbiage of commentary begets what in time becomes tradition. Glorious as tradition is, Wieseltier believes, it is not the only focal point of the Bible. "It should be possible," he says, "to read the Bible not only for what it tells about tradition, but also for what it tells about experience."[36] Buber and Rosenzweig would not have agreed more.

And so, if we want to get inside Leviticus, an historical perspective, valuable as it is, will only take us so far. We have to read it not as antiquarians looking at an artifact from Judaism's deep past but rather within the categories of the phenomenology of religious experience, where in its *parshiyot* we relive Judaism's origins. We have to read it much as we read the Passover Haggadah, not so much as a rehearsal of the past but as a recovery of it in the present.

Reading Leviticus is a reenactment. It represents a book where

> **the textualization of ritual is balanced by the ritualization of the text. . . . God speaks to Moses from the Tent of Meeting, and commands him to speak the forthcoming words to the People of Israel . . . the text obliquely commands its own reading. Readers are**

**given the opportunity to stand in the place of Moses while speaking these words to the people.**[37]

The issues then are still issues now: sacrifices individual and communal, purity and defilement, what we eat, sexual relationships, atonement, holiness. Here is hard-core Judaism—at the core of the Torah.

## A LIST OF THE 10 *PARSHIYOT* OF LEVITICUS

**The Kohanic ("Priestly") Handbook** covers the first five and a half *parshiyot*:

1. Va-yikra' (Lev. 1:1–5:26)
   - the laws of the sacrifices (preparation and ingredients)
   - the *olah* (burnt offering)
   - the *minchah* (grain offering)
   - the *zevach shelamim* (communion sacrifice)
   - the *hatat* (offering for an unintentional offense committed either by a *kohen*, the community, the leader, or an individual)
   - the *asham* (expiation offerings)

2. Tsav (Lev. 6:1–8:36)
   - the laws of the sacrifices (procedures)
   - the procedures for *olah, minchah, hatat, asham,* and the varieties of *zevah shelamim*
   - prohibitions of eating fat and blood
   - the *Kohanim*'s share of the meat
   - the consecration of Aaron and the *Kohanim*

3. Shemini (Lev. 9:1–11:47)
   - the first sacrificial service
   - the catastrophe of Nadab and Abihu
   - Aaron's response
   - restrictions on the *Kohanim*
   - the dietary laws: permitted and prohibited quadrupeds, birds, fish, and insects
   - impurity of reptiles and improperly slaughtered carcasses and animal corpses

4. Tazria' (Lev. 12:1–13:59)
   - impurity conferred by childbirth and the remedial sacrifice
   - impurity conferred by skin diseases and conditions (*tsara'at*)
   - *tsara'at* in fabrics and leather and purification procedures

5. Metsora' (Lev. 14:1–15:33)
   - purification procedures for *tsara'at* of skin diseases
   - *tsara'at* in houses and purification procedures
   - impurity conferred by discharges from the genitalia (men and women) and purification procedures and sacrifices

6. 'Aḥarei Mot (Lev. 16:1–18:30)
   - the Yom Kippur atonement ritual

**The H ("Holiness") Code** begins here:

   - the requirements for valid sacrifices
   - rules pertaining to the blood of sacrifices
   - prohibition of nonslaughtered meat
   - forbidden sexual relationships

and continues in:

7. Kedoshim (Lev. 19:1–20:27)
   - the specifics of the sanctified life
   - forbidden sexual relationships and their punishments

8. 'Emor (Lev. 21:1–24:23)
   - special holiness laws for *Kohanim* and the *Kohen Gadol*
   - sacred donations and who may partake of them
   - Sacred Time
   - the *Shabbat*
   - Passover
   - the *omer* offering and the Shavuot festival of firstfruits

*(continued)*

**A LIST OF THE 10 *PARSHIYOT* OF LEVITICUS,**
*continued*

- the *shofar* festival
- the Day of Atonement
- The Sukkot festival—booths and four species
- various Tabernacle laws: the menorah and the 12 loaves of bread
- the blasphemy incident and the prohibition against blasphemy

9. Be-har (Lev. 25:1–26:2)
- the sabbatical year
- the jubilee year
- other land issues: redemption of land in
- walled cities
- open areas
- Levitical properties
- economic laws regulating indebtedness and the treatment of debtors

Epilogue to the Holiness Code:

10. Be-ḥukkotai (Lev. 26:3–27:34)
- the consequences of obedience: blessings
- the escalating consequences of disobedience: suffering, punishment, and exile
- the hopeful conclusion: God will remember the people and the land

Appendix: Funding the Tabernacle
- assessments for pledges paid in silver
- donations of animals, houses, property
- taxes

Less than those in any of the other four books, the *parshiyot* of Leviticus do not lend themselves to reading on one's own, without the aid of the explanatory notes most *Humashim* provide. The material is simply too technical. Therefore, the reading steps I have suggested need to be modified for this book. What you want in the first two readings here is enough commentary that will give you the *peshat*, the plain sense of the text.

Commentaries that are more interpretively ambitious or elaborate should still be deferred until step 3, that is, after you have had your own encounter with the parashah.

The *parshiyot* of the Kohanic Handbook (the first five and a half *parshiyot*, chapters 1–16), though they are about as different from narrative fiction as one could possibly imagine, can be accessed in a way similar to it: by deploying what literary critics call our "willing suspension of disbelief." We put our modern sensibilities aside—vegetarians will have an especially hard time with this—and enter into the world of the ritual sacrifice of animals as a primary mode of communicating with and serving God. Once we do that we can review the handbook and its various instructions. The challenge is to ponder them and try to connect them to our reality.

The Holiness Code *parshiyot* should not require as strenuous a reading strategy. While there is much there that is anachronistic and problematic—the treatment of homosexuality being the most widely debated example—the general tenor of these laws still speaks to us with undiminished power. To illustrate this I have selected as our sample parashah one that comes at the end of the Holiness Code.

## A Guided Reading of *Parashat* Be-har

### Step 1: The First Reading

1. **The textual terrain**: As we expect in Leviticus, we are reading law here. But . . .

2. **The context**: The context is, at least on the surface, confusing. These are laws that "The LORD spoke to Moses on Mount Sinai" (Lev. 25:1)? I had been given to understand that the content of all of Leviticus was imparted to Moses in the *mishkan*.

3. **The parashah:** An initial perusal of the parashah yields these jottings.

- **The land** has a *Shabbat* just like people!

- **The jubilee year** starts on Yom Kippur. Seems like the whole society presses the Reset button on that day. Could we arrange something like this for our time? The words are already on the Liberty Bell (Lev. 25:10). The first thing would be to repair the crack in it. What would a contemporary jubilee year look like?

- **There is a moral economic system**: "When you sell . . . to . . . or . . . buy . . . from . . . your neighbor, you shall not wrong one another" (Lev. 25:14). Thus, insider trading is forbidden by the Torah. And all loans are interest-free (25:37).

- **"But the land must not be sold beyond reclaim, for the land is Mine; you are but strangers resident with Me"** (Lev. 25:23). In this world we are renters, not buyers, tenants, not landlords. This is another well-kept secret.

- **"If your kinsman is in straits and has to sell part of his holding, his nearest redeemer shall come and redeem what his kinsman has sold"** (Lev. 25:25). Family takes care of family.

- **When selling a home in a walled city** (Lev. 25:30), the buyback period is only a year. In the open country it's a lot longer—until the jubilee year. Why?

## Step 2: The Second Reading

The first reading left me wondering what all these laws are doing in the Holiness Code. But now it's clearer: holiness is not some abstract pietistic ideal but one that is lived out in quotidian reality. This is what the Holiness Code has been teaching. This parashah shows that quotidian reality encompasses not only the sphere of the individual life but the social sphere as well—society and the community.

But now new questions arise:

- What are the political implications of all this? How do institutions like the sabbatical year, the jubilee year, the whole vision of land ownership, play out in a modern, Western, secular, capitalistic society? Can they play out? Are the values of our society compatible in any way with those that underlie the laws in this parashah?

• Then there are environmental questions. The sabbatical and jubilee year laws rest on the understanding that the **land is a living organism and that it does not belong to us in perpetuity.** I assume that the land referred to is Eretz Yisra'el. But why not extend it to all of God's earth? Either way, I see this relationship to (the) land as a powerful principle embedded in the Torah. Why has it not been enunciated as such? In biblical terms, global warming is global warning. The passages elsewhere in the *Humash* about the land "spewing out" those who are fouling it up are the Torah's way of talking about pollution.

I'd like to find a commentary that addresses these matters.

---

# On Reading Numbers and Its 10 *Parshiyot*

Early on in this book I made the point that not only is the *Humash* an anthology of five canonical books, but that each book is itself an anthology of texts of various sorts. Nowhere do we see this more clearly than in Numbers. Its 10 *parshiyot* offer the reader the most diverse collection of material in the *Humash*. Here we find a potpourri of priestly regulations, laws, poems, fragments of lost epics, and lists. There are so many lists that we could describe Numbers as the original Book of Lists (see p. 167). And amid all this there is narrative—but not until we get about a third of the way into the book (the middle third of the 10 *parshiyot*), where the story that was broken off at the end of Exodus resumes.

So variegated is the material in Numbers and so loosely is it organized that many scholars have long regarded it as an incoherent jumble of texts and traditions that has no discernible beginning (it picks up right where Leviticus left off) and comes to no real conclusion. Others claim to see some organizing principles and unifying threads that bind the diverse texts together.

> In spite of its eclectic character, the Book of Numbers does constitute some kind of literary unit. . . . [It forms a unique repository of traditions associated with the wanderings of the Israelites and an indispensable link in the theology of Jewish history.[38]

The narrative sections bear this out, for they do progress in a meaningful order. They tell of a people adrift in the desert, adrift physically and spiritually. The experience in Egypt is receding in their minds—it is now remembered nostalgically—and the vision of the Promised Land is a chimera. In this harsh and uncertain environment Numbers shows us Israelites behaving badly (details below). One scholar has described Numbers as "the Book of Israel's Failings."[39]

And that may just be the point of this book. The juxtaposition of these failings with the Holiness Code and its vision of Israel as a "kingdom of *Kohanim* and a holy people" is striking. If Leviticus holds up the ideal, Numbers presents the real.

Yet the book is not completely mired in negativity. The two censuses it records mark out the two different realities that Numbers depicts. The first census (in chapter 1) is of the generation of the Exodus, a generation that, we will soon learn, will be condemned to die out in the desert. The second census (in chapter 26) counts those who come after, who will enter the land and settle its apportioned areas. So there is, as the *parshiyot* proceed, a taking leave of the people's failings and a focus on their resolve to make a future worthy of their ancestors and the promises made to them.

Numbers can be broken down into the following units:

- **Introduction: Final Tabernacle Details and Preparations for the March into the Desert** (Numbers 1–10): This is kohanic (P) material that continues Leviticus. Since it was not included in the latter book but placed at the opening of Numbers, it serves as a kind of prologue to the events in the desert that will shortly be recounted. A number of laws are embedded here that underscore the role of the *Kohanim* in promoting purity and echo the ideals of the Holiness Code. Then the march into the wilderness begins.

- **Israel's Failings: Complaints, Rebellion, and Disobedience in the Desert** (Numbers 11–21): Immediately the people begin grumbling. They clamor for food and water and are unhappy with Moses' leadership. Twelve scouts are sent out to reconnoiter the Land. Their majority report is disheartening and the people talk of abandoning the journey and returning to Egypt. For such despair they are fated to die in the wilderness. There is an attempt (unsuccessful) to overthrow Moses. And Aaron, too, is challenged.

  The years pass. It is now, apparently, the 40th year (Num. 20:1). Miriam and Aaron die, and Moses, too, we learn, will end his days in the desert along with the unhappy cohort he led out of Egypt. But then, inexplicably, the fortunes of the people improve. They inflict defeats on two nations that stand in their way, the Amorites and the Bashanites, and now Numbers begins to move in a more positive direction. These narratives are generally seen as a conflation of E and J versions of the events with the corresponding P account.

  But as is typical of Numbers, the stories in this section are interlarded with legal material (Numbers 15, 18, and 19) from the P school. It is these interruptions of the narrative flow that create the impression that Numbers is a random assemblage of stories and traditions. Such a view, I think, does not give enough compositional credit to the editor of Numbers or to the Redactor. One of the challenges of reading Numbers is to try to discover what connections there might be between the juxtaposed passages of narrative and law.

- **The Book of Balaam** (Numbers 22–24): Now we get another interpolated literary unit, a delightful story about a talking donkey who sees more than the vaunted seer who rides him. This narrative, possibly building on an earlier animal fable, is ascribed to the E source. Its inclusion here fits, or is made to fit, the context perfectly. Israel, as we learned in chapter 21, has vanquished the Amorites and the Bashanites and is now encamped on the borders of Moab. And Balak is the king of Moab who sets the plot in motion.

  We should not miss the humor in this story. The Torah is a serious book but it is not devoid of a sense of humor.

Also noteworthy here is the interplay between the prose narrative and the poetry of Bilaam's prophetic utterances about Israel (which invite comparison with Jacob's in Gen. 49:1–27).

• **Israel's Failings Continued, and the Second Census** (Numbers 25–26): The people are now near the end of their 40 years of wandering. But as if to bracket the whole desert experience, they again commit a licentious apostasy as they did at the beginning when they worshiped the Golden Calf, this time in idolatrous fertility rites with the Moabites at Beit Pe'or (the account is ascribed to J). The punishment here is similar: the execution of the main offenders and a plague. The subsequent census of those who survive (the accounts of these are ascribed to P) marks a new beginning.

• **Preparations for Entry into the Land** (Numbers 27–36): Attention now turns to what awaits the Israelites beyond the Jordan. We find a miscellany of details about this: the appointment of Joshua as Moses' successor, a battle against the Midianites and the disposition of its spoils human and material, the apportionment of the land among the tribes, the delineation of borders, the designation of six cities of refuge. This is all attributed to P as are two catalogues inserted here: of the sacrifices offered up in the Sanctuary (chapters 28 and 29) and the 42 way stations of the 40-year journey (chapter 33).

There is a nice symmetry to this unit. It begins and ends with the appearance before Moses of five women, the daughters of Zelophehad, of the tribe of Manasseh. The issue is whether they can inherit the territory of their father, who had died without any male heirs. What is initially offered them (in chapter 27) is later qualified, if not negated (in chapter 36). And there the book ends, summarily, without closure. It is a strange way to conclude a book. Unsatisfying.

Some Bible scholars understand the ending of Numbers not to be absent but deferred. They find it at the very end of Deuteronomy, in the last eight verses of chapter 34. I find this view persuasive, for the style of those verses is quite congruent with the last half of Numbers 27, and their content follows nicely from where that chapter ends. If, in the light of this conjecture, you reattach Deut. 34:5–12 to Num. 27:12–23, you will see what could be the true ending of Numbers. And construed thus, everything else in this unit is really an appendix, similar to the appendix to Leviticus (chapter 27) that follows its true conclusion (chapter 26). It's not hard to understand why the ending might have been deferred in this way. To have left it in here, in its original place as the end of Numbers, would have left no room or reason for Deuteronomy.

## A LIST OF THE 10 *PARSHIYOT* OF NUMBERS

**Introduction: Final Tabernacle Details and Preparations for the March into the Desert** covers the first two and a half *parshiyot:*

1. Be-midbar (Num. 1:1–4:20)
   - the first census
   - the marching order of the 12 tribes
   - the genealogy of the Levites, their duties and census

2. Naso' (Num. 4:21–7:89)
   - census and duties of the Levites (cont'd)
   - Holiness laws: sequestering the impure, penalty for theft, the ritual procedure for a suspected adulteress, the ritual procedure for a nazirite
   - the formula of the kohanic blessing
   - the offerings brought by the 12 tribal chieftains

3. Be-ha'alotekha (Num. 8:1–12:16)
   - the lighting of the menorah
   - the consecration of the Levites and their term of service
   - the "Second Passover" (for those impure at the first)
   - the navigator for the upcoming march: the Cloud of the Divine Presence
   - the two silver reveille trumpets
   - the march begins

*(continued)*

**A LIST OF THE 10 *PARSHIYOT* OF NUMBERS,**
*continued*

**Israel's Failings: Complaints, Rebellion, and Disobedience in the Desert** covers the rest of this and the next three *parshiyot:*

- the complaints begin—clamoring for meat
- challenges to Moses—alternative prophets Eldad and Meidad
- the quail
- challenges to Moses—by Miriam and Aaron
- Miriam's punishment

4. Shelaḥ-Lekha (Num. 13:1–15:41)
   - the scouting expedition of the 12 spies
   - their report and the people's reaction
   - the price of their despair
   - a failed assault
   - interlude of laws: of the sacrifices, of the challah bread, of sacrifices for inadvertent sins
   - narrative of the *Shabbat* desecrator
   - interlude: the law of fringes (tzitzit)

5. Koraḥ (Num. 16:1–18:32)
   - the uprising(s) against Moses by Korah (Levitical) and by Dathan and Abiram (Reubenite)
   - the punishment
   - the retrieval and refashioning of the fire pans
   - more complaints against Moses and Aaron and the punishment: a plague
   - Aaron's primacy reaffirmed: the miracle of the blossoming rod
   - interlude of laws: *Kohanim* and Levites reaffirmed
   - their duties and privileges

6. Ḥukkat (Num. 19:1–22:1)
   - the Red Heifer: purification and defilement

- defilement by a corpse and purification rite
- the death of Miriam
- clamoring for water
- Moses and Aaron's infraction and punishment
- the request to Edom and its denial
- the death of Aaron
- more complaints: the scourge of snakes and the brass serpent
- the Song of the Well and other poetic quotations
- victories against Sihon (Amorites) and Og (Bashanites)

**The Book of Balaam** is in the seventh parashah:

7. Balak (Num. 22:2–25:9)
   - Balak's invitation to Bilaam: refusals and acceptance
   - Balaam on the way: the talking donkey
   - Balaam's four utterances: blessings instead of curses

**Israel's Failings Continued, and the Second Census** covers the rest of the seventh parashah and all of the eighth:

- seduction and sin with the Moabites at Beit Pe'or
- Pinḥas takes action
- punishment and plague

8. Pinḥas (Num. 25:10–30:1)
   - Pinḥas rewarded with permanent kohanic status
   - the second census

**Preparations for Entry into the Land** covers the rest of the parshiyot.

- how the land will be apportioned
- a request by the daughters of Zelophehad
- Joshua installed as Moses' successor
- a master calendar and regimen of sacrifices

*(continued)*

**A LIST OF THE 10 *PARSHIYOT* OF NUMBERS,**
*continued*


9. Mattot (Num. 30:2–32:42)
   • interlude of laws: vows of women (single, mar-
     ried, widowed, divorced)
   • the war with Midian
   • harsh treatment of human captives and disposi-
     tion of the booty
   • inventory of the booty
   • the victory offering
   • a special arrangement for the two and a half
     tribes east of the Jordan


10. Mase'ei (Num. 33:1–36:13)
   • a list of the 42 places of encampment during the
     40 years
   • the boundaries of the land
   • designation of tribal apportionment supervisors
   • designation of 48 levitical towns
   • designation of 5 cities of refuge
   • laws of murder and manslaughter
   • the case of the daughters of Zelophehad revisited


This overview of Numbers reveals that the book's distinctive character lies in the way it fits together disparate textual elements. Narrative passages are punctuated by legal teachings; lists are duly recorded; and snippets of poetry intrude here and there. We don't start seeing this penchant for admixture until we are about midway through the third parashah, Be-ha'alotekha (specifically with Numbers 11). Up to that point Numbers is really an extension of Leviticus. For this reason I select as our sample parashah one that comes a bit later: *parashat* Koraḥ. Koraḥ, in content and in form, exhibits many features that characterize Numbers and its text presents some issues that are central to how we read the *Humash*.

# A Guided Reading of *Parashat* Koraḥ

## Step 1: The First Reading

1. **The textual terrain**: The parashah starts out with narrative. Then comes a series of directives by God to Moses and then— and this is unusual—by God to Aaron alone. This alerts me that I had better pay attention to Aaron here.

2. **The context**: *Parshiyot* just **begin**. Why couldn't the Redactor, or some other later editor, have considered the plight of readers who do not possess a knowledge of the whole before reading the parts? Why could they not have inserted at the outset of each parashah a note or two—what biblical scholars call a superscription—orienting the reader to what has come just before and what follows?

   My question is rhetorical, for by now I have discovered that such contextualizing notes exist in the commentary of many of the *Humashim* I noted in the previous section. It's just a matter of knowing where to find them in the particular *Humash* you are using. Having found them in mine, I see that the events told in Koraḥ occur sometime during the desert wanderings.

3. **The parashah**: Here is what I see and wonder about after a careful first read.

   • **What's going on in Numbers 16?** The story of the rebellion is confusing. Obviously Moses is being challenged and the rebels are punished, but the details seem to keep shifting. Take the complaint against Moses. At first we hear that it's because he and Aaron have arrogated all holiness (i.e., power) to themselves (Num. 16:3). Later the gripe is that Moses has brought them out of Egypt to die in the wilderness (v. 13), although Moses seems to think they have charged him with corruption (v. 15: "not a donkey of theirs have I carried off"). Then there's unclarity about Moses'—or God's—response to the challenges. At first Moses proposes a test of the fire pans: those whose incense God will accept are the holy ones (vv. 5–7, repeated in vv. 16 and 17). But later we see that the determination of guilt will be made by God in a different way: the culpable will be those swallowed up by the earth (v. 30). And finally, there seems to be a discrepancy in the site of these events. We are told that the fire pan contest takes place at the entrance to the Tent of Meeting (i.e., the Tabernacle, vv. 18 and 19). But then when the sinkhole opens up, the mutineers and their families are standing at the doorways of **their own tents** (v. 28), from which the rest of the community had been warned to get away (vv. 24–27). And if this is not enough confusion for one story, consider the last verse of chapter 16: the 250 men are consumed by fire. Had they not also been swept away when the earth opened up? Apparently not. They had been standing there with their fire pans all this time, patiently waiting for the contest.

- **Korah is right** when he says, "For all the community are all holy, all of them, and the LORD is in their midst" (Num. 16:3). All he's doing is affirming what the Torah has been telling us all along, that Israel is *"a kingdom of Kohanim and a holy people"* (Exod. 19:6). Am I missing something here?

- **Moses and Aaron question God** (Num. 16:22): What they say here echoes Abraham's reaction to God's proposed destruction of Sodom and Gomorrah in Genesis (Gen. 18:23 and 25): "Will you sweep away the innocent along with the guilty? . . . Shall not the Judge of all the earth deal justly?" So it's true: Jews can argue with God. And here is a further thought on this idea: Moses and Aaron are actually supporting Korah's point that there is holiness in the people!

- **The fire pans are refashioned** (Num. 17:1–5): This is very suggestive, but of what? It is recycling of the highest order, but I sense there's more than that here.

- **"You two have brought death upon the LORD's people!"** (Num. 17:6): This community is implacable. To say that to Moses and Aaron after what they've just witnessed? There is a fundamental disconnect between the people and their leaders. It's scary to think that any community is a potential mob.

- **Aaron's staff blossoms** (Num. 17:16–26): This tells me that when a leader's authority with her community has eroded, that leader has to produce concrete and visible evidence that she still has "the right stuff." It is altogether contemporary.

- **"Lo, we perish! We are lost, all of us lost!"** (Num. 17:27): This is mass hysteria, again an indication that a body politic is like an individual: underneath its surface lie irrational fears and forces.

- **" . . . any outsider who encroaches shall be put to death"** (Num. 18:7): Numbers, looks to be the legal response to the challenges to Moses and Aaron. This is a reaffirmation of the enfranchisement of the *Kohanim* and the Levites. It reads like the final refutation of Koraḥ's contention. There will be no equal access to the holy. But why not? Is holiness hereditary?

## Step 2: The Second Reading

- **What's going on in Numbers?** It's clear that there's a duality to this narrative: two different complaints against Moses, two different punishments meted out, two different locations for the punishment. Looks like a doublet. I shall need to see what source criticism has to say.

- **Koraḥ's claim** continues to intrigue me. He **has** a point. Holiness resides in everyone.

- **Aaron's staff blossoms and outsiders are viewed differently**: As I reread, I see that there is inherent in this parashah—and, I am realizing, not only in this parashah—a bias. The writer(s) have a bias. This story and its aftermath privilege Aaron and the *Kohanim* and, together with them, the Levites. (Is Koraḥ, who was a Levite, tacitly and retroactively being accommodated here?) Still, the laws of chapter 18 qualify the events told in chapter 16. They make it clear that the *Kohanim* and the Levites are the custodians, the sole custodians, of holiness. They run the *mishkan*. Outsiders are encroachers.

This bias is at odds with the Holiness Code of Leviticus, where all Israel are enjoined to realize their potential for a life of sanctity. It is at odds with Judaism as we know it today. When the Temple was destroyed Aaron and his clan went out of business.

Judaism moved in a more—how shall I say it?—egalitarian direction. Sure, in many synagogues they still give *Kohanim* and Levites the honor of the first two *aliyot* to the Torah.[40] But egalitarian is egalitarian. If women can get *aliyot* and lead the service and be ordained as rabbis, then the *Kohen* and *Levi* categories are anachronisms or, at best, honorific.

This parashah, then, upholds Aaron and his kohanic descendants as what we would call today "clergy." But Judaism really doesn't have clergy. Christianity has clergy. It preserved the "priestly" functions. Jews have rabbis. Rabbis are teachers; they're not clergy. (Does the IRS know this?)

And now, upon further reflection, I see that this parashah is rich not only in religious or theological implications but in social, political, and psychological ones. It can be read as a case study in the dynamics of leadership and the phenomenology of crowds. It impels me to reread Elias Canetti's formidable book *Crowds and Power* (1962). Somewhere in that vast and all-too-diffuse study there should be some light shed on what transpires here.

## A LIST OF THE LISTS IN NUMBERS

- census lists (chapters 1 and 26)
- the marching order of the 12 tribes (chapters 2 and 10)
- the genealogy of the Levites and their duties and census (chapter 3)
- inventory of the offerings brought by the 12 tribal chieftains (chapter 7)
- the names of the 12 spies (chapter 13)
- catalogue of the sacrifices to be offered daily, on *Shabbat*, on Rosh Hodesh, and on festivals (chapters 28 and 29)
- inventory of the spoils of the battle with the Midianites (chapter 31)

- the itinerary of the Israelites' 40-year trek in the wilderness (chapter 33)

- the borders of the Promised Land (chapter 34)

## On Reading Deuteronomy and Its 11 *Parshiyot*

Up to now the Torah has been very "priestly," or, as I've been calling it, kohanic. For the better part of the last three books, since the middle of Exodus to be precise, we've heard a lot about the *mishkan*, sacrifices, *Kohanim*, Levites, purity, and holiness. True, there have been several narrative interpolations that carried forward the saga of the people that emerged from Genesis and the first part of Exodus. But after the Sinai event, related at the midpoint of Exodus, the story line became a counterpoint, and the melody, so to speak, was carried by law and ritual prescriptions. But now we reach the book of Deuteronomy, in the words of the immortal Monty Python, "Now for something completely different."

Deuteronomy is different. The language is different, the style is different, the emphasis is different. Deuteronomy does not mention the *mishkan*. It is not concerned with sacrifices. Aaron and *Kohanim* are scarcely mentioned and when they are it is en passant. Deuteronomy is about Torah. The central event in the life of the people was not the investment of the Divine Presence in the sanctuary but the covenant at Sinai (always called Horev in this book) between God and Israel. The central figure is Moses. The central concern is with fidelity to the covenant and the biggest worry is not impurity but polytheism.

The book is organized as a series of farewell speeches by Moses at the end of his life, as the next generation of Israelites prepares to enter the Promised Land. Embedded in one of the speeches is a law code that forms the core of the book (Deut. 12:1–26:15).

Deuteronomy thus presents us with some key questions: What accounts for the striking differences between this book and the previous four? Do we take the book at face value and read it as the actual words of Moses as he reviews his career and the 40 years in the desert? Or is this book a brilliant act of textual ventriloquism whereby a writer from a time long after Moses puts a retrospective reading of the Israelite experience into the mouth of Moses so as to elucidate for his (the writer's) and future generations his vision of the Israelite project? How we answer these questions will shape the strategies by which we read this magnificent book. More than any other book of the Torah, indeed of the whole Tanakh, Deuteronomy forces the reader to declare herself on basic assumptions of authorship.

Traditionalists will ground their reading in the first alternative. They will hold that what we have in Deuteronomy is Moses speaking in his "late style" and the book is all of a piece with the previous four. All the points on which it is at variance with them—literary, legal, and historical—can be reconciled through principles of textual interpretation established long ago by Rabbinic tradition and still available to us.

Modernists, in contrast, hold up the many differences between Deuteronomy and the other four books as prima facie evidence that it was composed much later than them and in very dissimilar circumstances. They believe, as biblicists for the past two centuries have believed, that Deuteronomy was written around 622 B.C.E. (its ideas and ideology may go back further), that is, in the late First Temple period, the fateful years preceding the destruction of the Temple and the consequent exile to Babylonia. Deuteronomy, they conjecture, is "the scroll of Torah," *sefer ha-Torah* that the book of Kings tells us was "found" in the Temple by a *kohen*, who brought it to Josiah, the reigning Judean king, and read it to him (2 Kings 22:8–23:25). What Josiah heard hit him like a thunderbolt, for it presented a view of Torah and its practice that called into question the religious status quo. It triggered a major religious reform in how Torah was understood and observed in Judea from then on, and the effects of this reform are still with us.

Deuteronomy construed thus is a stand-alone text quite separate from J, E, and P.[41] It is coded D by Bible critics. "It is the least hypothetical of the documents that the documentary hypothesis claims as the original components of the Pentateuch."[42] D is understood to include not only Deuteronomy but the six books that continue the story beyond the entry into the land: Joshua, Judges, 1 and 2 Samuel, and 1 and 2 Kings. All these books reflect the style and the outlook of what scholars call "the Deuteronomic historian(s)."[43]

How did Deuteronomy become part of the *Humash*? The prevailing scholarly view is that in its original redaction the books of Deuteronomy and Joshua were added to an already existing four-book canonical anthology of J, E, and P, that is, books of Genesis, Exodus, Leviticus, and Numbers. What had been a Tetrateuch was now a Hexateuch. This makes sense, for the story of the Israelites properly climaxes with their entry into the land. After the fall of the First Temple, probably during the Babylonian exile, when the Torah was in its final phase of redaction, it was decided to end the Torah with the Israelites still outside the land (as the exiles were). The book of Joshua was dropped from the Torah, Deuteronomy remained, and the Hexateuch became a Pentateuch.

That more or less is the interpretive framework within which modernists read Deuteronomy. Obviously it is antithetical to what traditionalists believe. I have discussed in Part II the issues that these divergent assumptions of authorship raise and what they imply for the authority of the text.

Scholars differ, albeit slightly, on exactly how Deuteronomy is configured. The structure looks more or less like this:

- **Editorial Heading** (Deut. 1:1–5): These verses set the context in which the contents of the book that follows are presented.

- **Moses' First Retrospective Discourse** (Deut. 1:6–4:40): Moses here reviews all that transpired from the time the Israelites decamped from Sinai. He essentially recapitulates events told in Exodus and Numbers, except that what was narrated there in the third person is here given in the first person. It is worth comparing the two versions. Moses leaves out or occasionally changes some details told in the earlier books. He says, for example, that at Sinai "The LORD spoke to you out of the fire; you heard the sound of words but perceived no shape—nothing but a voice" (4:12). Yet the Exodus account has the 70 elders beholding the divine (chapter 24). And whereas Numbers had it that God instructed him to send out the spies (Num. 13:1–2), here he says it was the people who proposed it (Deut. 1:22).

  This section concludes with a brief appendix about the designation of the cities of refuge (Deut. 4:41–43), which is a partial repetition of Num. 35:9–15.

- **Moses' Second Retrospective Discourse** (Deut. 4:44–28:68): Here the focus is on the Revelation and the covenant at Horev (Sinai). Moses reiterates the Ten Commandments, but in words slightly but tellingly different from the Exodus version, and he puts it to the people that the covenant is theirs to uphold or contravene. Then, as if to explicate the content of the covenant, Moses presents an elaborate series of laws that covers a wide range of human endeavor—ritual, moral, civil, criminal, and societal. This unit (Deut. 12:1–25:16), the Deuteronomic Code, constitutes the heart of the book. It is bracketed by descriptions of a covenant-renewal ceremony projected to take place upon entry into the land, between two mountains, Gerizim and Ebal (11:29–32 and chapter 27). Like the Holiness Code in Leviticus, the Deuteronomic Code is followed by an epilogue that lays out graphically the rewards and punishments attendant upon keeping or violating these laws (the long chapter 28).[44]

- **Moses' Third Retrospective Discourse** (Deuteronomy 29 and 30): Like a lawyer in the final stage of stating his case, Moses here gives a summary statement of the terms of the covenant. Here he is at his most eloquent. The speech contains some of the finest flourishes of the book, with many quotable passages. Of particular note is the emphasis on the covenant as a living reality and the here-and-now nature of Torah.

- **The Grand Finale** (Deuteronomy 31–4): Deuteronomy and the Torah now approach closure. This section is a collage of material that effects this. There is first a narrative (chapter 31, *parashat* Va-yelekh), which describes Joshua's appointment as Moses' successor and Moses' commitment of the Torah to writing. The *Humash* is thus ending with the idea that it is a written text to be read and heard. Then we get the great poem (chapter 32, *parashat* Ha'azinu) called "The Song of Moses," though it undoubtedly comes from a period later than Moses but earlier than D. In its way this masterwork of Hebrew verse fittingly limns the relationship of God and Israel that Moses has been advancing all through Deuteronomy. The penultimate passage (chapter 33) is another poem, Moses' cryptic blessings of the tribes. Then comes the conclusion (chapter 34): Moses is given a last look at the land he will not enter, he dies, is buried (by whom? by God?), and is mourned by all Israel.

## A LIST OF THE 11 *PARSHIYOT* OF DEUTERONOMY

1. Devarim (Deut. 1:1–3:22)

**Editorial Heading**

- the place and time of the farewell speeches

**Moses' First Retrospective Discourse**

- review of the events from Horev (Sinai) to Kadesh (the first 11 days)
- the events after the departure from Kadesh toward Canaan (year 38)

2. Va-ethannan (Deut. 3:23–7:11)
   - Moses' plea to enter the land
   - God's expectations of Israel
   - appendix: the designation of three cities of refuge in Transjordan

**Moses' Second Retrospective Discourse**

- heading: the place and time of this speech
- the covenant at Horev
- iteration of the Ten Commandments
- elaboration of the first two commandments
- the *Shema*
- warnings against idolatry and intermarriage

3. 'Ekev (Deut. 7:12–11:25)
   - continuation of the polemic against idolatry
   - reflections on the relationship of God and Israel
   - recap of the Golden Calf episode
   - brief interlude: on the Levites
   - reflections on the land

4. Re'eh (Deut. 11:26–16:17)
   - the upshot of the speech: Israel's choice between blessing and curse

*(continued)*

## A LIST OF THE 11 *PARSHIYOT* OF DEUTERONOMY, *continued*

• the Deuteronomic Code: the designated place of sacrifices and other religious matters[45]

5. Shofetim (Deut. 16:18–21:9)
   • the Code continued: civil and religious authorities, judicial and military matters

6. Ki Tetse' (Deut. 21:10–25:19)
   • the Code continued: a miscellany of laws (mostly about civil and domestic life)

7. Ki Tavo' (Deut. 26:1–29:8)
   • the Code concluded: liturgical declarations (the firstfruits ceremony, the tithing declaration)
   • concluding statement: reciprocity between God and Israel
   • covenant ceremony on Mounts Gerizim and Ebal: blessings and curses
   • the consequences of obedience and transgression: blessings and curses

### Moses' Third Retrospective Discourse

• introduction: the context of this speech

8. Nitsavim (Deut. 29:9–30:20)
   • final summary and exhortation: the Torah, the land, the choice

### The Grand Finale

9. Va-Yelekh (Deut. 31:1–31:30)
   • Moses prepares for death: the appointment of Joshua
   • instructions about the Torah: public reading at sabbatical year assembly (*hak-hel*) and securing it in the Ark
   • summons to hear the Song

10. Ha'azinu (Deut. 32:1–32:52)
   • poem: the Song of Moses
   • conclusions to the Song
   • God's final instructions to Moses

11. Ve-zo't ha-berakhah (Deut. 33:1–34:12)
   • poem: Moses' farewell blessings of the tribes
   • Moses' death

Deuteronomy, then, presents a version or a stream of biblical religion that Stephen Geller calls "Deuteronomic-covenantal."[46] It stands as an alternative to the "Priestly-cultic" religion of the last half of Exodus, Leviticus, and much of Numbers. The Deuteronomic stream relates to God as a transcendent being, not as the immanent God of Priestly religion. It is focused less on mystery and sacrifice and more on understanding and inner commitment, less on fear of God and more on love of God. It sees Torah not as ritual procedure but as word and text. At the same time Deuteronomic religion is not tolerant; it is resolute and militant in its hostility to polytheism and polytheists. It is significant, I think, that the Redactor(s) of the *Humash* give(s) Deuteronomy the last word, as if to qualify the Priestly voice that has dominated the three preceding books. And if we look beyond the borders of the Torah into the books of the Prophets and the Writings, we see that the Deuteronomic voice and vision largely prevail there (except for the books of Ezekiel, which are anchored in the "Priestly" vision).

So Deuteronomy, though it looks and sounds like a review of Israel's past, actually looks ahead to the future. It contains so many of the fundamentals of what in time will become normative Judaism: the *Shema*; the insistence on the centrality of Torah; the importance of both mind and heart, and of explanation and commitment in understanding and living out Torah; and the idea that the covenant between God and Israel imposes obligations and **choices** on both parties. Guiding words in this book are not hard to pick up: "hearing," "listening," "your heart," "that you may long endure on the land," "today."

The first three *parshiyot* of Deuteronomy are uniform in their content. We hear only the voice of Moses addressing people. The keys to reading these portions are: (1) how to hear and evaluate Moses' version of the events he is recounting and their comparison to the versions in Exodus and Numbers; and (2) how to identify the concerns and issues that the Deuteronomist is placing in Moses' mouth.

The middle four *parshiyot* are taken up with the law code that is the centerpiece of this book. Reading them involves: (1) looking into the social and historical context of this diverse collection of rules and regulations; and (2) ferreting out from them the values and the vision that underlie them.

The last four *parshiyot* all communicate the sense of an ending, in different ways. Each of them should be read with an eye toward discovering how they do this.

The parashah I choose for modeling a reading is Re'eh. It effects the transition from Moses' monologue to the legal section and it raises issues that are typical and central for Deuteronomy.

---

## A Guided Reading of *Parashat* Re'eh

### Step 1: The First Reading

1. **The textual terrain and the context**: We are in the midst of Moses' second farewell speech.[47] It has been going on for several chapters. It reaches a climax here with his eloquent statement of "the bottom line"—"See, this day I set before you blessing and curse" (Deut. 11:26)—and then shifts into legal discourse.

2. **The parashah**: Here are my notes from an initial read-through:

   - **Free will and choice**: Both come through clearly here. With all the admonishments, incentives, and threats that Moses, and God via Moses, have repeatedly articulated to the people, what stands out here is the Torah's presupposition that in the end it comes down not to what people, and I suppose individuals, must do or should do but what they want to do and what they choose to do.

- **Intolerance**: " . . . the nations you are to dispossess. . . . Tear down their altars, smash their pillars . . ." (Deut. 12:2–3). There is no "live and let live" policy here. As much as I understand this, this is disturbing. It disturbs me because I fear this is the seed of the whole legacy of religious intolerance that has shed so much blood throughout history and continues unabated in our time. This passage has cost us, and not only us.

- **Idolatry**: The Torah is obsessed with idolatry. Why? Is this obsession to be understood only in its historical context? If so, idolatry is an anachronism, passé. Or is it still with us? Is it still an issue? (I recall now that the eminent Jewish thinker Emil Fackenheim [1916–2003] made a strong case that it is. I should reread his essay "Idolatry as a Modern Religious Possibility."[48])

- **"The place that the LORD your God will choose to establish His name"** (Deut. 16:6): What is this place? The Temple? Jerusalem? Why is the text so vague, so hestitant to name it?

- **"You shall not gash yourselves or shave the front of your heads . . ."** (Deut. 14:1): Would the Torah forbid body piercings? Mohawk haircuts?

- **The poor**: There is an interesting contradiction in the text. On the one hand: "There shall be no needy among you— since the LORD your God will bless you in the land that the LORD your God is giving you . . ." (Deut. 15:4). On the other hand: "For there will never cease to be needy ones in your land . . . (15:11).

- **The holidays**: There are interesting discrepancies in how they are described here compared to the two other places where the festivals are described (Exod. 23:10–12 and 14–17 and Lev. 23). Passover is presented as commemorating the Exodus. But Shavuot and Sukkot look to be agricultural festivals, of firstfruits and harvest, respectively. They are not connected to any historical events in the life of the people.

## Step 2: The Second Reading

A second reading deepens some concerns that the first one raised. I now find a connection between two issues that drew my attention: human autonomy and intolerance—a connection and a contradiction between them.

At the beginning of the parashah Moses tells the people that they have to make a choice between the blessings that accrue from obedience to God and the curses that will follow upon disobedience. There's an implicit respect here for human autonomy, a tacit acknowledgment that the critical element in human affairs is what philosophers call volition. This is in sharp disagreement with the Greek view that man and the gods, too, are controlled by fate, and with the later Calvinist idea of predestination.

But what the Torah grants in one passage it seems to revoke in the next. Idols and idolaters are to be extirpated. Not politely disagreed with or argued against but **exterminated**. This is theological cleansing. Why? I could understand this extreme reaction if the altars and Asherite pillars and sacred posts to be destroyed were those of errant Israelites, the results of a bad choice or a wrong choice. But these are the cultic artifacts of the surrounding nations. They are the modes of accessing divinity and serving it, chosen by those people with the very autonomy and free will that have just been affirmed. So why not respect them even if you disagree with them? Why not say, "We made our choice, you made yours" and let it go at that?

I fear that it comes down to a conflict between the exclusivism of antiquity and the pluralism of Western modernity. The former has been bequeathed to us by our ancestors and by tradition; the latter has been forged in the crucible of the Enlightenment. And I am left wondering: Is the former an atavism that we can ill afford in today's global village? Or is the latter an illusion, and modernity, and the Enlightenment itself, a chimera?

These questions block out the other important issues in the parashah. At least for now. Maybe I'll get to them next year. Or the year after.

# PART V

# Commentaries: A Concise Guide

**1.**
*Humash* Commentaries

**2.**
Other Historical-Critical
Commentaries

**3.**
The Great Medieval
Commentaries

**4.**
Synthetic Commentaries

**5.**
Midrash

**6.**
Women's Commentaries

**7.**
Web Resources

> Coming to the Bible through commentaries is much like looking at a landscape through garret windows, over which generations of unmolested spiders have spun their webs.
>
> —Henry Ward Beecher

If I agreed with Beecher there would be no need for this discussion. And to some extent I do agree with him. In the exchange between the reader and the text that takes place every time we open the *Humash*, the reader is ultimately in charge. It is what the reader sees and hears in the text that is pivotal. That is what Beecher means to say by his analogy—and I think he's right.

So why bother with commentary?

Because in reading the *Humash* we need all the help we can get. The landscape of the five books is sufficiently confusing—linguistically, rhetorically, and historically—that unaided the reader will not know what she is looking at even if all the cobwebs were swept from the windows and the reader were not up in the garrett but down at ground level. Commentaries can indeed obscure our view of the text, especially when they are tendentious or apologetic or didactic. But when they are responsible and carefully done they can illuminate the text in important ways. I would venture to say that Beecher never read Rashi. Had he done so, he might not have offered his analogy.

Beecher's analogy speaks to a basic question about biblical commentary: What is it for? Is its purpose to **explain** the text or to **interpret** it? One could argue that these are not clear-cut alternatives but two sides of the same coin. Is not every explanation an interpretation and vice versa? Hermeneutical theory (the theory of interpretation) usefully distinguishes between *exegesis*, the articulation (drawing out) of the text's objective meaning, and *eisegesis*, the meaning that is subjectively determined (put in) by the reader. In Part II, I discussed these two modes as they impinge on the act of reading. I noted that in reading the *Humash* there is an ongoing tension between them. My point in bringing them up here is to note that this same tension also operates in the writing of commentaries. This shouldn't surprise us since commentators are, first and foremost, readers, readers who make the results of their reading public.

In Jewish terms the *exegesis/eisegesis* dichotomy can be correlated with the difference between *peshat* and *derash*. Running through the whole history of *Humash* commentary from Rabbinic times to our own is a debate over what the commentator's task is: to elucidate the *peshat*, the plain meaning of the words of the text? Or to produce a *derash*, a meaning that is read out of—actually into—those words? On one side are the *pashtanim*, those who hold that the function of commentary is to provide the *peshat*; on the other are the *darshanim*, those who believe that to expound Torah involves going beneath the verbal surface of the text to discover and teach meanings and implications hitherto unknown. Virtually all commentators on the *Humash* are implicated in this debate and, whether they say so explicitly or not, take a position in it. Some, like the great medieval exegete Rashbam (Rabbi Shemu'el ben Meir, France, ca. 1085–ca.1174), are pure *pashtanim*; others, like the early modern Keli Yakar (Shlomo Ephraim of Luntshitz, 1550–1619, Poland), are brilliant *darshanim*. Most walk both sides of the expository street and mix the two modes in their writings.

The commentaries I note in the following discussion reflect this tension, even as the ones written in our time are couched in contemporary terms and language. But right here, two cautionary notes are in order.

First, **what follows is not a comprehensive listing.** The variety and volume of material is vast and proliferates by the year, if not even more frequently. Much of it exists only in Hebrew. I list here only commentaries written in English, of which there is also no shortage. I have chosen to note those that I believe stand the best chance of helping the novice or the intermediate parashah reader to appreciate and contemplate the individual pearls on the metaphorical necklace. If you are an advanced reader and/or you control Hebrew sources, you will probably know where to find the key commentaries, in Hebrew and in English, traditional and contemporary. But I think anyone at any level will find things of value in the commentaries listed here. Regardless of where you understand yourself to be, it is likely that as you progress, you will come upon other interesting and relevant sources. Be assured that they abound.

Second, **don't be overwhelmed or intimidated by the volume and range of commentaries**. It's possible that as you go through my capsule profiles, you will throw your hands up in frustration and wonder, "Where do I begin?" This is a fair question. My answer to it is this: begin with the one with which you feel most comfortable. Pick the commentary that sounds or looks most inviting to you and go from there. You may have to test-drive a few of them. Chances are one of the *Humash* commentaries will be of most value to you in the early going. You may or may not ever have to branch out from there. You will know when you need to get a second opinion on the meaning of a verse or a passage or a story—or a third and a fourth. As I've said, parashah reading is a lifelong project. Every yearly cycle is a different experience. One year you may want to key into a historical approach and focus on source criticism to see what you can learn from it. Another year you may want to work with Rashi and see what he does with the text. And so on. To paraphrase a Rabbinic word to the wise: you are not called upon to learn the whole Torah; but neither should its breadth and depth deter you from immersing yourself in it today.

# 1.
# *Humash* Commentaries

The commentaries mentioned here are all excellent and worth consulting. Each one has some feature or features that recommend themselves to anyone at any level. The following are all found in volumes that provide the Hebrew text and an English translation. The weekly *parshiyot* are clearly demarcated and labeled.

- *The JPS Torah Commentary:* This five-volume set published by Jewish Publication Society between 1989 and 1996 contains the traditional Hebrew text, the new JPS translation (NJPS), and commentary prepared by leading authorities on the *Humash*. The layout and format are clear and informative. Each parashah is introduced and commented upon verse by verse. Problems and complexities are flagged in the discussion and dealt with at length in instructive excurses located at the back of the volume. Each volume contains a superb comprehensive introduction to the book in question.

  Genesis and Exodus were done by Nahum M. Sarna. They incorporate much of what can be found in his previous writings on those two books.[1] Leviticus was done by Baruch A. Levine. The commentary on Numbers by Jacob Milgrom is the tour de force of the set, followed closely by the commentary on Deuteronomy by Jeffrey H. Tigay. The focus is primarily historical, in the two Sarna volumes, alas, almost exclusively so. The latter three volumes range more widely in the sources they bring and in the critical tools and perspectives they employ.

  The only disadvantage to this invaluable commentary is that it comes in five separate volumes. Thus the reader of any one of them does not have immediate access to the rest of the *Humash*—unless the other four are at hand.

> Nahum Sarna, ed. *The JPS Torah Commentary: Genesis.* Philadelphia: The Jewish Publication Society, 1989.
>
> Nahum M. Sarna, ed. *The JPS Torah Commentary: Exodus.* Philadelphia, New York, and Jerusalem: The Jewish Publication Society, 1991.
>
> Baruch A. Levine, ed. *The JPS Torah Commentary: Leviticus.* Philadelphia: The Jewish Publication Society, 1989.
>
> Jacob Milgrom, ed. *The JPS Torah Commentary: Numbers.* Philadelphia and New York: The Jewish Publication Society, 1990.
>
> Jeffrey H. Tigay, ed. *The JPS Torah Commentary: Deuteronomy.* Philadelphia: The Jewish Publication Society, 1996.

- **W. Gunther Plaut, *The Torah: A Modern Commentary:*** Here is a commentary that does it all. The layout and the format of the revised edition are clear and user friendly, a major improvement over the first edition, which was done with no regard for the regimen of weekly readings. Here each parashah is introduced contextually and then synopsized. Then, as you read through the text, individual verses are glossed with brief explanatory remarks. At the conclusion of each portion come a series of short essays, followed by a section titled "Gleanings." The essays deal with the salient issues raised by the parashah and summarize readably complex scholarly debates. At every turn they face up to the conflicts and continuities between the Jewish present and the biblical past. They are a marvel of lucidity, and of intellectual rigor and probity. The "Gleanings" section offers a digest of source material relating to that parashah from the Midrash, classical commentaries, Jewish thinkers, ancient and modern poets, and other religious traditions. Before each book, besides Plaut's general introduction to it, is an additional discussion by William W. Hallo that looks at that book in its relation to ancient Near Eastern literature.

> W. Gunther Plaut, gen. ed. and David E. S. Stein. *The Torah: A Modern Commentary*, rev. ed. New York: Union for Reform Judaism, 2005.

• *Etz Hayim: Torah and Commentary:* The layout in this book is based on a double agenda: (1) of explicating the *peshat*, and (2) of engaging in *derash*. The intent here is to give each its due, in a way that enables the reader to see and appreciate the difference between the two interpretive modes. Thus on each page, under the Hebrew text and the English translation (the NJPS version), are not one but two separate commentaries bifurcated by a line. Above the line is *peshat*, below the line is *derash* material. The *peshat* comments focus on individual verses and are abstracted from the *JPS Torah Commentary*, as are the introductions to each book. Both, however, lack the fullness of discussion of the original. The *derash* section offers a potpourri of interpretive comments from the Midrash and other classical Jewish sources. It is in this section that one finds, at the beginning of each parashah, some brief remarks that set its context. *Etz Hayim* also offers a third kind of commentary. Occasionally, at the bottom of some pages, there is a box titled "Halakhah L'Ma'aseh," that is, how a particular verse applies with respect to Jewish law (*halakhah*). The comments here are brief and studiously nondidactic, reflecting the understanding of the editors that the Conservative perspective, which underlies this commentary, lacks a clear consensus on some halakhic matters.

   David Lieber, sen. ed., et al. *Etz Hayim: Torah and Commentary.* New York: The Rabbinical Assembly, 2001.

• **Richard Elliot Friedman, *Commentary on the Torah with a New English Translation:*** Friedman is one of those rare academicians who can inhabit the domains of high biblical scholarship and at the same time transpose its findings into the less arcane discourse of nonspecialists. He did that with *Who Wrote the Bible?* and his other books, and here he has applied his talents and learning to the venerable enterprises of translation (discussed in Part IV) and commentary.

One would think that Friedman would trade on his expertise in historical and source criticism. But not here; he eschews it almost completely. He wants a commentary that explains the many aspects of the text that source criticism does not address and in a way that avoids the dry-as-dust style of much scholarly writing on the Bible. The result is a series of observations and insights, many of them personal, that feel fresh and attuned to the intellectual and spiritual concerns of contemporary liberal Judaism. Friedman is aware that his is not the first or the only attempt to open up the *Humash* to the modern reader. He is thus very selective in the verses and passages he chooses to discuss. His commentary is not as exhaustive or as comprehensive as the others, but for many readers this will be a plus. When Friedman does remark on the text, it is always in order to highlight a point or an issue that he feels has not been noticed or addressed in other commentaries. He also has a fine feel for the *Humash* as an holistic book and many of his remarks help the reader develop a "big picture" perspective.

> Richard Elliot Friedman, *Commentary on the Torah with a New English Translation*. San Francisco: HarperSanFrancisco, 2001.

• *The Chumash: The Stone Edition:* This *Humash*, published in a dozen editions in the ArtScroll series, features a commentary that it describes as "anthologized from the rabbinic writings." The copious commentary, written by rabbis with deep talmudic learning, synthesizes a vast range of Rabbinic midrashic interpretation. Stone is particularly good at explaining the details of the legal material in Exodus and Deuteronomy and the sacrificial detail in Leviticus. But the apologetic and almost medieval approach it takes toward narrative details makes this a *Humash* to use selectively.[2] This *Humash* also contains Rashi's commentary, but in Hebrew only.

> Rabbi Nosson Scherman, gen. ed. *The Chumash: The Stone Edition*. Brooklyn, N.Y.: Mesorah Publications Ltd., ArtScroll Series, 1993 and following.

• **Aryeh Kaplan:** *The Living Torah:* The main attraction here, as noted in Part IV, is the fluid yet accurate translation, but the concise notes on individual verses at the bottom of the page are worth consulting. They do not constitute a commentary but they are always informative. In keeping with Kaplan's Orthodox orientation, Rabbinic and medieval Jewish sources are cited, with occasional references to the Septuagint (the ancient Greek translation of the *Humash* done around 250 B.C.E.) and Josephus (a Jewish historian in Roman times, around 37–100 C.E.).

Aryeh Kaplan, ed. and trans. *The Living Torah*. New York and Jerusalem: Maznaim Publishing Corp., 1981.

The following commentaries are appended to an English translation of the *Humash* text. The reader who wishes to look at or compare the Hebrew original will need to have it at hand in a separate volume.

- *The Jewish Study Bible:* Here we have not only the Pentateuch but the entire TANAKH in one volume. The translation is the NJPS version. The weekly portions are marked off and labeled. The commentaries on the individual books were done by major scholars and edited by Adele Berlin and Marc Zvi Brettler. They appear in the margins of each page and go passage by passage, with frequent notes on individual verses. The JSB is concise, unfailingly informative, and encyclopedic in the array of material it cites. It is particularly good at referring the reader to verses and passages elsewhere in the TANAKH, in rabbinic literature, and in the prayer book that have a bearing on the one(s) being discussed. Maps show up when needed. At the end of the book are 25 essays on three general topics: Jewish interpretation of the Bible as it has evolved through the ages, the role the Bible plays in Jewish life and thought, and the various backgrounds against which the Bible can be read. These essays alone make this book worth having.

  Adele Berlin and Marc Zvi Brettler, eds. *The Jewish Study Bible*. Oxford and New York: Oxford University Press, 2004.

- **Everett Fox, *The Five Books of Moses:*** The centerpiece of this book is Fox's translation, described in Part IV. But Fox also offers a commentary that is useful for those literarily inclined, less so for those looking for a historical-critical approach. Fox is strong on illuminating the structural and thematic elements of each book. His concise and always interesting notes on the text and his glosses on individual words bridge the gap between the Hebrew original and the English as he has rendered it. The notes also succinctly harvest points and insights made by the major scholars of each book, all of whose works Fox clearly has mastered. The individual *parshiyot* are not demarcated.

Everett Fox, trans. *The Five Books of Moses*. New York: Schocken Books, 1995.

• **Robert Alter,** *The Five Books of Moses:* On the surface this is a book quite similar to that by Fox. It is first and foremost a translation project; the primary goal of the commentary is to highlight the literary and rhetorical aspects of the text. But Alter goes about it in his distinctive elegant and erudite style. For those who want to put themselves in the hands of a consummate close reader, this commentary is for you. Alter explicates the text from the inside, taking pains to show how words and phrases work to produce meaning. He is particularly helpful in pointing out intertextual references so as to show how the *Humash* is one big verbal echo chamber, a key matter for any *Humash* reader to see. Additionally he offers judicious helpings of comments that explain the social and cultural context of the stories and the laws. The individual *parshiyot* are not labeled.

Robert Alter, trans. *The Five Books of Moses*. New York and London: W. W. Norton & Co., 2004.

# 2.
# Other Historical-Critical Commentaries: The Anchor Bible Series

If you want to see the historical-critical study of the Bible at its most authentic and impressive best, the Anchor Bible series is the place to go. The Anchor Bible project, published by Doubleday (now part of Random House), began decades ago as an attempt to produce the finest and most authoritative scholarly treatment in English of both Old and New Testaments, and it is still going strong. By now most of the books in both canons, including most of the five of the Pentateuch, have been covered, and the end is in sight. Each of the books is the product of a prominent specialist. Each one includes a comprehensive introduction, an original English translation, detailed notes on the verses, and an analytic commentary on each chapter or group of chapters. The focus is strictly historical and linguistic, and discussions are thorough to a fault. There is, however, no Hebrew text and the weekly portions are not specified.

The Genesis volume was done by the late E. A. Speiser. It came out in 1964 and established itself as one of the flagship volumes in the whole series, a reputation it has not relinquished. At this writing it is being updated by Ronald S. Hendel. Exodus was done by William H. C. Propp. Jacob Milgrom's Leviticus has to be one of the most prodigious works of biblical scholarship done in modern times. Its three volumes, published between 1991 and 2001, run collectively to over 2,700 pages, and surely represent the most exhaustive, if not exhausting, treatment of this difficult book ever done. The Numbers commentary by Baruch A. Levine is in two volumes. Deuteronomy is the work of Moshe Weinfeld, perhaps the leading authority on that book. The first volume covers chapters 1–11 and came out in 1991; another two on the rest of the book are in process.

The Anchor Bible commentary is not for beginners and even if you are an advanced reader it is probably not the first commentary you will want to consult. The specialists write in their own language and style and at times they can be numbingly technical (Speiser's Genesis excepted). Reading them, one has to remind oneself that it is a religious and spiritual text that is being put under the critical microscope. But if you want to get to the bottom of the historical and linguistic dimensions of the text, this is where to look. The volumes are most likely to be found in libraries. Some of them are out of print, though used copies are often available online.

E. A. Speiser. *Genesis*. Garden City, N.Y.: Doubleday and Co., 1964.

William H. C. Propp. *Exodus 1–18: A New Translation with Notes and Comments*. New York: Doubleday, 1999.

———. *Exodus 19–40: A New Translation with Introduction and Commentary*. New York: Doubleday, 2006.

Jacob Milgrom. *Leviticus 1–16: A New Translation with Introduction and Commentary*. New York: Doubleday, 1991.

———. *Leviticus 17–22: A New Translation with Introduction and Commentary*. New York: Doubleday, 2000.

———. *Leviticus 23–27: A New Translation with Introduction and Commentary*. New York: Doubleday, 2001.

Baruch A. Levine. *Numbers 1–20: A New Translation with Introduction and Commentary*. New York: Doubleday, 1993.

———. *Numbers 21–36: A New Translation with Introduction and Commentary*. New York: Doubleday, 2000.

Moshe Weinfeld. *Deuteronomy 1–11: A New Translation with Introduction and Commentary*. New York: Doubleday, 1991.

# 3.
# The Great Medieval Commentaries

Medieval commentaries were written in manuscripts. You had to read them with the *Humash* text nearby, though I daresay many a reader in those days did not need such a "crib." After Gutenberg, though, the major commentaries were published all together, laid out on the printed page in the margins above, below, and beside the Hebrew text and the Aramaic version *(Targum)*. This format came to be called *Miqra'ot Gedolot* ("The Big Book of Scripture"), known in English as the Rabbinic Bible, and it is available and is as widely used today as it was centuries ago. *Miqra'ot Gedolot* al-

A page of the *Miqra'ot Gedolot*. The *Humash* text is in the upper right quadrant.

lows you to read the major commentaries in tandem with the text. It enables you to see quickly see how each one operates, where they agree and disagree—if you read Hebrew.

If you don't, you were out of luck until very recently. There is now under way a project that carries the *miqra'ot gedolot* concept over into English. This is the series being put out by The Jewish Publication Society titled *The Commentators' Bible: The JPS Miqra'ot Gedolot.*

- *The Commentators' Bible: The JPS Miqra'ot Gedolot:* This landmark development opens new vistas of commentary for the reader who doesn't know Hebrew. Now, for the first time, one can read, in exactly the same page layout, the Torah text in Hebrew, the JPS English translation (the NJPS and the 1917 versions), and the comments of the big four: Rashi, Rashbam, Ibn Ezra, and Ramban all translated into a smooth English (see the photo on the next page). There are also additional comments selected from other important medieval and early modern exegetes and interpreters. All this—the translation, the superb notes, the excellent introductory material, and the editing—is the brainchild and fruit of the hard work of Michael Carasik.

At this writing only Exodus exists in this exciting new format. As the succeeding volumes come out, *The Commentators' Bible* will surely take its place as a staple of all serious Torah study for those who cannot savor the classical medieval commentators in their original Hebrew form.

> Michael Carasik, ed. and trans. *The Commentators' Bible: The JPS Miqra'ot Gedolot: Exodus.* Philadelphia: The Jewish Publication Society, 2005.

The four major commentaries, discussed in Part III, have all been translated into English and each one can be read and studied on its own. The following translations of them all come in five-volume sets.

- **Rashi:** The commentaries of Rashi are available in English in three formats. The most useful version is:

  > *The Sapirstein Edition Rashi.* New York: Mesorah Publications Ltd., ArtScroll Series, 1998.

EXODUS 1:6–10  SHEMOT                                                שמות א שמות

NJPS   brothers, and all that generation. [7]But the Israelites were
fertile and prolific; they multiplied and increased very greatly, so
that the land was filled with them.

[8]A new king arose over Egypt who did
not know Joseph. [9]And he said to his
people, "Look, the Israelite people are
much too numerous for us. [10]Let us deal
shrewdly with them, so that they may not

OJPS   died, and all his brethren, and all that generation. [7]And
the children of Israel were fruitful, and increased abundantly, and
multiplied, and waxed exceeding mighty;
and the land was filled with them.

[8]Now there arose a new king over Egypt,
who knew not Joseph. [9]And he said unto
his people: "Behold, the people of the children of Israel are too many and too mighty
for us; [10]come, let us deal wisely with them,
lest they multiply, and it come to pass, that,

וְכָל־אֶחָיו וְכֹל הַדּוֹר הַהוּא: [7]וּבְנֵי
יִשְׂרָאֵל פָּרוּ וַיִּשְׁרְצוּ וַיִּרְבּוּ וַיַּעַצְמוּ בִּמְאֹד
מְאֹד וַתִּמָּלֵא הָאָרֶץ אֹתָם: ס

[8]וַיָּקָם מֶלֶךְ־חָדָשׁ עַל־מִצְרָיִם אֲשֶׁר לֹא־
יָדַע אֶת־יוֹסֵף: [9]וַיֹּאמֶר אֶל־עַמּוֹ הִנֵּה עַם
בְּנֵי יִשְׂרָאֵל רַב וְעָצוּם מִמֶּנּוּ: [10]הָבָה
נִתְחַכְּמָה לוֹ פֶּן־יִרְבֶּה וְהָיָה כִּי־תִקְרֶאנָה

RASHI   7 Fertile. Their women did not
miscarry, and they did not die as infants.
Prolific. They would have sextuplets.

8 A new king arose. Rab and Samuel
dispute over whether this was literally a new
king, or the old king (whose death is not
recorded) issuing new decrees. Who did
not know Joseph. If it was the old king, this
would mean that he acted as if he did not
know him.

9 He said. It was Pharaoh who initiated
the plan.

10 Let us deal shrewdly with them.
The text literally says lo, which could mean
"with it" (the people); but our Sages interpret it as dealing shrewdly "with Him," with
the Savior of Israel. Knowing that God
punishes measure for measure, they thought: If we kill the children by fire, we can be killed
by fire; if by the sword, we can be killed by the sword. But it is safe to kill them by water,

ABARBANEL'S QUESTIONS   + It would seem that
v. 8, "A new king arose over Egypt who did not know
Joseph," should immediately follow v. 6, "Joseph
died." Why does the text insert the verse about the
Israelites' fertility (which we know about already,
anyway, from Gen. 47:27) in between them? + Since
Pharaoh already thought that the Israelites were "too
numerous for us" (v. 9), why does v. 10 say that he was
worried that they would increase? + What does "the
event of war" (v. 10) have to do with it? Why wasn't
Pharaoh afraid they themselves would conquer Egypt?
+ Why would Pharaoh worry that the Israelites would
"get them up out of the land" (OJPS)? He should be
delighted that they would leave!

RASHBAM   6 All that generation. The
70 people.

7 Fertile. With regard to conception.
Prolific. With regard to birth. Thus the
womb would not miscarry. The root meaning of the word is "crawl," as if it meant here
"to produce crawlers"—for little children,
like all small creatures, crawl on the ground.
Multiplied. Rather, they "got big"; the little
ones grew up and did not die in childhood.
Increased. They did not die as grown men,
but lived long and increased very greatly,
to the extent that the land was filled with
them, as the Temple court "was filled with
the radiance of the Presence of the LORD"
(Ezek. 10:4) and "the skirts of His robe filled
the Temple" (Isa. 6:1). [A]

10 Let us deal shrewdly with them.
So that they do not increase. For if they
increase, then in the event of war with our
enemies, they may join our enemies in

[A] Rashbam's Hebrew comment is ostensibly grammatical,
though somewhat confusing. One wonders whether the examples chosen are meant to suggest that the Israelites' increase of population filled Egypt with the Divine Presence.

NAHMANIDES   them to the stars, is midrashic. It is certainly true with respect to the
love God showed for them by repeating their names over and over again. But the literary
connection is as I have explained. That is why Exodus literally begins by saying "And
these are the names"—to establish the link with Genesis.

10 Let us deal shrewdly with them. Pharaoh and "the sagest of his advisers" (Isa.
19:11) did not consider slaying them outright, for to do so without cause would be an enormous betrayal of a people that had come down to Egypt in the first place by command of
the previous king. Moreover, the Egyptian people (for he consulted their opinion as well)
would not have let the king commit such gratuitous violence, especially since the Israelites
were "too numerous" (v. 9) and could fight a mighty battle against them. Instead, Pharaoh
said, they should act cleverly, so that the Israelites would not sense that they were acting
out of enmity toward them. So he set them to do forced labor, as is the custom for those

IBN EZRA   6 All that generation.
Since the text has already mentioned the
death of Joseph and all his brothers, this
phrase must mean "all the Egyptians of that
generation." This is proven by the fact that
the king in v. 8 "did not know Joseph." A
reference does not indicate a period of time.

biblical "generation" is a genealogical reference (i.e., father and son are two generations);
it does not indicate a period of time.

7 Prolific. The verb used is the same used in the story of Noah and his sons; it is translated "swarm" in Gen. 8:17 and "abound" in
Gen. 9:7. It may mean that the women gave birth to twins or more; I myself have seen a woman who gave birth to quadruplets, and there
is medical evidence for up to septuplets. But the story in The Chronicles of Moses about Jewish mothers giving birth in the fields like
animals (and angels bringing the boys to them after they were grown) is nonsense; this is neither a holy book nor one of authentic
tradition. [B] Very greatly. Those who are impressed by the fact that the numerical value of this expression in Hebrew, used in Gen.
17:20 with reference to Ishmael, is the same as that of "Muhammad"—what do they do with this verse, where exactly the same phrase is
applied to Israel? God forbid that Moses should speak in numerological riddles! The land was filled with them. "Land" has the sense of
"the whole land of Egypt" (rather than "the earth," which the Hebrew word could also mean). [C]

8 A new king arose. "A new king" means just what it sounds like it means—there is no need to add the complication of an old king
with new decrees here. But "arose" implies that he was not related to the previous king.

9 His people. The Egyptians.

10 Let us deal shrewdly with them. That is, let us seek a wise course that will prevent them from increasing. In the event of war.

[B] The Chronicles of Moses fills in the details of Moses' biography with many fanciful elements.   [C] In his long commentary Ibn Ezra revised this view, taking "land" to mean the land of
Goshen (that is, the region of Rameses in Goshen; see Gen. 47:11) where the Israelites lived in Egypt.

ADDITIONAL COMMENTS   6 All that generation. Had any at all of the Egyptians who knew Joseph still been alive, the new king
(v. 8) would not have been able to do what he did (Gersonides).

7 Fertile and prolific. In accordance with God's promise (Gen. 46:3), "I will make you there into a great nation" (Hizkuni).
Increased. In size (Gersonides).

8 A new king arose. If this is the old king, then "arose" implies that he "rose" against Israel like an enemy (Hizkuni). Who did not
know Joseph. Though he was undoubtedly recorded in the annals in connection with the imposition of the 20% agricultural tax (Gen.
47:26), it never occurred to the new Pharaoh that he could have been a Hebrew (Sforno).

10 Let us deal shrewdly with them. Let us enslave them now, when it is unnecessary, so they are enslaved if it ever becomes

A page from *The Commentators' Bible: The JPS Miqra'ot Gedolot*. The
*Humash* text appears across the top of the page.

Along with the Torah text in Hebrew and in English translation is Rashi's commentary, translated and annotated by Yisrael Herczeg. The English translation of the Five Books follows Rashi's interpretations. The literal translation of Rashi's comments are highlighted and interwoven with explanatory words and phrases. This treatment communicates nicely the flow of the commentary. Additional notes highlight other features of Rashi's work.

A similar presentation of Rashi is the version of:

> I. M. Rosenbaum and A. M. Silbermann. *Pentateuch with Targum Onkelos, Haphtaroth and Rashi's Commentary.* Jerusalem: Feldheim, 1985.

This is a reprinting of a work that was originally published in 1930 in London and has been popular ever since.

If you want to see Rashi's comments broken down into small bits with no explanatory material, then the translation to use is:

> Abraham ben Isaiah and Benjamin Sharfman. *The Pentateuch and Rashi's Commentary: A Linear Translation into English.* Brooklyn, S.S. & R. Publishing Co., 1949.

This version displays on the top half of each page, phrase by phrase, the Hebrew text of the Torah and, facing it, the English translation of same. Then, on the bottom half of the page, again phrase by phrase and facing each other, are the Hebrew and English translation of Rashi.

* **Ibn Ezra:** The work of Ibn Ezra has been translated by H. Norman Strickman and Arthur M. Silver, in five volumes:

> *Ibn Ezra's Commentary on the Pentateuch: Genesis (B'reishit).* New York: Menorah Publishing Co., 1988.

> *Ibn Ezra's Commentary on the Pentateuch: Exodus (Shemot).* New York: Menorah Publishing Co., 1997.

> *Ibn Ezra's Commentary on the Pentateuch: Leviticus.* New York: Menorah Publishing Co., 2004.

*Ibn Ezra's Commentary on the Pentateuch: Numbers.* New York: Menorah Publishing Co., 1999.

*Ibn Ezra's Commentary on the Pentateuch: Deuteronomy (Devarim).* New York: Menorah Publishing Co., 2001.

The comments are annotated with good explanatory material. The only drawback here is that the Hebrew is not given. Nor is the text of the Torah, either in Hebrew or in English; only the words on which Ibn Ezra is commenting are cited. So these books have to be used with a *Humash* at hand.

- **Ramban:** Ramban's commentary on all five books exists in English in the translation of Charles B. Chavel:

  Ramban (Nachmanides): *Commentary on the Torah: Genesis,* trans. Charles B. Chavel. New York: Shilo Publishing House, 1999.

  Ramban (Nachmanides): *Commentary on the Torah: Exodus,* trans. Charles B. Chavel. New York: Shilo Publishing House, 1973.

  Ramban (Nachmanides): *Commentary on the Torah: Leviticus,* trans. Charles B. Chavel. New York: Shilo Publishing House, 1974.

  Ramban (Nachmanides): *Commentary on the Torah: Numbers,* trans. Charles B. Chavel. New York: Shilo Publishing House, 1975.

  Ramban (Nachmanides): *Commentary on the Torah: Deuteronomy,* trans. Charles B. Chavel. New York: Shilo Publishing House, 1976.

The comments are accompanied by Chavel's brief explanatory footnotes. Ramban's original Hebrew is not given; neither is the text of the Torah in Hebrew or in English.

A newer, improved version that offers more guidance and fuller notes on Ramban's method and elliptical style is under way in the burgeoning ArtScroll Series:

*The Torah: With Ramban's Commentary Translated, Annotated, and Elucidated.* New York: Mesorah Publications.

This project continues ArtScroll's achievement with Rashi and is similarly laid out. The work when complete will run to eight volumes. To date four volumes are out, covering Genesis and Exodus. Like its predecessor volume on Rashi, ArtScroll Ramban offers the Ramban's comments both in English translation and in the original Hebrew together with the Torah text in Hebrew and English translation. Unfortunately, what the editors omit from their translation are all of Ramban's numerous comments on the kabbalistic implications of the verse or phrase he is discussing. Each time they come to such a comment they resort to a formulaic note on the order of "Ramban's next comment discusses the deep kabbalistic concepts implicit in [the phrase or verse under discussion] and is not within the scope of this elucidation." They do, however, indicate where the excised comment begins in the Hebrew. Presumably the editors chose to delete such comments from their translation in accordance with the traditional view that kabbalistic knowledge is not a mass commodity.

- **Rashbam:** Rashbam's commentary has been translated, edited, and annotated in four volumes by Martin Lockshin. Lockshin's notes are helpful in pointing out where and why Rashbam is offering a reading opposed to his grandfather's. His introduction places Rashbam in the context of the history of medieval Jewish biblical exegesis. The volumes are:

    *Rabbi Samuel ben Meir's Commentary on Genesis.* Judaic Studies 5. Lewiston, Lampeter/Queenston: The Edwin Mellen Press, 1989.

    *Rashbam's Commentary on Exodus.* Brown [University] Judaic Series 310. Atlanta, Ga.: Scholars Press, 1997.

    *Rashbam's Commentary on Leviticus and Numbers.* Brown [University] Judaic Series 330. Atlanta, GA.: Scholars Press, 2001.

    *Rashbam's Commentary on Deuteronomy.* Brown [University] Judaic Series 340. Atlanta, GA: Scholars Press, 2004.

# 4.
# Synthetic Commentaries

Another way to access in a single reading from one book both the riches of the Midrash and the work of the medieval commentators is to consult two parashah-by-parashah commentaries that, deservedly, are treasured by experienced readers. I call them synthetic because they each reference and integrate a wide range of sources: Rabbinic midrash, medieval commentaries, and those who continued those modes of interpretation in the early modern and modern eras.

- **Nehama Leibowitz** (1905–97): Known to her many students in Israel and her readers the world over simply as "Nehama," Leibowitz was in her time arguably the leading teacher of how to delve into a parashah. Leibowitz shows lucidly the different ways in which the midrash and the medieval Hebrew commentaries handle issues in each parashah and what the commentaries, major, minor, and in-between, have done over the centuries with those lines of interpretation.

  The years have not diminished the value of her work to anyone who wants to inquire into a weekly Torah portion. Her discussions (in Hebrew) of each one of the 54 *parshiyot*, originally circulated in mimeographed pages over many years. They were eventually collected and published in five Hebrew volumes. In the 1970s, they were translated and adapted from the Hebrew by Aryeh Newman and published (in many printings) by the World Zionist Organization, Department for Torah Education and Culture in the Diaspora (Jerusalem). Each of the books features several discussions of each parashah. The titles are:

*Studies in B'reishit (Genesis)*
*Studies in Shemot (Exodus)—2 volumes*
*Studies in Va-yikra' (Leviticus)*
*Studies in Bamidbar (Numbers)*
*Studies in Devarim (Deuteronomy)*

• **Avivah Gottlieb Zornberg:** Though she has published only on the *parshiyot* of Genesis and Exodus, Zornberg's treatment of them represents an exquisite, though at times overwhelming, elaboration of Leibowitz's approach. In her own right a popular teacher of *Humash* in Jerusalem today, Zornberg brings to her reading a thorough command of midrash and commentaries, a deep grounding in English and Western literatures, culture, and literary and psychoanalytic theory, and an acute poetic and religious sensibility. But a word of caution: her discussions of each parashah are demanding. They wend their way over a vast intellectual terrain, too vast, I fear, to be absorbed week after week—unless one has a lot of time on one's hands. They are best taken in small bites, and the division of the discussions into discernible parts makes such an approach possible.

*Genesis: The Beginning of Desire.* Philadelphia and Jerusalem: The Jewish Publication Society, 1995.

*The Particulars of Rapture: Reflections on Exodus.* New York and London: Doubleday, 2001.

# 5.
# Midrash

What about reading Midrash so as to see directly what the Rabbis said about the Torah verses without mediation by later *darshanim*? In translation this could be disappointing and frustrating. Midrash is a form of poetry and, like poetry, it does not travel well to other linguistic systems. It is so rooted in the Hebrew language to attain its effect and meaning that to read it in any language other than Hebrew produces a relatively small return for one's efforts. The wordplay that is at the heart of the midrashic process just doesn't work in English.

But if you are undeterred, here are two possibilities that will open up this textual field to you.

- **The Soncino Midrash Rabbah:** *Midrash Rabbah* is not a discrete work but a composite collection of Rabbinic commentary on several books of the TANAKH. The translation is best described as serviceable.

    *The Soncino Midrash Rabbah,* vols. 1–5. London: Soncino Press, 1939.

- **Mekhilta De-Rabbi Ishmael:** *Mekhilta* covers only the middle part of the book of Exodus, but it displays well the Rabbis' repertoire of interpretational methods.

    *Mekhilta De-Rabbi Ishmael.* Trans. and ed. by Jacob Z. Lauterbach, 2nd bilingual ed. Philadelphia: Jewish Publication Society, 2004.

Translations of other midrashic texts are also extant. They mostly serve scholarly needs and will be instructive only to the most determined nonspecialists. They are generally available in university libraries. If you are going to read midrashic text, it is best to do so with a teacher.

That said, there are two collections of midrash on the *Humash* that do communicate its content, if not its method, to the non-Hebrew reader.

• *Louis Ginzberg, Legends of the Jews:* This is one of the greatest works of scholarship in any language and of any age. In seven volumes, two of them notes alone, Ginzberg collected a vast array of midrashic texts on the TANAKH and wove it all into a unified whole starting with Genesis and going through to Esther. The work thus presents a continuous and coherent telling of the biblical books as interpreted by the midrashic tradition in all its diversity. The first three volumes cover the *Humash*. Ginzberg wrote the work in German. Most of the English translation was done by Henrietta Szold. The Jewish Publication Society put the work out between 1909 and 1939 and it has been reissued many times since then.

• *The Book of Legends: Sefer ha-Aggadah.* This was edited by the great Hebrew poet Hayim Nahman Bialik (1873–1934) and Yehoshua Hana Ravnitsky (1859–1944) and appeared in Hebrew between 1908 and 1911. This, too, is a monumental work, as Bialik and Ravnitzky, working together in the early years of the 20th century, combed the corpus of Rabbinic literature in order to compile what they believed were the essential texts of the midrashic tradition in its aggadic (as opposed to its halakhic) mode. They took what they found and presented it quite differently from Ginzberg. Whereas Ginzberg synthesized all the texts into a seemingly seamless sequential narrative whole, Bialik and Ravnitzky took an anthological approach. They did order some of the material according to the biblical chronology, but they also organized it around a wide spectrum of themes. The result is that in this collection one can see (though not always) discrete midrashim more clearly than in Ginzberg's, where the individual texts all blend together into a narrative. Bialik and Ravnitzky also rewrote the texts, taking them out of the Rab-

binic Hebrew of the original and casting them in an early
20th-century literary Hebrew.

Upon publication *Sefer ha-Aggadah* became a staple in homes
and schools in prestate Palestine and wherever else Hebrew
was read and taught. In 1992 Rabbi William G. Braude translated the tome and the English version was published by
Schocken Books (New York).

# 6.
# Women's Commentaries

As issues of gender and sexuality have moved to the forefront in human and cultural studies, the effects of this development on how the Bible is read have been enormous and fruitful. Gender and feminist criticism is a burgeoning field and today it is by no means confined to Christian and secular academic circles, as it was a decade or two ago. There is now available an impressive body of gender and feminist scholarship and interpretation of the TANAKH by Jewish women.[3] Most of this consists of books and collections of essays, which are certainly valuable but of less immediate utility to a weekly parashah reader than a commentary. At this writing there are two such that I can note:

> The Women's Torah Commentary: New Insights from Women Rabbis on the 54 Weekly Torah Portions. Ed. Rabbi Elise Goldstein. Woodstock, Vt. Jewish Lights Publishing, 2000.

> Judith S. Antonelli. In the Image of God: A Feminist Commentary on the Torah. Northvale, N.J., and London: Jason Aronson Inc., 1995.

A significant addition will be the forthcoming publication of The Torah: A Woman's Commentary by the Women of Reform Judaism. Edited by Dr. Tamara Cohn Eskenazi and Rabbi Andrea Weiss, and involving a consortium of leading woman rabbis and scholars, this project will result in a commentary on the Humash by women that integrates virtually all of the approaches to the text that have been outlined in this book.

Two other important works deserves mention:

- *The Women's Bible Commentary:* This book offers a superb introduction to feminist perspectives on the Bible. It is the fruit of an interfaith project of some of the leading women in the field of Bible scholarship, Jewish, Roman Catholic, and Protestant. Though there is more here than a weekly parashah reader needs—the book contains individual chapters on all the books of the TANAKH, the Apocrypha, and the New Testament—of relevance are the first five chapters on each of the books of the *Humash.* Each chapter begins with an excellent summary of the particular book's historical background and how it relates to the concerns of women and feminist studies. The commentary that follows picks up specific passages, stories, characters, verses, and laws in the book that relate to women and reads them through a feminist lens. This organization requires the reader of a given parashah to look through the chapter on the book in which the parashah occurs in order to see if anything in the parashah is discussed. The volume is all commentary; there is no biblical text.

  The Women's Bible Commentary. Eds. Carol A. Newsom and Sharon H. Ringe, expanded ed. Louisville, Ky. Westminster John Knox Press, 1998.

- *Tikva Frymer-Kensky, Reading the Women of the Bible:* This book is not a formal commentary but can be used as one. It exemplifies what is achieved when a great biblical scholar reads the *Humash,* and the whole TANAKH, through the lens of gender.

  Tikva Frymer-Kensky. Reading the Women of the Bible: A New Interpretation of Their Stories. New York: Schocken Books, 2002.

The following books are not only works of commentary but also of contemporary midrash. They could have been listed in the section above on midrash. They show how powerful a force feminism is in feeding the wellsprings of the midrashic process today. Only in the first one is each parashah treated separately; the latter three books are arranged more thematically but can easily be coordinated to specific *parshiyot.*

  Ellen Frankel. The Five Books of Miriam: A Woman's Commentary on the Torah. New York: G. P. Putnam's & Sons, 1996.

*Lifecycles: Jewish Women on Biblical Themes in Contemporary Life*. Eds. Debra Orenstein and Jane Rachel Litman. Woodstock, Vt. Jewish Lights Publishing, 1998.

Jill Hammer. *Sisters at Sinai: New Tales of Biblical Women*. Philadelphia: The Jewish Publication Society, 2004.

Vanessa Ochs. *Sarah Laughed*. New York: McGraw-Hill, 2005.

# 7.
# Web Resources

The Internet offers an amazing assortment of commentaries on the weekly portions. It is a major resource for any parashah reader. There is something in cyberspace for everyone, no matter how you define yourself in relation to Jewish tradition or outlook and no matter what your level of Jewish literacy and background may be.

When you click into a URL, you may, in some cases, have to browse a bit to find the link to the parashah commentaries they contain.

Many sites offer commentaries written for the current week as well as archives from previous years catalogued by parashah. Some sites provide links of their own to other commentary Web locations. The result is an almost inexhaustible supply of material that will fuel your investigation now and into the future.

Each of the major denominations offers websites that treat the parashah from its particular viewpoint. Many synagogues do the same, and so do many rabbis. The number of sites and URLs I could list here is indeterminate.

But before you go surfing, I'll make one suggestion: don't mine the Web's treasures until you have looked into some of the commentaries noted above.

Here are a few URLs that I've found useful and/or interesting. They reflect my own proclivities. In time I hope you will compile your own list. It won't take you long.

- **myjewish learning.com:** a comprehensive website that covers virtually every subject or issue relating to Judaism and the Jewish people, including the weekly Torah portions. The site is transdenominational.

- **kolel.org:** a website maintained by Kolel, the Adult Center for Liberal Jewish Learning in Toronto. The discussions of the weekly portions are concise and at the same time substantial. The site also provides much other instructional material for parashah readers.

- **tanach.org:** guided study of the weekly portions by the master teacher Rabbi Menachem Leibtag. He leads you systematically and thoroughly through the text and brings in a wide array of traditional commentaries. It may be too technical for some beginners, but it is a very rewarding site. It is sponsored by Yeshivat Har Etzion in Israel.

- **hillel.org/jewish/thisweek:** Discussions are authored by Hillel and campus rabbis from all over the continent. The site is sponsored by the Meyerhoff Center for Jewish Learning of Hillel: The Foundation for Jewish Campus life. It is transdenominational.

- **radicaltorah.org:** a variety of approaches, all focusing on the social action implications of the portion being discussed.

- **e-parsha.com—The Electronic Torah Warehouse:** If you want to see the big picture—and I do mean the big picture—as far as what the Web offers in the way of commentary and text, go to e-parsha.com. This meta-site may well be the eighth wonder of the world. It was compiled and is maintained by Rabbi Joshua Cypess, currently the rabbi of Young Israel in New Haven, Connecticut. e-parsha.com will direct you almost anywhere you want to go in the field of Torah commentary. Though the perspective is modern Orthodox, Cypess lists a huge array of websites of parashah commentaries from all over the spectrum, including those with non-Orthodox points of view, both institutional and individual.

# Afterthoughts

Each of the 54 portions, from the beginning of Genesis to the end of Deuteronomy, is a precious and exquisite pearl. Each of them has its place on the necklace to which it belongs. How many necklaces are there? Five? One? It doesn't matter. The necklaces or the necklace is the Torah—which, in its totality, adorns the body of Israel.

Each time we read a parashah we string another pearl onto its necklace. One by one we read them, week by week, from the time of the first frost through the dead of winter into the budding of spring and over the flowering of summer.[1] We fill up the necklace(s).

Question: Are we proceeding in a linear fashion? Or in a circular one? The answer is: both.

Consider the strange fate of the last parashah in the Torah, Ve-zo't ha-berakhah, which details the final blessing and the death of Moses. We never read it in its entirety on a *Shabbat* as we do the other 53 (though in some years the first verses are read on the previous Monday and Thursday). Only on the morning of Simchat Torah do we read this portion through to the end of Deuteronomy, and then, as soon as we have done so, we roll right back to the beginning of Genesis. All year we had been moving in a straight line, or so we thought, from one parashah to the next, and it turns out that all along we were going in a circle.

This manner of reading, our stringing the pearls, reflects a distinctly Jewish worldview. In this worldview the shape of human history and of the whole human experience is linear—but only apparently. Man was expelled from mythic Eden into the travails of this material world, and since then human history has moved—and continues to move—forward, year by year, progressing, however imperceptibly, from the imperfection of the present toward a Redemption in the future. But, Judaism holds, one day history as we know it will end, and we will enter—or return to—a postmessianic Eden. What we think is a straight line is in reality a circle.[2]

If this perspective on time is overly speculative and "man" is an abstraction, consider then the individual human experience. Each of us at birth is cast out of the bliss of the womb, thrown into the arena of human endeavor, with all its challenges, struggles, and glories. Year by year we live until such time as we return to the womb of earth and pass into a reality of which no one on this side of it can rightfully or meaningfully speak.

So, too, goes our life in community. Congregations, *havurot*, study groups—societies—all show the same trajectory. They begin with vision and aspiration, actualize them as they develop, decline as energy and enthusiasm are depleted—and then gird up to renew themselves.

What feels linear is in fact circular.

This is how we read the Torah, and, maybe, why we read it this way. Within the inexorable linearity of the progression of the years of our lives, there is the recurring cycle of the weekly portions. That moment when we finish Deuteronomy and immediately begin reading Genesis, again, is one of the most extraordinary moments in the Jewish calendar. In my view it is right up there with Yom Kippur and the Passover seder. Indeed, I see it as the culmination of the holiday sequence that begins with Rosh Hashanah, inaugurating the Jewish new year, and continues with Yom Kippur, on which we reboot our selves, so to speak. Simchat Torah marks off the beginning of the new cycle within which our renewed lives will unfold.

This means that with each passing year, as we string the pearls again and again, we should be reading and understanding Torah on a deeper and deeper level.

The very last thing Moses instructs all the people is:

> **Therefore, write down this poem and teach it to the people of Israel; put it in their mouths, in order that this poem may be My witness . . . since it will never be lost from the mouth of their offspring. . . .**
> **(Deut. 31:19, 21)**

Moses is referring to the great poem in *parashat* Ha'azinu. But the Rabbis understand his words to mean something more far-reaching:

> **Rabbah said: Even though one's ancestors have bequeathed to him a Torah scroll, he is commanded to write his own, as it is written, "Therefore, write down this poem . . ." (Babylonian Talmud, *Sanhedrin* 21b)**

On the basis of this statement Maimonides writes in his encyclopedic code **The Mishneh Torah**:

> **It is a positive commandment for every single Jew to write a Sefer Torah for himself . . . and if he writes it in his own hand it is as if he received it from Mount Sinai.**[3]

This is the last of all the commandments given in the Torah.

How can we fulfill it? We can, I suppose, take the teaching at its word and actually write our own personal scroll. Or, as the Talmud suggests, and the commentary in the *Etz Hayim Humash* notes, we can

> **commission a ritual scribe (*sofer*) to write even one letter on [our] behalf [for to do so] is considered to have fulfilled this mitzvah (Babylonian Talmud, Menahot 30a). Many congregations that acquire a new Torah scroll celebrate its completion (*Siyyum Seifer Torah*) by having individuals who have contributed to its purchase fill in a letter of the Torah.**[4]

I think there is still another way: we can read the Torah through, week by week, parashah by parashah.

For reading is a way of making the text our own. Reading is, in its own way, an act of (re)writing. As a latter-day sage of Israel has said to all who open the Book:

**You are the one who writes and the one who is written.**[5]

# Notes

## How to Read This Book

1. These readerships, in all their diversity, reside largely in North America and other parts of the English-speaking world, but not in Israel. This is because Israeli culture is intrinsically different from that of North America and is at a different cultural moment. That is a short explanation. For a fuller one, see Uriel Simon's extraordinarily insightful and important essay, "The Bible in Israeli Life" in *The Jewish Study Bible*, ed. Adele Berlin and Marc Zvi Brettler (Oxford and New York: Oxford University Press, 2004), 1990–2000. The whole issue of the differential between North American Jews and Israeli Jews in how they relate to the *Humash* deserves investigation and explication.

2. The only other book I know that comes close in purpose to this one is George Robinson's *Essential Torah: A Complete Guide to the Five Books of Moses* (New York: Schocken Books, 2006). It appeared just after I had completed the manuscript of this book. Thus I did not see it while writing, nor have I drawn on it in any way since. I cover a lot of the same ground as Robinson, and in certain cases make very similar observations. I suppose this is inevitable when two authors treat the same subject. So though they overlap, these are ultimately two very different books. They differ in scope, objective, and discursive approach. Robinson's discussion is wide-ranging and comprehensive, covering all aspects of the Pentateuch; mine is focused on the weekly Torah portions and treats the *Humash* only as it pertains to reading them. Robinson does cite various opinions and offers good suggestions on "how to study Torah," but he does not present a specific step-by-step methodology of dealing with the weekly parashah as a discrete textual unit. He does treat the 54 *parshiyot*—such treatment takes up half his book—but his discussion consists of a short synopsis of and his own commentary on each. Robinson pragmatically favors *Humash* study in a group setting; I set more stock in and privilege the individual reading experience and focus on its dynam-

ics and mechanics. My approach is anchored in phenomenology and reader-response theory. All told, I see *Essential Torah* and this book as two different performances of the *Humash*, complementing and not duplicating each other.

## A Note to the Christian Reader

1. Martin Buber, "Two Foci of the Jewish Soul," in *Israel and the World: Essays in a Time of Crisis* (New York: Schocken Books, 1963), 39.

## Part I: Preliminaries: What Are We Talking About?

1. The Hebrew calendar follows the lunar year, which contains 354 days consisting of 12 lunar months (about 50 weeks). Judaism, however, requires that the lunar year be synchronized with the 365-day solar year, for if it is not, the annual imbalance of about 11 days will eventually accrue, and the result will be that Passover, which must be observed in the Northern Hemisphere's spring (Exod. 23:15, 34:18, and Deut. 16:1), will eventually occur during the winter or earlier. The two systems are, therefore, balanced by intercalation. Approximately every third year a 13th lunar month is added to the lunar year. This occurs 7 out of every 19 lunar years. Such lunar leap years contain 54 weeks. In the 12 "regular" lunar years of 50 weeks, certain weekly portions are combined and read as a "double-headers."

2. The four modes are known acronymically in Hebrew as PaRDeS (**prds**), the word for orchard. Just as an orchard affords those who enter into it multisensual delights, so biblical interpretation offers all who engage in it a rich field for the mind, heart, and spirit and the perennial human quest for beauty, meaning, and truth.

3. Gilgamesh was a king in Mesopotamia around 2750 B.C.E. Over succeeding centuries legends about him accumulated and were written down. An early version, written in Sumerian, an ancient sacred language, dates from about 2100 B.C.E. A later revised version, discovered on cuneiform tablets in 1844 near the present Iraqi city of Mosul (near ancient Nineveh), is in Akkadian (a Semitic language that is a precursor to biblical Hebrew) and dates from about 1700 B.C.E. A very readable English rendering of the epic is Stephen Mitchell's *Gilgamesh: A New English Version* (New York, London, etc.: Free Press, 2004).

4. See Richard Elliot Friedman, *Who Wrote the Bible?* 2nd ed. (San Francisco: HarperSanFrancisco, 1996), 54–60.

5. See, for example, Leon Kass, *The Beginning of Wisdom: Reading Genesis* (New York and London: Free Press, 2003), 151–67.

6. Ismar Schorsch, "Coming to Terms with Biblical Criticism," *Conservative Judaism* 57:3 (Spring 2005): 18f.

7. Gabriel Josipovici, *The Book of God: A Response to the Bible* (New Haven, Conn., and London: Yale University Press, 1988), 34.

8. "Sefer Breishit Introductory Shiur: The Importance of 'Parshiot,'" Tanach Study Center, http://www.tanach.org. Click on "Archive," then "Sefer Breishit Introductory Shiur."

9. This is true even of the five portions that open each book of the *Humash*. In the case of B'reishit, the first parashah in Genesis, one could say that the connections are extra-Pentateuchal. They are with parallel stories in Mesopotamian literature.

10. Everett Fox, *Now These Are the Names: A New English Rendition of the Book of Exodus* (New York: Schocken Books, 1986), xxxvi.

11. The Masoretes (scribes who in 8th- or 9th-century Palestine standardized and fixed the received Hebrew text and pronunciation of the TANAKH—see p. 47) speak of the TANAKH as comprising not 39 but 24 books. They get this number by regarding Samuel, Kings, and Chronicles as one book (a net loss of three), by combining Ezra and Nehemiah into one (a net loss of one), and by lumping the 12 Minor Prophets together into one book (a net loss of 11).

12. Discovering the connection between the Torah reading and the haftarah is an interesting interpretive exercise. Sometimes it can furnish some clues about what was seen by the Rabbis as central to the Torah portion. Michael Fishbane's introductions to the *haftorot* in the *Etz Hayim Torah* are especially valuable for showing the connections.

13. David Stern, "Introduction: The Anthological Imagination in Jewish Literature," *Prooftexts* 17:1 (January 1997): 2f.

14. Obviously God is beyond gender. I use the conventional masculine form of the biblical writers and hope that this note will suffice to obviate the need to jump through verbal hoops each time God's attributes and actions are invoked here.

## Part II: Reading and Hearing

1. I follow here the dichotomy made long ago by Milton Steinberg in his *Basic Judaism*. This seems a much more accurate and useful way to describe the theological differences between religionist Jews today than the denominational "Orthodox-Conservative-Reform" division or even the binary opposition of "Orthodoxy" and "non-Orthodoxy." Steinberg's unsurpassed assessment of the divide is worth repeating. He writes: "Manifestly, an abyss separates the modernist from the traditionalist in their respective views of Torah. But an abyss, no matter how broad and deep, is a cleft in the earth's surface. The walls to either side will be of similar composition; they will be joined by a common ground below and may be even further united by a bridge from above. . . . And both stand on the same ground, are made of the same stuff, and surmount their disagreements in arches of shared

purpose" (Milton Steinberg, *Basic Judaism* [New York: Harcourt Brace, 1947], 30).

2. It remains a hypothesis because until we find the actual source texts it cannot be conclusively proved. But the consensus itself is a staple of contemporary biblical scholarship even as such details as the dating and the nature of the various sources continue to be debated and revised among biblicists. An excellent account of the whole matter by one of the leading American exponents of the documentary hypothesis is Richard Elliot Friedman's *Who Wrote the Bible?* 2nd ed. (San Francisco: HarperSanFrancisco, 1996).

3. For an English translation of the Pentateuch where each of these sources is printed in a different color ink, see Richard Elliot Friedman, *The Bible with Sources Revealed: A New View into the Five Books of Moses* (New York: HarperSanFrancisco, 2003).

4. See Stanley Fish, *Is There a Text in This Class? The Authority of Interpretive Communities* (Cambridge, Mass., and London: Harvard University Press, 1980).

5. Source critics have found that for P, the priestly strand of the Pentateuch, seeing is primary. It stresses the visual. The people behold the divine glory. It is the Deuteronomic strand, D, that emphasizes "hearing" and "listening" and the divine word that is spoken into the people's ears.

6. *Mekhilta* 9:1.

7. Joshua R. Jacobson, *Chanting the Hebrew Bible: The Art of Cantillation* (Philadelphia: The Jewish Publication Society, 2002), 366.

8. Ibid., 368. Jacobson is referring to Hanoch Avenary's article on "Masoretic Accents" in the *Encyclopedia Judaica*, vol. 11, cols. 1098–1111.

9. The haftarah has its own trope melodies, which adds to the preparative burden.

10. The translation project began in 1925 and was a fruitful collaborative one until Rosenzweig's untimely death in 1929. Buber continued to work on it for nearly 40 years, until 1962.

11. Dan Avnon, *Martin Buber: The Hidden Dialogue* (London, Boulder, New York, and Oxford: Rowman & Littlefield, 1998), 52.

12. Ibid.

13. Ibid., 53.

14. Cited from Buber's *Werker*, vol. 2, *Schriften zur Bibel* (Munich: Kösel-Verlag, 1964), 1131, in Robert Alter, *The Art of Biblical Narrative* (New York: Basic Books, 1981), 93. The translation is Alter's.

15. Robert Alter translates Deut. 34:6 as "And he was buried in the glen in the land of Moab." Alter believes that "the third-person singular verb without specified grammatical subject is not infrequently used in biblical Hebrew in place of a passive verb. Many interpreters have understood this ostensibly active verb to mean that God (an-

thropomorphically) buried Moses. That possibility cannot be dismissed, but God's acting as a grave digger for Moses seems incongruous with the representation of the deity in these narratives, and thus construing the verb as a passive is more likely" (Robert Alter, *The Five Books of Moses* [New York and London: W. W. Norton & Co., 2004], 1058). For other readings of this enigmatic verse, see also Richard Elliot Friedman's *Commentary on the Torah with a New English Translation* (San Francisco: HarperSanFrancisco, 2001), 678.

16. My reading is prompted by this passage in the Babylonian Talmud: "Why was Moses buried facing Beit Pe'or? In order to atone for what happened at Pe'or" (Babylonian Talmud, *Sotah* 14a).

17. Note also how Exod. 1:1–5 picks up Gen. 46:8ff.

18. NJPS translates "yet Pharaoh remained stubborn," but here and in many of the following verses I follow Robert Alter and Richard Elliot Friedman, who in their respective translations hold up the literal meaning of the phrases so as to foreground the "guided word" effect that the Hebrew is creating.

19. NJPS translates "Pharaoh is stubborn."

20. NJPS translates "a very severe pestilence."

21. For an even fuller list of verses in Exodus where the k-b-d, "heavy," root in deployed, see Friedman, *The Bible with Sources Revealed on Exodus 7:14* (p. 130). But somehow Friedman misses the verses in the Song of the Sea where the writer's verbal artistry is used precisely to show God verbally hoisting Pharaoh by his own petard.

22. To see how a highly skilled reader identifies "guiding words" and explicates their implications, see Robert Alter, *The Art of Biblical Narrative* (New York: Basic Books, 1981). This book is an essential resource for any parashah reader in training, as is Alter's commentary to his translation of the Pentateuch, *The Five Books of Moses* (New York and London: W. W. Norton & Co., 2004). Another lucid presentation of biblical narrative style is Joel Rosenberg's excellent essay "Biblical Narrative" in *Back to the Sources: Reading the Classic Jewish Texts*, ed. Barry W. Holtz (New York: Summit Books, 1984), 31–81.

23. See Adele Berlin's essay "Reading Biblical Poetry" in *The Jewish Study Bible* ed. Adele Berlin and Marc Zvi Brettler (Oxford and New York: Oxford University Press, 2004), 2097–2104. Holtz, *Back to the Sources* has two fine discussions of these matters: Murray H. Lichtenstein's "Biblical Poetry," 105–127, and Edward Greenstein's essay "Biblical Law," 83–103.

24. *The Art of Biblical Narrative*, 93. The English translation of the Pentateuch that most consciously seeks to replicate what Buber and Rosenzweig were trying for in German is that of Everett Fox, *The Five Books of Moses* (New York: Schocken Books, 1995). Alter's own version also tries to do this, too.

25. Shemariyahu Talmon, quoted in Avnon, Martin Buber, 230 (note 28).

26. Franz Rosenzweig, "The Unity of the Bible: A Position Paper vis-à-vis Orthodoxy and Liberalism," in Scripture and Translation, trans. Lawrence Rosenwald with Everett Fox (Bloomington and Indianapolis: Indiana University Press, 1994), 23.

27. Martin Buber, "People Today and the Jewish Bible," in Rosenwald and Fox, Scripture and Translation. In the interests of stylistic readability I have here and there changed their punctuation and paragraphing, and in one case taken a word from the translation of this piece by Olga Marx, found under the title "The Man of Today and the Jewish Bible," in Martin Buber, Israel and the World: Essays in a Time of Crisis (New York: Schocken Books, 1963), 89–102. The piece is part of a series of lectures delivered by Buber in 1926.

28. Avnon, Martin Buber, 13.

29. Ibid.

30. Here I follow the Marx translation (Israel and the World, 94) with one borrowing from Rosenwald and Fox, Scripture and Translation, 8.

31. Rosenwald and Fox, Scripture and Translation, 13. For the Marx version of this passage see Israel and the World, 102.

## Part III: Some Major Approaches to Reading a Parashah

1. For alternative methodological schemas, see Adele Berlin and Marc Zvi Brettler, "The Modern Study of the Bible" in The Jewish Study Bible (Oxford and New York: Oxford University Press, 2004), 2084–96, and Benjamin Edidin Scolnic, "Traditional Methods of Bible Study" and "Modern Methods of Bible Study" in Etz Hayim: Torah and Commentary (New York: The Rabbinical Assembly, 2001), 1494–1503.

2. This was apparently an interesting reformulation of what Heschel had written a few years earlier: "Religion consists of God's question and man's answer. . . . Unless God asks the question, all our inquiries are in vain" (God in Search of Man [New York and Philadelphia: Meridian Books and the Jewish Publication Society, 1959], 137).

3. For an excellent historical presentation, see Cyrus H. Gordon and Gary A. Rendsburg, The Bible and the Ancient Near East, 4th ed. (New York and London: W. W. Norton & Co., 1997). The impact of archaeology on biblical study is well treated in Hershel Shanks, Ancient Israel: From Abraham to the Roman Destruction of the Temple, 2nd ed. (N.p.: Prentice Hall, 1999). For anthropological analysis of Leviticus, see Mary Douglas, "The Abominations of Leviticus" in Purity and Danger (London: Routledge & Kegan Paul, 1969), 41–57.

4. Do the Rabbis of the Talmud already open the door to the idea

that the *Humash* is not a "perfect" text? They pick up on the fact that the tablets of the Ten Commandments that Moses presented were **not** the originals but facsimiles. The originals had been shattered when Moses descended from Mount Sinai and saw the Israelites worshiping the Golden Calf (Exod. 32:19). What happened to the broken fragments? "The [second set of] tablets and the shards of the [first] tablets were placed in the Ark [of the Tabernacle]" (Babylonian Talmud, *Bava Batra* 14b). On that same page the Rabbis also say that Joshua, not Moses, wrote the last eight verses of the Torah (Deut. 34:5–12), since Moses could not have written about his own death.

5. Richard Elliot Friedman, *Who Wrote the Bible?* 2nd ed. (San Francisco: HarperSanFrancisco, 1996).

6. Richard Elliot Friedman, *The Bible with Sources Revealed: A New View into the Five Books of Moses* (New York: HarperSanFrancisco, 2003).

7. *Who Wrote the Bible?* 76–79.

8. Friedman notes that there is another polemical point hidden inside the Golden Calf story. The northern *Kohanim* from whose circles the story originated had been excluded from serving in the two temples that Jeroboam, the first king of the breakaway kingdom, set up at Dan and Beth El, temples in which he set up cast-iron golden calves as footstools on which the Israelite God was seated.

9. *The Bible with Sources Revealed*, 261.

10. There is more to this story than what source criticism discloses. As we shall see below, feminist criticism raises other crucial issues.

11. For a longer list, see Friedman, *The Bible with Sources Revealed*, 28–30.

12. Ibid., 35. I would caution the reader not to regard this statement as the last word on the subject. In Part IV, when we look at the book of Deuteronomy, we will see that it is the source that articulates a theology of transcendence, and it is P, by regarding the in-dwelling of the Divine Presence in the *mishkan* as the culminating moment in the Israelite experience, that foregrounds God's immanence.

13. For a development of this point, see Israel Knohl, *The Divine Symphony: The Bible's Many Voices* (Philadelphia: The Jewish Publication Society, 2003).

14. For a full discussion of these issues, see David Damrosch, *The Narrative Covenant: Transformations of Genre in the Growth of Biblical Literature* (San Francisco: Harper & Row, 1987).

15. See his *The Art of Biblical Narrative* (New York: Basic Books, 1981) and *The Art of Biblical Poetry* (New York: Basic Books, 1985).

16. *The Art of Biblical Narrative*, 132.

17. Gabriel Josipovici, *The Book of God: A Response to the Bible* (New Haven, Conn., and London: Yale University Press, 1988), 14.

18. NJPS notes that the Hebrew reads "Medanites," though it and

many translations of Gen. 37:36 render the word as "Midianites" on the assumption that Medanites and Midianites are essentially the same. A glance at Gen. 25:2 reveals that the two are distinct groups.

19. Robert Alter, *The Five Books of Moses* (New York and London: W. W. Norton & Co., 2004), 212.

20. I am indebted to Professor Gary Rendsburg for pointing out this reading to me. See Edward L. Greenstein, "An Equivocal Reading of the Sale of Joseph," in *Literary Interpretations of Biblical Narratives*, ed. K. R. R. Gros Louis, vol. 2 (Nashville: Abingdon, 1982), 119–21; and Gary A. Rendsburg, "Confused Language as a Deliberate Literary Device in Biblical Hebrew Narrative," in *Journal of Hebrew Scriptures* 2:6 (1999). http://www.arts.ualberta.ca/JHS/Articles/article_12.htm.

21. See Joel Rosenberg, "Biblical Narrative" in *Back to the Sources: Reading the Classic Jewish Texts*, ed. Barry W. Holtz (New York: Summit Books, 1984), 52–62.

22. *The Art of Biblical Narrative*, 159.

23. The conventional distinction between poetry and prose is not easily applied to biblical literature. Parallelism is evident in many passages that are not "poetry" in the strict sense of the term (e.g., Gen. 15:15, 16:10–12).

24. See Murray H. Lichtenstein, "Biblical Poetry," in *Back to the Sources: Reading the Classic Jewish Texts*, ed. Barry W. Holtz (New York: Summit Books, 1984), 119ff.

25. John Barton, *Reading the Old Testament*, rev. and enlarged ed. (Louisville, Ky: Westminster John Knox Press, 1996), 40.

26. Ibid., 42.

27. For a reading of the 54 *parshiyot* that imaginatively presents the perspectives of many of these female biblical personae, see Ellen Frankel, *The Five Books of Miriam: A Woman's Commentary on the Torah* (New York: G. P. Putnam's & Sons, 1996).

28. Ilana Pardes probes this narrative and asks whether Miriam's "role was far greater than recorded" here. The episode serves as the point of departure of her inquiry into "[whether]" . . . one can find antithetical female voices by paying attention to underexamined fragments on the margins of biblical historiography" (*Countertraditions in the Bible: A Feminist Approach* [Cambridge, Mass. and London: Harvard University Press, 1992], 11).

29. See the comments of Tikvah Frymer-Kensky on this passage in the *Women's Bible Commentary*, ex. ed., ed. Carol A. Newsom and Sharon Ringe (Louisville, Ky.: Westminster John Knox Press, 1998) 67.

30. See the last section of *Devarim* [Deuteronomy] *Rabbah* on *parashat* Ve-zo't ha-berakhah and *Midrash Tanhuma* on *parashat* Va-ethannan #6. A Hebrew conflation of these two sources is in Bialik

and Ravnitsky's' massive and invaluable anthology of midrash, *Sefer ha-Aggadah*, 76b–79b. This work was translated into English by Willam Braude as *The Book of Legends* (New York: Schocken Books, 1992) and the passage on Moses' death is on 101b–104b (#137).

31. This point has been picked up by many modern scholars, but it was already noted in the midrash *Bereshit Rabbah* and is cited by Rashi in his comment on Gen. 39:1. For all the references, see Gary A. Rendsburg, *The Redaction of Genesis* (Winona Lake, Ind: Eisenbrauns, 1986), 94.

32. David Stern, "Midrash and Jewish Interpretation," in *The Jewish Study Bible*, ed. Adele Berlin and Marc Zvi Brettler (Oxford and New York: Oxford University Press, 2004), 1874.

33. Mishnah Soferim.

34. In Hebrew the root of the verb "to kiss" (n-sh-q, נשק) is very close, and undoubtedly related, to the root of the verb "to bite" (n-sh-kh, נשך).

35. The other nine are: Gen. 16:5, 18:9, 19:33, 37:12, Num. 3:39, 9:10, 21:30, 29:15, Deut. 29:28. See Joshua R. Jacobson, *Chanting the Hebrew Bible: The Art of Cantillation* (Philadelphia: The Jewish Publication Society, 2002), 383f.

36. See Heschel's monumental *Heavenly Torah as Refracted Through the Generations*, trans. Gordon Tucker (New York and London: Continuum, 2005).

37. See, for example, Rashi's comment on Deut. 29:12.

38. Edmond Jabès, *The Book of Questions*, vol. 1, trans. Rosmarie Waldrop (Middletown, Conn.: Wesleyan University Press, 1976), 18.

39. It was also a response to the Karaites and the Christians, both of whom, in their respective ways, challenged the meanings Rabbinic interpretation had assigned to the text. See Edward L. Greenstein, "Medieval Bible Commentaries," in *Back to the Sources: Reading the Classic Jewish Texts*, ed. Barry W. Holtz (New York: Summit Books, 1984), 220–26.

40. Translations are by Michael Carasik in *The Commentators' Bible: The JPS Miqra'ot Gedolot—Exodus* (Philadelphia: The Jewish Publication Society, 2005), 134.

41. In his translation of Rashbam, Martin Lockshin reads the term as *confanon*. See Martin I. Lockshin, *Rashbam's Commentary on Exodus: An Annotated Translation*, Brown Judaic Studies 310 (Atlanta, Ga.: Scholars Press, 1997), 183.

42. So it is identified in a note in the Hebrew in the HaMa'or *Humash*. See also Charles Chavel's note in his translation of Ramban's (Nachmanides') *Commentary on the Torah: Exodus* (New York: Shilo Publishing House, 1973), 244.

43. *The Zohar: Pritzker Edition*, trans. and comment. Daniel C. Matt (Stanford, Calif.: Stanford University Press). When complete this

project will comprise 12 volumes. At this writing four have appeared covering all the *parshiyot* of Genesis and the first half of Exodus.

44. *The Zohar: Pritzker Edition*, vol. 2, 7 and 9 *passim*.

45. Ibid., Matt notes 46 and 62.

46. Cited in Rabbi Mordecai HaKohen, *'Al Ha-torah* [in Hebrew], vol. 1 (Jerusalem: Orot Publishing Co., 1956), 38, adapted from Luntschitz's *'Olelot Ephraim*.

47. *The Zohar: Pritzker Edition*, vol. 2, 193f.

48. Ibid., Matt note 600.

49. Ibid., Matt notes 601, 602, 603, and 604.

50. Ibid., 198 and Matt note 638.

51. Ibid., 194f.

52. Ibid., Matt notes 608, 609, 610.

53. See, for example, his *Moses: The Revelation and the Covenant* (1945 and published in English translation in many editions) where, in attempting to write a biography of Moses, Buber uses biblical criticism as his point of departure.

54. For a fine Hasidic commentary on the *Humash*, see Arthur Green, *The Language of Truth: The Torah Commentary of the Sefat Emet Rabbi Yehudah Leib Alter of Ger* (Philadelphia: The Jewish Publication Society, 1998).

55. Told by the late Lubavitcher Rebbe on 19 Kislev 5718 (December 12, 1957), on the occasion of the 159th anniversary of Rabbi Schneur Zalman's release from prison—http://www.chabad.org/library/article.asp?AID=63845. In Buber's adaptation of this story, the narrative continues: "When the chief of the gendarmes [*sic*] heard his age mentioned, he pulled himself together, laid his hand on the rav's shoulder, and cried, 'Bravo!' But his heart trembled" (Martin Buber, *Tales of the Hasidim: The Early Masters* [New York: Schocken Books, 1947], 269).

56. This is the point at which many Israeli Jews could enter the conversation with the *Humash*. See Uriel Simon's discussion of "Existential *Peshat* as a Possible Response to Current Needs" in his essay "The Bible in Israeli Life" in *The Jewish Study Bible*, ed. Adele Berlin and Marc Zvi Brettler (Oxford and New York: Oxford University Press, 2004), 1998ff.

## Part IV: How to Read a Weekly Torah Portion

1. See Alister McGrath, *In the Beginning: The Story of the King James Bible and How It Changed a Nation, a Language, and a Culture* (New York: Anchor Books, 2001).

2. *The Torah: The Five Books of Moses*, 3rd ed. (Philadelphia: The Jewish Publication Society of America, 1992). The three volumes, with revisions, were combined into a single one as *TANAKH: The Holy Scriptures* (Philadelphia, New York, and Jerusalem: The Jewish Pub-

lication Society, 1988). This is now available in various editions, some with the Hebrew, some without, and in various sizes. The bilingual edition is to be preferred.

3. *The Contemporary Torah: A Gender-sensitive Adaptation of the JPS Translation*, ed. David E. S. Stein and Carol L. Meyers (Philadelphia: The Jewish Publication Society, 2006).

4. Adele Berlin and Marc Zvi Brettler, eds., *The Jewish Study Bible* (Oxford and New York: Oxford University Press, 2004).

5. Everett Fox, *The Five Books of Moses* (New York: Schocken Books, 1995). Fox also offers a fine commentary that I will note in Part V.

6. Robert Alter, *The Five Books of Moses* (New York and London: W. W. Norton & Co., 2004).

7. Richard Elliot Friedman, *The Bible with Sources Revealed: A New View into the Five Books of Moses* (New York: HarperSanFrancisco, 2003). The purpose of this version is to illuminate the approach of source criticism. See my discussion of this in Part III. Friedman's translation together with the Hebrew original is Richard Elliot Friedman, *Commentary on the Torah with a New English Translation* (San Francisco: HarperSanFrancisco, 2001). See Part V for my discussion of the commentary.

8. New York and Jerusalem: Maznaim Publishing Corp., 1981.

9. Brooklyn: Mesorah Publications, Ltd. This first appeared in 1993 and has had several printings.

10. W. Gunther Plaut, gen. ed., and David E. S. Stein, *The Torah: A Modern Commentary*, rev. ed. (New York: Union for Reform Judaism, 2005).

11. David Lieber, sen. ed., *Etz Hayim: Torah and Commentary* (New York: The Rabbinical Assembly, 2001).

12. See Tur and Shulchan Arukh, *Or ha-Chayyim*, section 285 #2.

13. I wonder if those who advise reading the *Humash* with a study partner (*havruta*) or partners are confusing it with Talmud study, which is traditionally done that way. Such possible confusion overlooks the intrinsic difference between the two kinds of text. Talmudic text fairly requires two or more readers to process it; the Bible is more explicitly vocative on the individual level and so needs to be read both in solitude and communally.

14. For a comprehensive list of the features on biblical narrative, see Joel Rosenberg, "Biblical Narrative," in *Back to the Sources: Reading the Classic Jewish Texts*, ed. Barry W. Holtz (New York: Summit Books, 1984), 37–51.

15. For a full consideration of these matters, see Murray H. Lichtenstein, "Biblical Poetry," in Holtz, *Back to the Sources*, 105–27.

16. Edward Greenstein, "Biblical Law," in *Back to the Sources*, 84.

17. A good place to begin is chapter 10 of Cyrus H. Gordon and Gary A. Rendsburg, *The Bible and the Ancient Near East*, 4th ed. (New

York and London: W. W. Norton & Co., 1997), 153–67.

18. Greenstein, "Biblical Law," 84. See also 99.

19. There are in some years *Shabbatot* where there is a difference between what is read in Israeli and Diaspora synagogues. This is because the second day of *yom tov* is not observed in Israel, and so when it falls on a *Shabbat*, the regularly scheduled parashah is read, while in Diaspora the special reading assigned for the second day of *yom tov* is read. Eventually the two schedules do get realigned.

20. Richard Elliot Friedman, *Who Wrote the Bible?* 2nd ed. (San Francisco: HarperSanFrancisco, 1996), 159 and 223–25.

21. *Zohar* II, 206a.—206b. On this basis we might have expected that we should be required to stand during the Torah reading, since there were no chairs at Sinai. One does see this in some very traditional synagogues, where it is a congregational or a personal custom to do so. The codes and their commentaries debate the question and rule that the requirement to stand during the Torah reading applies only to the Reader and those on the *bimah*. See Tur and Shulchan Arukh, *Or ha-Chayyim*, section 141 #1.

22. See Part I, where this image is introduced with other nuances.

23. Richard Elliot Friedman, *The Bible with Sources Revealed: A New View into the Five Books of Moses* (New York: HarperSanFrancisco, 2003), 76.

24. Lawrence Kushner, *God Was in This Place & I, i Did not Know: Finding Self, Spirituality and Ultimate Meaning* (Woodstock, Vt.: Jewish Lights Publishing, 1991).

25. In Gen. 15:13 "God said to Abram, 'Know well that your offspring shall be strangers in a land not theirs; and they shall be enslaved and oppressed four hundred years.' "

26. Ramban (Nachmanides), *Commentary on the Torah: Exodus*, trans. Charles B. Chavel (New York: Shilo Publishing House, 1973), 3–5.

27. Richard Elliot Friedman, *Who Wrote the Bible?* 2nd ed. (San Francisco: HarperSanFrancisco, 1996), 174–87.

28. Franz Kafka, *Letter to His Father* (New York: Schocken Books, 1953), 77. Kafka wrote the letter in 1919 when he was 36. His father apparently never received it.

29. But see Mary Douglas, *Leviticus as Literature* (Oxford and New York: Oxford University Press, 1999).

30. Wesley J. Bergen, *Reading Ritual: Leviticus in Postmodern Culture* (London and New York: T & T Clark International, 2005), 6.

31. Leon Wieseltier, "Leviticus," in *Congregation: Contemporary Writers Read the Jewish Bible,* ed. David Rosenberg (San Diego, New York, and London: Harcourt Brace Jovanovitch, 1987), 38. This essay is one of the best introductions to Leviticus.

32. Ibid.

33. This is based on a comment made en passant in the Babylon-

ian Talmud (*Eruvin* 2a).

34. Wieseltier, " Leviticus," 37, 29.

35. Ibid., 30.

36. Ibid., 29.

37. Bergen, *Reading Ritual*, 7.

38. William W. Hallo, "Numbers and Ancient Near Eastern Literature," in *The Torah: A Modern Commentary*, ed. W. Gunther Plaut and David E. S. Stein, rev. ed. (New York: Union for Reform Judaism, 2005), 896. More recently Mary Douglas has proposed that Numbers looks like a hodgepodge only if we insist on reading it linearly. When we apprehend the book's structure as a series of rings, its structure is quite coherent. See her *Thinking in Circles: An Essay on Ring Composition* (New Haven, Conn.: Yale University Press, 2007).

39. Shemaryahu Talmon, "The 'Desert Motif' in the Bible and in Qumran Literature," in *Biblical Motifs: Origins and Transformations*, ed. Alexander Altmann (Cambridge, Mass.: Harvard University Press, 1966), 46.

40. This practice is prescribed in the Mishnah (Gittin 5:8).

41. The first word may already be a clue to this. The first words of the previous three books, Exodus, Leviticus, and Numbers, all begin in the Hebrew with a conjunction, signified by the letter *vav* ו, "and" in English. (A technical note to fastidious grammarians: these three *vav*s could be seen as "consecutive" or "conversive" *vav*s. But they may also be "conjunctive," which is how I am reading them.) These "and"s serve to staple each new book to the one preceding it, so as to bind all four books (including Genesis) into one. By all rights the first word of Deuteronomy should begin like that, too. It should read "And these are the words that Moses spoke . . . ," ואלה הדברים אשׁר דבר משׁה. Instead it reads: "These are the words that Moses spoke . . . ," אלה הדברים אשׁר דבר משׁה. There is no conjunctive *vav* in the first word. Could this be a subtle verbal hint by the Redactor(s) of the *Humash* that Deuteronomy is a late addition?

42. William W. Hallo, "Deuteronomy and Ancient Near Eastern Literature," in *The Torah: A Modern Commentary*, ed. W. Gunther Plaut and David E. S. Stein, rev. ed. (New York: Union for Reform Judaism, 2005), 1148.

43. Thus compare 2 Kings 14:5–6, which, in describing the actions of Amaziah, king of Judah (798–769 B.C.E.), cites Deuteronomic law: "Once he had the kingdom firmly in his grasp, he put to death the courtiers who had assassinated his father the king. But he did not put to death the children of the assassins, in accordance with what is written in the Book of the Teaching of Moses, where the LORD commanded, 'Parents shall not be put to death for children, nor children be put to death for parents; a person shall be put to death only for his own crime' " (Deut. 24:16).

44. The mini-code in Exodus 21–23 ends in a similar fashion except that it is more positive: it details only the blessings of obedience, not the consequences of trespass. See Exod. 23:23–33.

45. There is no obvious principle or logic behind the arrangement of the long series of laws in the Deuteronomic Code. In this outline I follow the general categories given in *The JPS Torah Commentary: Deuteronomy*, ed. Jeffrey H. Tigay (Philadelphia: The Jewish Publication Society, 1996), 446–48. See also Plaut, *The Torah: A Modern Commentary*, 1255.

46. See Stephen A. Geller, "The Religion of the Bible," in *The Jewish Study Bible*, ed. Adele Berlin and Marc Zvi Brettler (Oxford and New York: Oxford University Press, 2004), 2031–35.

47. The Plaut *Humash* regards this parashah as the beginning of a separate, third farewell speech that continues through the succeeding three *parshiyot*, Shofetim, Ki Tetse', and Ki Tavo', that is, to the end of the law code.

48. In the still important anthology *The Religious Situation: 1968*, ed. Donald R. Cutler (Boston: Beacon Press, 1968), 254–87. Also relevant is Moshe Halbertal and Avishai Margalit, *Idolatry*, trans. Naomi Goldblum (Cambridge, Mass.: Harvard University Press, 1992).

## Part V: Commentaries: A Concise History

1. *Understanding Genesis: The Heritage of Biblical Israel*, new ed. (New York: Schocken Books, 1970); and *Exploring Exodus: The Origins of Biblical Israel* (New York: Schocken Books, 1996).

2. For example, in commenting on Gen. 24:59, where Rebekah and her nurse are dispatched back to Canaan with Abraham's servant, the Stone *Humash* explains the presence of the nurse by citing a Rabbinic view that Rebekah is three years old at this time. How this understanding squares with the prodigious feats of hospitality that Rebekah has performed—giving drink to the servant, running up and down the hill to water his camels, and then running to tell her family of the caravan's arrival—is not explained. The commentary adds only Ibn Ezra's view that Rebekah "was older, but it was customary for the nurse of a girl's infancy to remain with her as her servant throughout her life." The reader is still left befuddled and/or bemused.

3. A thorough survey of the field noting its major figures and their works is in Adele Reinhartz's essay "Jewish Women's Scholarly Writings on the Bible" in *The Jewish Study Bible*, 2000–2005.

## Afterthoughts

1. In the northeastern United States, where I live, there are four distinct seasons. Readers in other climatic zones may adapt this sen-

tence as they wish, or they may simply disregard it.

2. One of the postulates of post-Einsteinian physics is that time is curved.

3. Book 2, Sefer Ahavah, the laws of tefillin, mezuzah; and sefer Torah 7:1. In this second comment Maimonides is citing the Babylonian Talmud, *Menachot* 30a.

4. *Etz Hayim*, 1177.

5. Edmond Jabès, *The Book of Questions*, vol. 1, trans. Rosmarie Waldrop (Middletown, Conn.: Wesleyan University Press, 1976), front matter.

# Works Cited

Throughout these pages I have referred to several books that in various ways open up the world of the Bible. They have been crucial resources for me and they will be no less valuable to you. In addition to them, I want to note a few more that are, if not required reading, then highly recommended for anyone who wants a basic presentation of the "what," the "where," the "when," and the "how" of the remarkable 39-volume anthology that is the TANAKH. The following books are not commentaries or readings of the weekly portions but excellent treatments of key aspects of the *Humash* and the TANAKH.

Alter, Robert. *The Art of Biblical Narrative*. New York: Basic Books, 1981.

———. *The Five Books of Moses*. New York and London: W. W. Norton & Co., 2004.

Avnon, Dan. *Martin Buber: The Hidden Dialogue*. London, Boulder, New York, and Oxford: Rowman & Littlefield, 1998.

Barton, John. *Reading the Old Testament*. Rev. and enlarged ed. Louisville, Ky.: Westminster John Knox Press, 1996.

Bergen, Wesley J. *Reading Ritual: Leviticus in Postmodern Culture*. London and New York: T & T Clark International, 2005.

Berlin, Adele. "Reading Biblical Poetry." In Adele Berlin and Marc Zvi Brettler, eds., *The Jewish Study Bible* (Oxford and New York: Oxford University Press, 2004), 2097–2104.

Berlin, Adele, and Marc Zvi Brettler, eds. *The Jewish Study Bible*. Oxford and New York: Oxford University Press, 2004.

Buber, Martin. "The Man of Today and the Jewish Bible." In *Israel and the World: Essays in a Time of Crisis*. New York: Schocken Books, 1963.

———. "Two Foci of the Jewish Soul." In *Israel and the World: Essays in a Time of Crisis*. New York: Schocken Books, 1963.

Buber, Martin, and Franz Rosenzweig. *Scripture and Translation*. Trans. Lawrence Rosenwald with Everett Fox. Bloomington and Indianapolis: Indiana University Press, 1994.

Carasik, Michael, ed. *The Commentators' Bible: The JPS Miqra'ot Gedolot—Exodus*. Philadelphia: The Jewish Publication Society, 2005.

Damrosch, David. *The Narrative Covenant: Transformations of Genre in the Growth of Biblical Literature*. San Francisco: Harper & Row, 1987.

[de Leon, Moses?]. *The Zohar: Pritzker Edition*. Vols. 1 and 2. Trans. Daniel C. Matt. Stanford, Calif.: Stanford University Press, 2004.

Fish, Stanley. *Is There a Text in This Class? The Authority of Interpretive Communities*. Cambridge Mass., and London: Harvard University Press, 1980.

Fox, Everett. *The Five Books of Moses*. New York: Schocken Books, 1995.

———. *Now These Are the Names: A New English Rendition of the Book of Exodus*. New York: Schocken Books, 1986.

Frankel, Ellen. *The Five Books of Miriam: A Woman's Commentary on the Torah*. New York: G. P. Putnam's & Sons, 1996.

Friedman, Richard Elliot. *The Bible with Sources Revealed: A New View into the Five Books of Moses*. New York: HarperSanFrancisco, 2003.

———. *Commentary on the Torah with a New English Translation*. San Francisco: HarperSanFrancisco, 2001.

———. *Who Wrote the Bible?* 2nd ed. San Francisco: HarperSanFrancisco, 1996.

Geller, Stephen A. "The Religion of the Bible." In *The Jewish Study Bible*, ed. Adele Berlin and Marc Zvi Brettler. Oxford and New York: Oxford University Press, 2004.

Green, Arthur. *The Language of Truth: The Torah Commentary of the Sefat Emet Rabbi Yehudah Leib Alter of Ger*. Philadelphia: The Jewish Publication Society, 1998.

Greenstein, Edward L. "Biblical Law." In *Back to the Sources: Reading the Classic Jewish Texts*, ed. Barry W. Holtz. New York: Summit Books, 1984.

———. "Medieval Bible Commentaries." In *Back to the Sources: Reading the Classic Jewish Texts*, ed. Barry W. Holtz. New York: Summit Books, 1984.

Hallo, William W. "Deuteronomy and Ancient Near Eastern Literature." In *The Torah: A Modern Commentary*, ed. W. Gunther Plaut and David E. S. Stein, rev. ed. New York: Union for Reform Judaism, 2005.

———. "Numbers and Ancient Near Eastern Literature." In *The Torah: A Modern Commentary*, ed. W. Gunther Plaut and David E. S. Stein, rev. ed. New York: Union for Reform Judaism, 2005.

Heschel, Abraham Joshua. *Heavenly Torah as Refracted Through the Generations*. Trans. Gordon Tucker. New York and London: Continuum, 2005.

Jabès, Edmond. *The Book of Questions*, vol. 1. Trans. Rosmarie Waldrop. Middletown, Conn: Wesleyan University Press, 1976.

Jacobson, Joshua R. *Chanting the Hebrew Bible: The Art of Cantillation*. Philadelphia: The Jewish Publication Society, 2002.

Josipovici, Gabriel. *The Book of God: A Response to the Bible*. New Haven, Conn., and London: Yale University Press, 1988.

Kafka, Franz. *Letter to His Father*. New York: Schocken Books, 1953.

Kass, Leon. *The Beginning of Wisdom: Reading Genesis*. New York and London: Free Press, 2003.

Kushner, Lawrence. *God Was in This Place & I, i Did Not Know: Finding Self, Spirituality and Ultimate Meaning*. Woodstock, Vt.: Jewish Lights Publishing, 1991.

Leibtag, Menachem. "Sefer Breishit Introductory Shiur: The Importance of 'Parshiot,'" Tanach Study Center, http://www.tanach.org.

Lichtenstein, Murray H. "Biblical Poetry." In *Back to the Sources: Reading the Classic Jewish Texts*, ed. Barry W. Holtz, 105–27. New York: Summit Books, 1984.

Pardes, Ilana. *Countertraditions in the Bible: A Feminist Approach*. Cambridge, Mass. and London: Harvard University Press, 1992.

Plaut, W. Gunther, gen. ed., and David E. S. Stein. *The Torah: A Modern Commentary*. Rev. ed. New York: Union for Reform Judaism, 2005.

Ramban (Rabbi Moses ben Nahman, Nachmanides). *Commentary on the Torah: Exodus*. Trans. Charles B. Chavel. New York: Shilo Publishing House, 1973.

Reinhartz, Adele. "Jewish Women's Scholarly Writings on the Bible." In *The Jewish Study Bible*, ed. Adele Berlin and Marc Zvi Brettler. Oxford and New York: Oxford University Press, 2004.

Rosenberg, Joel. "Biblical Narrative." In *Back to the Sources: Reading the Classic Jewish Texts*, ed. Barry W. Holtz. New York: Summit Books, 1984.

Sarna, Nahum M. *Exploring Exodus: The Origins of Biblical Israel*. New York: Schocken Books, 1996.

———. *Understanding Genesis (The Heritage of Biblical Israel)*. New ed. New York: Schocken Books, 1970.

Schorsch, Ismar. "Coming to Terms with Biblical Criticism." *Conservative Judaism* 57:3 (Spring 2005).

Steinberg, Milton. *Basic Judaism*. New York: Harcourt Brace, 1947.

Stern, David. "Introduction: The Anthological Imagination in Jewish Literature." *Prooftexts* 17:1 (January 1997).

Talmon, Shemaryahu. "The 'Desert Motif' in the Bible and in Qumran Literature." In *Biblical Motifs: Origins and Transformations*, ed. Alexander Altmann. Cambridge, Mass.: Harvard University Press, 1966.

Tigay, Jeffrey H., ed. *The JPS Torah Commentary—Deuteronomy*. Philadelphia: The Jewish Publication Society, 1996.

Wieseltier, Leon. "Leviticus." In *Congregation: Contemporary Writers Read the Jewish Bible*, ed. David Rosenberg. San Diego, New York, and London: Harcourt Brace Jovanovitch, 1987.

# *Index*